Cambridge Studies in Social Anthropology

General Editor: Jack Goody

69

THE ABANDONED NARCOTIC

A list of books in the series will be found at the end of the volume.

The abandoned narcotic
Kava and cultural instability in Melanesia

RON BRUNTON

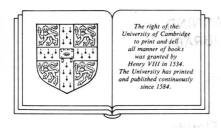

The right of the
University of Cambridge
to print and sell
all manner of books
was granted by
Henry VIII in 1534.
The University has printed
and published continuously
since 1584.

CAMBRIDGE UNIVERSITY PRESS

Cambridge
New York   Port Chester
Melbourne   Sydney

Published by the Press Syndicate of the University of Cambridge
The Pitt Building, Trumpington Street, Cambridge CB2 1RP
40 West 20th Street, New York, NY 10011, USA
10 Stamford Road, Oakleigh, Melbourne 3166, Australia

First published 1989

Printed in Great Britain at The Bath Press, Avon

British Library cataloguing in publication data

Brunton, Ron.
The abandoned narcotic: kava and cultural instability
in Melanesia. – (Cambridge studies in social anthropology).
1. Vanuatu. Kava. Social aspects.
I. Title.
394.1

Library of Congress cataloguing in publication data

Brunton, R. (Ron).
The abandoned narcotic: kava and cultural instability
in Melanesia / Ron Brunton.
        p.   cm. – (Cambridge studies in social anthropology: 69).
Revision of thesis (Ph.D.) – La Trobe University, 1988.
Bibliography.
ISBN 0 521 37375 1
1. Tanna (Vanuatu people) – Drug use. 2. Kava (Beverage) – Vanuatu.
3. Kava ceremony – Vanuatu. 4. Rivers, W. H. R. (William Halse
Rivers), 1864–1922. 5. Tanna (Vanuatu people) – Social conditions.
I. Title. II. Series: Cambridge studies in social anthropology: no. 69.
DU760.B84 1989
394.1′4 – dc20   89–31240 CIP

ISBN 0 521 37375 1

CE

Contents

Illustrations and tables

Acknowledgements

Part of this book is based on ten months' fieldwork in Vanuatu, mainly in Irakik and surrounding areas of Tanna, but also among Tannese living and working in Efate. This fieldwork was undertaken during a number of visits between 1972 and 1980, with an additional brief visit in 1986. I am truly grateful to the many Tannese who made my research possible, but especially to three men, all of whom sadly are now dead: David Nasu, who was willing to take the risk of allowing me to stay at Irakik, and argued my case in the face of some opposition to my research; Jake Yasu who was perhaps my closest friend on Tanna and a highly intelligent informant; and Jake Yahoi, whose knowledge of traditional culture was unrivalled in the area in which I worked. I would also like to thank Jimmy Rauh, Pelpel, Wara, Lemai, Mary Tangap, Yawilum and Mouk of Irakik, Mowiagin, Yasgapel, Yewus and Poita of Lomtihekel, Yewus, Nasei and Yemakse of Inapukil, Nias of Laruanu, Matua, Napwat and Nuknow of Loutahiko, Kumei, Sotei and Nasei of Lounapkaulanges, and Nakau of Lounekeuk, for the generosity of their assistance and hospitality. While what I have written may be very different to what they desired, I hope they will accept that I have tried to remain true to what they told me.

A number of expatriates helped me in various ways. I would particularly like to thank Keith Woodward, Gordon and Liz Norris, David and Socorro Browning, Tessa Fowler, Bob, Kath and Russell Paul, and Pere Sacco, who at different times did much to make my visits both successful and enjoyable.

As will be clear from the numerous references to personal communications, especially in the first half of this book, I have been very dependent on the goodwill of a large number of people. I would particularly like to thank those who went to the trouble of providing me with written answers to questions or access to their unpublished papers and/or material, or who allowed themselves to be subjected to lengthy interviews: Michael Allen, Wal Ambrose, Byron Bender, Joel Bonnemaison, Nancy Bowers, Mark Busse, Wee-Lek Chew, Geoff Dennis, Bob Depew, Tom Dutton, R. N. Duve, Don Gardner, Jacques Guy, Gerard Haberkorn, Allan Hanson, Terry Hayes, Alan Healey, E. E. Henty, Robin Hide, Kirk Huffman, Ian

Hughes, Alan Jones, David Kausimae, Roger Keesing, Jack Keitade, Raymond Kelly, Mait Kilil, Bruce Knauft, Peter Lawrence, Don Laycock, Monty Lindstrom, Tom Ludvigson, John Lynch, Holly McEldowney, Romola McSwain, Mac Marshall, Louise Morauta, Nigel Oram, Malcolm Ross, Bob Rubinstein, Buck Schieffelin, Graham Scott, Daniel Shaw, Christopher Smith, Matthew Spriggs, Robert Theodoratus, Darrell Tryon, Roy Wagner, David Walsh, Pamela Watson, James Weiner, Fred Westbrook, Geoff White, Mike Wood, Doug Yen, and Michael Young. I would also like to thank the staff of the Rijksherbarium in Leiden, the Botany Division of the Department of Scientific and Industrial Research, New Zealand, the Queensland Herbarium, the Australian National Herbarium and the National Herbarium of Victoria. My father-in-law, Emile Rod, kindly offered to translate a number of French texts, and some of the more difficult German ones. He did an excellent job, and I am deeply appreciative of all the time that he spent on it.

Of all the researchers who assisted me, there is one whom I must single out for special mention. In a lengthy correspondence that began in 1984, Vincent Lebot was extraordinarily generous in sharing his knowledge about the botany of kava. I had the pleasure of meeting him during my visit to Vanuatu in 1986, when he spent many hours showing me the results of his work, providing me with additional information, and commenting on my ideas.

This book is a revised version of my Ph.D. thesis, presented to the Department of Sociology at La Trobe University in 1988. I am very grateful to my supervisor, Martha Macintyre, for the warmth of her encouragement and the intelligence and good sense of her advice and comments. I would also like to thank my examiners, Michael Allen, Terry Hays and Michael Young, for their generous and constructive criticisms and suggestions.

My wife Tess, my mother and my step-father were unstinting in their support and forbearance during the course of my research. They know how much it was appreciated.

1

Introduction: W. H. R. Rivers and kava

In 1914 W. H. R. Rivers published *The History of Melanesian Society*, his heroic attempt to unravel the complexities of Oceanic cultures. Noting that the distribution of the two major drugs in Oceania appeared to be almost mutually exclusive, he suggested that they had been brought by two separate – though culturally related – waves of immigrants, the kava-people and the betel-people. Both these peoples brought other elements of culture with them, and the interaction of the immigrants with the original population and each other, together with processes of internal development, had produced the great cultural diversity that characterized the region.

Rivers thought that both the kava-people and the betel-people had migrated into the Pacific from south-east Asia. The kava-people came first, and as well as kava they brought shell money, the bow and arrow, the wooden gong, the pig, and the fowl. They also had secret societies, and associated with these were a cult of the dead, totemism, and the practice of taboo. The betel-people came later, and they also brought the custom of head hunting (1914, vol. 2: 226–7, 250–60, 533).

Betel chewing requires at least three ingredients: the nut of the areca palm (*Areca catechu*), the leaf, catkin or stalk of the betel pepper (*Piper betle*), and lime.[1] Rivers believed that, because it was a complex practice, combining substances with no obvious common associations, it must have developed in stages. First the betel leaf was chewed, then the other ingredients were added later, one at a time. Either the kava-people left their homeland before the other ingredients had been discovered, or these were not initially available to them in their travels. But they did find *Piper methysticum* – the kava plant – in Oceania, and Rivers supposed that they substituted this for the betel pepper, first chewing the leaves, then discovering 'that the root furnished a more potent means whereby to procure the desired effect' (ibid.: 256). At a later stage people learnt to make a drink from the plant, and this became the universal way of consuming kava.

---

[1] Some people add other substances, such as tobacco, cloves, gambier (*Uncara gambir*) and sap from the breadfruit tree, to the betel quid (Theodoratus 1953: 31, 44–5, 51 and *passim*; Crawford 1981: 97).

1

When the betel-people finally arrived in Melanesia, they brought betel chewing with them as a fully developed practice. To Rivers it seemed obvious that it had a number of advantages over kava: the constituents of betel were freely available, easy to carry about, and ready to be used immediately, whereas the supply of kava was rarely plentiful, the drink required prolonged preparation, and its use was restricted. Consequently, he believed that in the places where the betel-people came into contact with the kava-people, the use of kava was gradually abandoned in favour of the superior drug (ibid.: 252–5).

Rivers' work stimulated an interest in kava as an important marker of past migrations (e.g. Churchill 1916; Haddon 1916, 1920; Riesenfeld 1950; Schmitz 1960). But this was relatively short lived in British and Common-wealth anthropology. With the dominance of structural-functionalism after the 1920s, the questions Rivers raised were pushed to the margins of the discipline, appropriate for ethnologists and folklorists, but not social anthropologists. Detailed accounts of kava use continued to appear, particularly in the writings of those who had worked in Polynesia (e.g. Firth 1967; Newell 1947). Yet anthropologists who studied people who drank kava, either at the time of their fieldwork or in the past, sometimes did not even think it necessary to mention the fact in their publications. As the late Peter Lawrence, who was one of them, told me: 'When I was studying the Garia [in the late 1940s and 1950s] these things were only incidentals.'[1] It was only in the 1970s, following the development of more general interests in both psychoactive substances and the interpretation of ritual, that anthropological interest in kava revived. Nevertheless, as we will see, there is still a surprising degree of confusion in the literature, even in regard to rather straightforward matters.

While Rivers was given credit for his contributions to the development of kinship studies, his speculations on Oceanic culture history were ridiculed. Of course, from a contemporary perspective, nearly three-quarters of a century after the functionalist revolution, and as a result of the accumu-lation of high-quality ethnographic data and the increased anthropological sophistication that followed, it is easy to criticize his work. There was a circularity to his arguments; for instance, he identified specific institutions as belonging to the kava-people on rather tenuous grounds, and then supposed that wherever these institutions were found he had evidence for the earlier presence of the kava-people. He made unrealistic assumptions about the coherence of cultural complexes and consequently neglected

---

[1] Lawrence eventually referred to the Garia's use of kava in his monograph (1984: 224). Other anthropologists who have informed me that they worked among people who used kava, but who have not yet mentioned this in their publications, are Romola McSwain, Louise Morauta, and Buck Schieffelin.

indirect diffusion. He also made unwarranted generalizations regarding areas about which his knowledge was very limited.

These objections are well rehearsed, but they should not blind us to his insights. He raised important questions about the cultural similarity of widely separate areas of the Pacific, and he showed considerable sensitivity to the dynamics of leadership and change in Melanesian societies. Michael Allen has recently shown that Rivers' speculations about secret societies and descent systems can be a productive starting point for further inquiries (1981a, 1984). Similarly, I think that Rivers identified genuine anthropological problems relating to kava, as well as contributing possible ideas towards their resolution.

Rivers had a simple but compelling insight about kava: its geographical distribution is strange, and huge distances separate kava-drinking regions (see Map 1). From this he inferred that it had once been far more widespread (1910: 734). Of course, this is not an inescapable inference; the psychoactive properties of *Piper methysticum* could have been discovered independently in a number of different places. If this were the case, the problem would dissolve. There would be no justification for thinking that the spread of kava had ever been more extensive, and no point in speculating why a drug, so highly valued in many cultures, should have been abandoned by others. The purpose of this book is to argue that independent discovery is extremely unlikely, and that the problem of kava is but one aspect of the broader and more fundamental anthropological problem of cultural stability in stateless societies. The first part of the book presents botanical, linguistic and ethnological evidence which strongly suggests that Rivers was correct in thinking that kava was once drunk much more widely in Melanesia. In the second part, I attempt to explain why kava would have disappeared from many Melanesian societies before European contact. This explanation takes as its starting point one of Rivers' conjectures, and draws heavily on my own research, as well as that of others, on the island of Tanna, in southern Vanuatu. I describe the kava ritual – and the modifications it is known to have undergone – in the context of Tannese social organization and its structural weaknesses, and discuss the extent to which certain characteristics of Tannese society and culture are found in other Melanesian societies. I argue that there are sufficient grounds to justify using the known history of kava on Tanna as a model for what may have occurred much more widely in Melanesia.

Before I begin the actual reconsideration of Rivers' work, I intend to discuss two more general issues. Firstly, some information on kava and its properties is necessary. This occupies the remainder of the present chapter. Then, in Chapter 2, I discuss the precise geographical distribution of kava drinking in the Pacific, both to indicate the extent of the problem it raises, and to clear away some of the inaccuracies and confusion that exist in the literature.

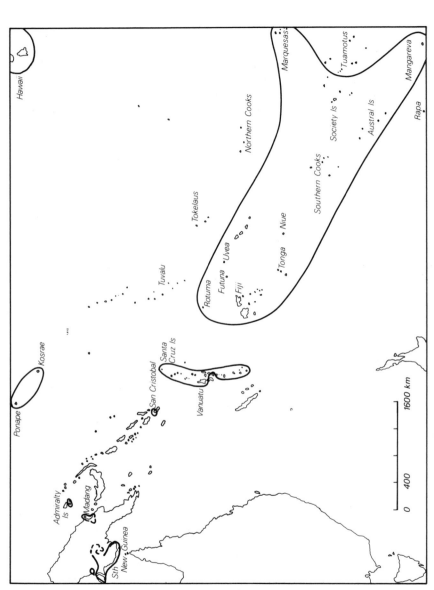

Map 1   *Traditional distribution of kava in the Pacific*

Piper methysticum, the plant from which kava is made, is a shrub that may grow to a height of between one and six metres. The drink is most commonly prepared from the roots, but in some places the stalks also are used. Methods of preparation vary according to whether the plant is used fresh or dried, and whether it is chewed, grated or pounded. Water is usually added to the pulverized root, although some people are reported to drink the undiluted juice – for example, the Kolopom Islanders of Irian Jaya (Serpenti 1969: 33–4). Kava is drunk soon after it is made, and there is no question of any fermentation taking place.

The psychoactive constituents and effects of *Piper methysticum* have been a topic of scientific investigation for well over a hundred years, at least since the French pharmacists Cuzent and Gobley independently published the results of their analyses in the late 1850s (Cuzent 1858: 644–6; Steinmetz 1960: 33). However, even relatively recent anthropological literature demonstrates uncertainty as to whether the plant contains any significant psychoactive constituents. For instance, in a widely read article Elizabeth Bott wrote that Tongans 'treat kava as if it were strong stuff. And so it is, but the strength comes from society, not from the vegetable kingdom' (1972: 207). Her authority for this statement was C. R. B. Joyce, a reader in Psycho-Pharmacology at the University of London, who reviewed the literature for her and concluded 'The whole situation is a remarkable example of the placebo phenomenon in a wide and important setting' (ibid.: 234). Yet recent pharmacological research leaves no doubt that *Piper methysticum* contains a number of active alpha-pyrones whose properties include soporific, anti-convulsant, muscle relaxant and local anaesthetic effects (Duffield and Jamieson 1988; Duve 1976, 1981; Lebot and Cabalion 1986: 53–73; Shulgin 1973; Smith 1979, 1983).

However, there is still uncertainty about some details which are of ethnographic relevance. The alpha-pyrones in kava have a low water solubility (Meyer 1967: 133) and this has led some writers to state that kava prepared by chewing has very different effects from kava prepared by grating or pounding. They suggest that saliva acts as an emulsifying agent, or in some other manner on the pyrones, enabling them to be readily absorbed by the body (e.g. Shulgin 1973: 60; Steinmetz 1960: 23–4, 29–31, 39; see also Lewis and Elvin-Lewis 1977: 439). But from my own experience I suspect that there is little, if any, difference in the effects of kava prepared by the alternative techniques. I have drunk kava prepared both by chewing and by grating on many separate occasions in Vanuatu, and with both I have experienced feelings of tranquillity, difficulty in maintaining motor co-ordination, and eventual somnolence.[1] Discussions with fieldworkers such

[1] In case it is countered that the only conclusion that can be drawn from my experiences with kava prepared by different techniques is the importance of expectations and settings in structuring the subjective experience of drugs, two points should be noted. On the basis of

as Michael Allen and Gerard Haberkorn, who have drunk kava in those northern Vanuatu communities where it is grated, confirm my own experiences.

The research of Buckley and his associates suggests that kava may also have active constituents which are water soluble, and this could explain the similarity of effects. They isolated an amorphous solid they called F_1, which was neither an alpha-pyrone nor an alkaloid. Laboratory tests on rats showed that F_1 was a depressant, whose effects were considerably stronger on the spinal-motor system than on the cerebral-cortical system (Buckley, Furgiuele and O'Hara 1967). Although they stated that they were attempting to isolate the pharmacologically active components of this solid, they do not appear to have produced any further publications. Recent work by Duffield and Jamieson on the aqueous kava extract indicates that while there are some pharmacological effects, these cover a narrower range of activities and are generally weaker than the effects produced by the alpha-pyrones.[1] They conclude it is very likely 'that the action of kava, as prepared for human ingestion, is indeed due to the water insoluble components' (1988: 7). Consequently, if I am correct in thinking that the techniques of preparing kava do not really govern its effects, the obvious inference is that the body absorbs the alpha-pyrones contained in material in suspension in water or saliva. Nevertheless, the question still appears to be open, and this serves to highlight Marshall's recent comments about the need for extensive psychological and physiological research on kava, in both field and experimental settings, using a wide range of varieties (1987: 25).

what I had read, the first time I drank grated kava I fully expected that its effects would be *different* from the effects of chewed kava. Also, I drank grated kava only in bars or other westernized settings which were quite unlike those in which I drank chewed kava.

[1] Duffield and Jamieson suggest that the earlier work by Buckley and his associates may have given misleading results because their extracts were not free of pyrone contamination (1988: 3).

2

The traditional distribution of kava drinking

Most writers who are interested in comparative aspects of kava include some discussion about its distribution, although there have been no attempts to do this systematically, and to evaluate the sources on which statements have been based. Consequently, mistakes which have crept into the literature, either through carelessness or misinterpretation, tend to be confidently repeated by later writers. This is particularly true of Melanesia.

Melanesia

A search of the literature shows that kava is variously stated to have been used in the following parts of Melanesia: some of the islands in the Admiralty group; New Britain; New Ireland; parts of Madang Province; the Lower Sepik; a number of places in the Huon Gulf area; over a wide area of southern New Guinea, including south-east Irian Jaya and a large part of the Fly (formerly Western) Province of Papua New Guinea; San Cristobal and a number of places in the south-east Solomon Islands; Vanuatu; Fiji. Each of these areas will be discussed in turn.

Admiralty Islands

Kava was drunk on the south-eastern islands of Baluan and Lou (Ambrose, personal communication; Bühler 1935: 23; Mead 1934: 341, 344; Nevermann 1934: 220; Parkinson 1907: 373–4; the latter two writers refer to kava drinking only on Lou). As well, Schwartz (1962: 239) and Bühler state that kava was used on the small island of Pam, which lies between the two other islands and shares a common language with them (Wurm and Hattori 1981: Map 14). In a later article co-authored with Romanucci-Ross, Schwartz adds Rambutyo to this list (1979: 257).[1] Holly McEldowney was told by the people of Baun village on Lou that they thought that the people of

[1] Schwartz and Romanucci-Ross leave Pam out of this later list, stating that kava was drunk only in Baluan, Lou and Rambutyo (1979: 257). The omission of Pam may be due simply to its small size and population.

Rambutyo once drank kava, as they had seen the special stones used to mash the kava root there (personal communication).

New Ireland and New Britain

Holmes states that kava drinking is found in both New Britain and New Ireland, but neither presents his sources nor specifies the societies involved (1979: 30). A similar claim is made by Ford (1967: 162), who almost certainly obtained his information from an article by Lester (1941–2: 101), as the same paragraph includes sentences which are almost direct, though unacknowledged, quotations from this article. However, Lester's survey of kava-drinking peoples contains a number of errors,[1] and there is simply no field evidence to back up his assertion. To the best of my knowledge no ethnographer – or anyone else – has described kava drinking in either of these two islands. Perhaps the most charitable suggestion is that Lester misinterpreted reports of *Piper methysticum* found growing wild in New Britain (Schumann and Lauterbach 1976 [1901, 1905], vol. 2: 238), and being used as a constituent of betel mixture in New Ireland (Abel 1906, 1907; cited in Riesenfeld 1950: 649).

Madang

Miklouho-Maclay was the first person to record the use of kava in this region (Map 2). He stated that 'all the natives of the Maclay Coast [the area around Bongu where he was based] do not use the *keu* (kava], in some villages this stimulant and its effect are known, but the use of it has not been adopted; in some others, it is not known at all' (1886a: 351). Unfortunately, he does not seem to have attempted a precise delineation of its distribution, although it is possible to gain some information by examining his diary. Kava is mentioned as being grown or prepared in the villages of Male, Koliku Mana, Bongu, Gorendu, and Englam Mana (1975: 112, 117, 165, 175, 214). A comparison of the maps accompanying his diary with Map 7 of the *Language atlas of the Pacific area* shows that the first two villages were inhabited by speakers of the Male language, the next two by speakers of Bongu, and the last by speakers of Yangulam. Werner briefly describes kava drinking in Kadda (1911: 152) which, on the basis of his map (ibid.: 49), appears to be in the Pulabu language area about 10 km inland from Bongu (Wurm and Hattori 1981: Map 7). However, the people of Bai village on the Gowar River, about 25 km east of Englam Mana, did not drink kava, had no name for it, and refused it when it was offered to them at feasts in other villages (Miklouho-Maclay 1975: 271).

[1] For example, he states that kava was not drunk in Papua, nor in some islands in Vanuatu which are known beyond doubt to have used it.

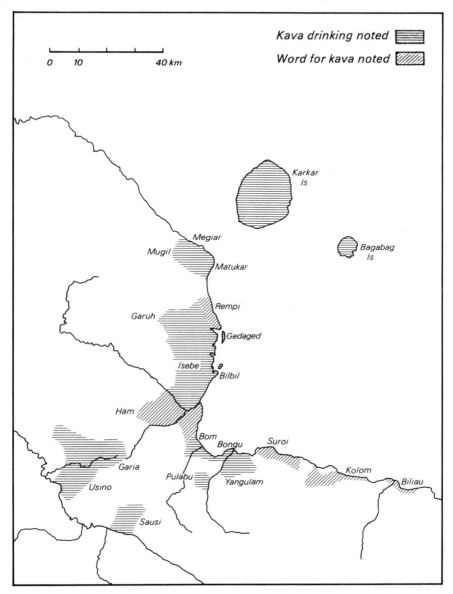

Map 2 *Traditional distribution of kava in Madang*

Hagen reported kava drinking among the Bom-speaking people of Bogadjim village (1899: 245–6). In the area around Madang, kava was drunk by the coastal and island people speaking the Austronesian Gedaged and Bilbil languages (Hannemann 1944: 7–8; see also Aufinger 1939: 279–80). Morauta, who studied seventeen interior villages situated between the Gum and Biges Rivers, inhabited by speakers of four non-Austronesian languages (Garuh, Kamba, Isebe, Amele), states that these people drank kava traditionally, although she did not record any contemporary use (personal communication). The people of Karkar Island and Bagabag Island also used kava traditionally, although the latter no longer drink it (Romola McSwain; Stephanie Fahey; Mait Kilil; personal communications).

In the hinterland of Madang province kava drinking has been recorded for the Garia,[1] the Usino, and for Yonopa village on the Ramu River in the Sausi language area (Lawrence 1984: 224; Conton 1977: 156–7; Eisler 1979: 82; Aufenanger and Höltker 1940: 101).

Although Miklouho-Maclay's statement that some of the people in the area knew of kava without drinking it themselves means that word lists are a less reliable form of information, he provides words for 'kava pepper' in the following languages in addition to the ones mentioned above: Biliau, Erima, Kolom, Rempi, Suroi and Songum (1951, vol. 3: 175, 182–3). Mager, who worked as a missionary in the area for a number of years, also gives words for kava in Biliau and Kolom, as well as in Ganglau and Ham (1952: 5).[2] Kasprus, who was a missionary in the Mugil area from 1932 until 1936, lists words for kava in the Megiar and Mugil (his Saker) languages, but not for neighbouring Matukar, Garus, Murupi and Rempi languages (he called the latter three the Em, Ate and A'e dialects of Garus), although he states that there was almost no cultural difference between the Megiar and Matukar (1942–5: 719–20, 750). As noted above, Miklouho-Maclay listed a word for kava in Rempi. Mait Kilil has confirmed that at least the Megiar, Mugil and Matukar peoples traditionally drank kava (personal communication).

Lower Sepik

Riesenfeld states, without indicating his sources, that kava was used 'perhaps on the Lower Sepik' (1950: 447). I have not been able to find any

---

[1] Lawrence states that it is 'a toxic drink made from wild ginger' (1984: 260). As we will see later, ginger is used as an intoxicant in parts of Papua New Guinea and may have been confused with *Piper methysticum* in at least one other account. However, from the description Lawrence has given of the drink (personal communication), and the presence of *Piper methysticum* among the Garia's neighbours, it is certain that it is *Piper methysticum*.

[2] These are not necessarily the language names used by these authors. I have adopted the names used by Z'graggen (1975).

corroborating evidence for this. However, there is a slight possibility that it was used by the Boiken-speaking people around Wewak. Gerstner records that they used at least two kinds of intoxicating gingers. One, called *hasabi*, was chewed in conjunction with other plants before dancing feasts (1954: 463). There are two aspects of this report which open the possibility that it was *Piper methysticum*. Firstly, although Gerstner states that the different gingers he lists in his article are all varieties of *Zingiber officinale* (1954: 463), he appears to be mistaken in the case of *komiŋ*, which is almost certainly a turmeric (*Curcuma spp.*, Sterly 1967b: 239). Gerstner would not be the only writer to have confused *Piper methysticum* with a *Zingiber*: as indicated in p. 10, n. 1, Lawrence made this mistake. Secondly, *hasabi* is a possible cognate of *isa*, the Garia word for kava (Lawrence 1984: 224), and the Usino word *kisa* (E. Henty, personal communication).[1]

A second possibility is that Riesenfeld had in mind references by Mead and Fortune to *Piper methysticum* among the Mountain Arapesh. Thus Mead lists a tree called *mushas* whose leaves are 'used as a substitute for pepper mythisticum' [sic] (1970 [1940]: 368), and Fortune gives the word for *Piper methysticum* in his Arapesh dictionary (1942: 39). But it seems that both had confused *Piper methysticum* with *Piper betle*, possibly as a result of reading an inaccurate article by Chinnery (1922; cf. im Thurn 1922). Thus Fortune says that *Piper methysticum* is a vine, and in a later publication Mead states that *mushas* is used as a substitute for betel pepper leaf (1971 [1947]: 516).

Huon Gulf

Riesenfeld included the Bukawa, Jabim, Tami, and the people of Cape Cretin and Finschhafen in his list of kava drinkers (1950: 447). Again, no authority is cited for this statement, but Speiser included the first three peoples in his list (1934: 148), and Haddon records that de Clercq and Schmeltz included the last two places in their table of kava distribution. Haddon states that their work contains inaccuracies but makes no further comment (1916: 147). Certainly, Warburg reported that *Piper methysticum* grew quite widely in the area, but added ' I have not heard that the natives of this place utilize the plant' (1890: 283; my translation). Zöller stated that at least one group did, but his phrasing indicates that he was not absolutely sure of this (1891: 253).[2] However, Neuhauss, in a book which is recognized as an early authority on the peoples and languages of the Huon Gulf region, and which contains essays on the Bukawa, Jabim and Tami, explicitly states

[1] The implications raised by possible cognates, and the relation between words for kava and words for ginger, are discussed in the next chapter.

[2] 'Der Genuss der Kawa, den ich mit Sicherheit in der Astrolabe-Bai und, wenn ich mich recht erinnere, auch bei den Jabim festgestellt habe . . .' (The use of kava, which I certainly found in Astrolabe Bay, and *if I remember correctly* [my emphasis] also among the Jabim . . .)

that kava was drunk only in the Astrolabe Bay area (1911: 276). Further-more, the extremely comprehensive Jabim dictionary compiled by the Revd H. Zahn, whose three decades of work in the area commenced in the last century, gives a Jabim word for a Piper species 'used to make an intoxicat-ing drink by the Tamol people' (1982: 27), the term Biro and others used for the people around Bongu and Bogadjim in Astrolabe Bay (Biro 1901: 102–4). It goes without saying that had the Jabim been kava drinkers, this would be a most eccentric gloss. Consequently, I believe that we are justified in concluding that there was no basis for Riesenfeld's and Speiser's inclusion of the area in their lists.

The only other people in the Huon Gulf area said to drink kava are the Umboi Islanders. This claim comes from Schmitz (1960: 91) who provides no authority for it, and to the best of my knowledge no one else makes it. It is possible that he based it on a Bilbil version of the Kilibob-Manumbu myth in which Manumbu sails to Umboi (Garani) and plants a lot of kava (Dempwolff 1911: 81).

Southern New Guinea

This is the major kava-drinking region in New Guinea and covers a large part of the Fly (formerly Western) Province, with an extension well into Irian Jaya (Map 3). Specific descriptions of kava use in this region are much more detailed than those available for the Madang area or the Admiralties. In 1938 Nevermann published an article summarizing the available infor-mation as well as adding material from his own observations. He indicated that the territory within which kava was drunk extended along the south coast from the Gogodala and Kiwai areas to Cape Valsch on Kolopom (Frederik-Hendrik) Island, and north through the areas of the Wiram (Suki language), Je-nan in Irian Jaya (Yey language; see also van Baal 1982: 8), Marind-anim, and Yelmek. Nevermann's map excluded the western swamp area of Kolopom Island around Kalilam village as he stated that he did not know whether kava was used there (1938: 189). Serpenti states that kava was introduced into the western area after the Dutch government had established its presence on the island (1965: 53). Nevermann also indicated that the people he called the Sohur (Yaqay), who lived around the Mappi River, formed a separate pocket of kava drinkers (1938: 181). Boelaars confirms that the Yaqay used kava and suggests that they may have adopted it from the Marind (1981: 54).

Within the region Nevermann defined there were considerable variations in the importance of kava and the frequency of its use. It is not really certain whether we can talk about a continuous area, or one with pockets within which kava was not drunk. A part of the problem stems from the fact that the Papuan Administration made kava drinking illegal in 1911 (Wolfers

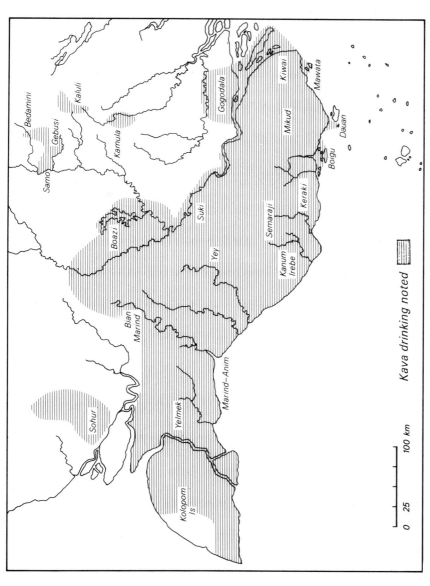

Map 3   *Traditional distribution of kava in Southern New Guinea*

1975: 39), so people tended to deny any knowledge of it, even when it was found growing in their gardens (Williams 1936: 427).[1] Williams thought that kava was a 'foreign element' (ibid.) among the Keraki (Nambu language) and their neighbours, the Semaraji and Gambadi (Rouku, Tonda and Peremka languages) and the Mikud (Idi language?).

There were also variations in the believed antiquity of kava drinking within the region. The Gogodala claim that they were the first people to use kava, and that they introduced it to the Kiwai (Crawford 1981: 97). This tallies with the account the Kiwai gave to Landtman, although they are also said to have learnt its use from the people on the coast south of the Fly (1927: 106). The Mawata people on the coast west of the Binaturi River said that they had adopted kava drinking from the Masingle, whom they partially dispossessed of their land (ibid.; Haddon 1916: 148). Nevertheless, the Mawata called kava *komata* or *gamoda*, and these words are obviously related to the Kiwai *gamada*, whereas the Masingle word was *sie*. Kava was said to have always grown in the area (Landtman 1927: 66).

More recent research has shown that other people in the region also drank kava. Although Haddon claimed that kava was unknown among the Torres Strait Islanders (1912: 141), Lawrie has recorded a Boigu tale referring to the drinking of kava (called *gamada*) on Dauan (1970: 231). Jeremy Beckett says that when he was working in the Torres Straits in the 1960s the Boigu had the reputation of still using *gamada* (personal communication).

The Boazi language speakers who live around Lake Murray in Papua New Guinea, to the north-east of the Je-nan, drank kava traditionally (Mark Busse, personal communication). It is not known whether the Pari (Pa) language speakers who live between the Lake Murray and Nomad areas drink kava; however they used a Piper species for medicinal purposes called *woti* (Skingle 1970: 224) – which is clearly related to *wati*, the Boazi and Marind-anim word for kava. Their northern neighbours the Awin did not drink kava (Bob Depew, personal communication).

In the Nomad area there are a number of peoples who drink kava: the Gebusi (Knauft 1987: 82–9), the Samo (Shaw 1981) and the Bedamini (Sørum 1980: 276, 1982: 54). But the Etoro, the immediate eastern neighbours of the Bedamini, do not appear to use kava (Ray Kelly, personal communication),[2] and Tom Ernst says that he has never come across

---

[1] Williams states 'recently the restriction has been lifted' (1936: 427), although he suggests that people had not yet realized this. However Wolfers writes that the prohibition was not repealed until 1962 (1975: 137). In the early 1960s Serpenti found the same secretiveness about kava among the Kolopom Islanders, even though the Dutch government also had ended its ban on kava (1965: 49).

[2] Kelly says that he is reluctant to make an absolute statement on the matter as he did not investigate ritual to any extent, and had kava been used in male initiation ceremonies, in curing, or by mediums, it might have escaped his notice. The plant was not present in any of the gardens he examined.

evidence of its use among the Onabasulu to the south-east (personal communication). However, the Kaluli, who are the southern neighbours of the Onabasulu, did drink kava and grew it in their gardens (Buck Schieffelin, personal communication).

The Kamula, who live in the area south of Mount Bosavi around Crater Lake and Keseki, traditionally drank kava, which they called *kawata*. The Kamula, like the Sohur, and possibly the people of the Nomad area and the Kaluli, may have formed a pocket of kava users. Although their present-day territory extends nearly to the Aramia River, just above Gogodala, this is the result of a postwar southward migration (Wood 1982: 241–2, and personal communication). Crawford states that the non-Gogodala people on the northern bank of the Aramia drank kava only as a recent Gogodala introduction, and that traditionally there was no trade in a northerly direction from the Aramia (1981: 53).[1] Yet Wood has told me that there is no evidence to suggest recent introduction. The Kamula's affinities are to the people of the Great Papuan Plateau (Crawford 1981: 59), although their language is classified as a family-level isolate of the Central and South New Guinea Stock (Wurm 1982: 132).

A few examples from people to the east of Mount Bosavi should also be mentioned in this section. The Foi of Lake Kutubu and the Mubi River used a plant in ritual which Williams said was *Piper methysticum* 'or a kind of pepper very similar to it' (1976: 284; see also Weiner 1988: 52, 112). The Lae herbarium has a specimen identified as *Piper methysticum* which was collected at Lake Kutubu in 1946/7, and the vernacular word given for it was *takorabu*, the same as one of the words received by Williams. The specimen was supposed to have been cultivated and used to make a drink (E. Henty, personal communication), but as important details, such as the name of the collector, are not known about the specimen, we have to be careful about assuming that kava was drunk at Lake Kutubu in the face of denials by Williams and Weiner. Williams was told that the plant originally had been brought to Lake Kutubu from Hai and Kasua. He was unable to identify these places (1976: 284). However, the Kasua live immediately south of the Great Papuan Plateau, and Hai could be Haivaro, a Kasua-speaking village south-east of Mt Bosavi (Freund 1977: 24). Freund makes no mention of kava in his study of the Kasua. As the co-author of a bibliography of kava in the Pacific, he is likely to have had the interest to note it were the plant still in obvious use (Freund and Marshall 1977).

Much further to the east, Wagner reports that the Daribi of Simbu Province use *Piper methysticum* in a number of magical contexts (1972:

[1] By 'non-Gogodala people' Crawford appears to mean the Kamula and 'other closely related people' (1981: 35, 39), although Reesink shows Bainapi speakers as occupying the territory between the Gogodala and the Kamula (1976: 37). The Bainapi language is a member of the Bosavi family (Wurm 1982: 136), and the people migrated south to their present location from the area between the Soari and Wawoi Rivers in 1941 (Reesink 1976: 11).

153–4). While there may be doubts about the botanical identification (Roy Wagner, personal communication), the Daribi word for the plant is *kerare*, which clearly appears to be related to the Keraki word for kava, *kurar* (Williams 1936: 427). Robin Hide was told by the people of Yuro, a bilingual Daribi/Pawaia settlement, that up until the 1930s they used to make a drink for male initiates from a plant known as *hamu* in the Pawaia language. He tried to ascertain whether *hamu* was *Piper methysticum* but received contradictory replies (personal communication; see also Egloff and Kaiku 1978: 23–4).

Solomon Islands

Fox reported that the Arosi of San Cristobal formerly drank kava 'but that with the coming of the betel nut kava drinking passed away' (1924: 216–17). Although writers such as Riesenfeld (1950: 650) have suggested that Fox's observations may have been unduly influenced by Rivers's speculations about the presence of the 'kava-people' in the Solomons, there is sufficient detail in Fox's account to make this unlikely, unless we are to assume that he consciously falsified his data. He also claimed that the fact of previous kava drinking had 'been confirmed by a number of independent witnesses' (ibid.: 217). Eckardt states that bowls of kava were prepared for large feasts in Bauro, which adjoins the Arosi area, and Uji (1881: 349). Uji could be Ugi (or Uki Ni Masi), an island off the north coast of San Cristobal, with linguistic affinities to South Malaita (Tryon and Hackman 1983: 39). Unfortunately Eckardt provides no further information, but his statement does give added credence to Fox's account.

In his dictionary of the 'Are'are language on Malaita, Geerts gives as the gloss for the word *kakawa* 'a tree, its roots being sucked is intoxicating' [sic] (1970: 47). David Kausimae, an 'Are'are politician to whom I wrote requesting further information, has informed me that *kakawa* is the same plant as that used by the Fijians 'to produce intoxication'. Tryon has also been told by old Malaitans living in Fiji that the plant Fijians use to make kava grew on Malaita as well. He was given the words *kwakokwako* and *kwaŋga* as the names for this plant (personal communication). The first is probably from Kwara'ae (see Whitmore 1966: 146). Furthermore, on neighbouring San Cristobal, *ba'enakakawa* is the word for a particular variety of *Piper methysticum* (Fox 1978: 86). But the question of whether the 'Are'are actually used kava remains open. Geoff Dennis, a long-time resident of the Solomons to whom I also wrote, said that he has been told that 'Are'are chiefs once drank kava. Yet, according to Kausimae, the 'Are'are did not use it.

Rivers reported that kava was drunk in Vanikoro and Utupua (1914, vol. 1: 226–7) and this was confirmed by Davenport, who stated that 'kava is an indispensable item for every . . . feast' (1968: 214). Kava was used also on Tikopia, where it was poured as a libation to the gods. But although these rites were of central importance, kava was rarely drunk. Occasionally a participant might drink to slake his thirst, and some, though not all, spirit mediums drank kava while in trance. Firth was told that at one time kava was drunk in a ceremonial manner, although there is no confirmation of this in traditional tales (1970: 204). In nearby Anuta – which, like Tikopia, is a Polynesian outlier – the basic religious rite is also called *kava*, and it shows many similarities to the Tikopian version. No kava is actually used, however, and the plant does not grow on the island (Firth 1954: 102).[1] But according to a traditional Anuta tale, kava was once drunk (Firth 1970: 204). The people of Graciosa Bay on Santa Cruz Island told Doug Yen that they had drunk kava within living memory, although they claimed to have been the only people within their immediate area who did (personal communication). According to Fox, the people of Taumako, another Polynesian outlier in the Santa Cruz group, also drank kava but only on special occasions such as funerals. (1971: 190).

Although kava was not drunk on other Polynesian outliers in the Solomons, there are echoes of a former familiarity. In Rennell and Bellona, *kaba*, which is a reflex of the Proto-Polynesian term for kava, **kawa* (see Biggs 1978: 708), was 'an important offering of cooked tubers of bananas, usually accompanied with the drinking of coconut water, commonly called *kaba ki hage* and dedicated to [the god] Tehu'aigabenga' (Elbert 1975: 112). In Ontong Java *'ava*, also a reflex of **kawa* (see Biggs 1978: 708), was the word for burial place (Ian Hogbin, personal communication), a not unexpected association given the role of kava in funerals and communication with the ancestors. The cognate *kawa* had the same meaning in the Polynesian outlier of Nuguria in Papua New Guinea (Ray 1916: 45).

Vanuatu

The one island in Vanuatu (Map 4) where there is no evidence of kava having been drunk traditionally is Ambrym, although in both south-west and south-east Ambrym wild kava (*bəralmɛn*, Lonwolwol; *veramei*, SE Ambrym) was used in magic and ritual (Mary Patterson, personal communication; Paton 1973: 14; 1979: 20; Bob Tonkinson, personal communication). In Malekula the precise distribution is uncertain. The Big Nambas have long been thought to have been the only traditional kava drinkers, although the plant was used ritually in parts of the south-west of the island, and in the Small Islands off the north-east coast (Deacon 1934: 318, 373–4,

---

[1] Kirch and Yen state that it no longer grows on Tikopia either (1982: 36, 358). Firth writes that during his 1966 visit he was told that the kava plant had not been cultivated since the abandonment of the rites in which it was used, and had consequently died out (1970: 201).

650; Layard 1942: 376, 557). However Kirk Huffman states that his research has revealed that kava was drunk in north-east Malekula, and by men who had reached the highest ranks of the graded society in the south-west of the island (personal communication). MacDonald recorded that people living north of Pangkumu on the central east coast called kava *meruh*, which appears cognate with words for kava in neighbouring islands, but he provided no further information (1889: 240).

The situation on Espiritu Santo is also not completely clear. Baker, who travelled widely on the island, made the comment that little or no kava was drunk (1929: 72), but Harrisson, who claimed to have made a complete census of Espiritu Santo, stated that it was drunk everywhere with the exception of the area around Mt Turi, which is in the interior of the eastern half (1936a: 246; 1936b: 333). Speiser states that the short-statured people in mountain areas didn't drink kava (1923: 162), but Harrisson visited these areas and did not exclude them from his general comments, and the people at Wunapenini are specifically mentioned as drinking kava (1936a: 248–9). Ludvigson, who worked in the Ari valley in the centre of the island, refers to the men as being 'habitual users' of kava, and gives no indication that it was a recent adoption (1981: 227). Some of the confusion could be due to the fact that in parts of the island only men who had reached high ranks of the graded society were permitted to drink; because of depopulation and other disruptions following contact, men were no longer in a position to take these grades (Speiser 1913: 144; 1923: 162; Harrisson 1936a: 250; 1936b: 333).

Lester, who, as already mentioned, is the source of a fair amount of misinformation about the distribution of kava in Melanesia, stated that kava was not drunk on Paama, and possibly Aoba (1941–2: 101). As far as Aoba is concerned he was simply wrong (Allen 1981b: 127; Rodman 1973: 189; Speiser 1923: 163), and he was also incorrect about Paama (Terry Crowley, personal communication).

Harrisson implies that kava was used only ritually on Malo (1936b: 333). However, older Maloese say that it was drunk traditionally (Bob Rubinstein, personal communication; see also Speiser 1923: 162–3). For the Banks Islands, Codrington commented that kava drinking was so recent that it had not yet spread to Santa Maria (Gaua) Island by the 1880s (1891: 351), although Rivers states that Codrington misinterpreted the situation and that kava had originally been used and then abandoned (1914, vol. 1: 86). Speiser states that kava drinking had not been observed on Epi (1923: 163), but this is contradicted by Michael Young (personal communication).

Elsewhere in Vanuatu the situation is clearer, and there appears to be no dispute about the presence of kava drinking in the Torres Islands, Maewo, Pentecost, and all the islands from the Shepherds south to Aneityum.

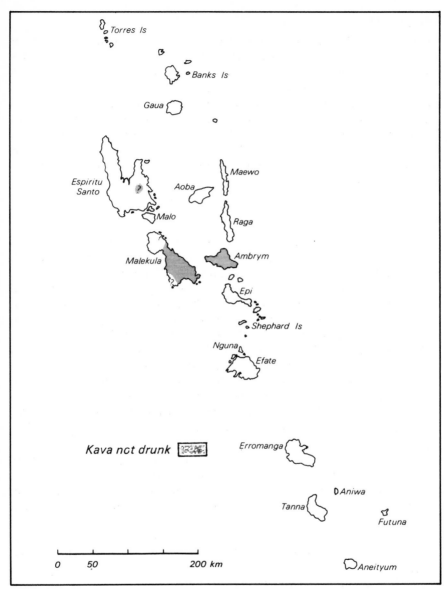

Map 4   *Traditional distribution of kava in Vanuatu*

Fiji

There is no real controversy about the traditional use of kava throughout Fiji, although Riesenfeld, taking his cue from Thomson (1908: 341), states 'in Thomas Williams' time [kava drinking] had not become general in Vanua Levu and part of Viti Levu' (Riesenfeld 1950: 647), to support his suggestion that it was a late introduction into Fiji. Yet, insofar as this implies that there were places where kava was not drunk, it misconstrues the point Williams was making. Williams' precise words were that kava 'is not so commonly in use on Vanua Levu and some parts of Viti Levu, as it is on other islands, where it is frequently the case that the Chiefs drink it as regularly as we do coffee' (Williams and Calvert 1859: 111).

Polynesia

The question of the distribution of kava drinking in Polynesia is not as complicated as is the case in Melanesia. Essentially, kava was drunk throughout Polynesia with the exception of Easter Island, New Zealand, the Chatham Islands and Rapa. Kava was also absent from the flat coral atolls (although it is possible that some of the Tuamotus were an exception). These are unsuitable for *Piper methysticum* as the plant requires an environment with high rainfall and rich, well drained soil (Lebot 1983: 87; Lebot and Cabalion 1986: 114). Nevertheless, as the literature contains a few inconsistencies and uncertainties about the presence of kava in some parts of Polynesia, a specific enumeration is warranted. For convenience of presentation the listing is alphabetical. I have not included the Polynesian outliers as these are dealt with – if only by implication in some cases – under the headings of Melanesia and Micronesia.

Austral Islands: Very isolated volcanic islands. The people of Tubuai drank kava traditionally, but missionaries abolished the custom after their arrival in 1822, and there is virtually no information about its use. By the time of Aitken's fieldwork very few plants were to be found on the island (1930: 42).

Chatham Islands: No evidence of kava. The climate was 'too cold for sweet potato and other Polynesian food plants to grow' (Te Rangi Hiroa 1945: 112).

Easter Island: No kava (Metraux: 1940: 159).

Futuna: Kava (Burrows 1936).

Hawaii: Kava (Titcomb 1948).

Mangareva: Ferdon states that kava was 'not believed to have been a contact period crop in Mangareva' (1981: 185). However, Ferdon's ideas about the diffusion of kava in this part of the Pacific are not very well based, as he argues – mistakenly, as I will show in the next chapter – that it arrived in Tahiti not long before the group was discovered. Although Te Rangi Hiroa does not list kava as one of the economic flora of Mangareva, drinking is mentioned in Mangarevan chants and he does state that kava was used in funeral ceremonies and was provided by priests for the initiation of seers (1938: 439, 446, 449, 489). He also infers that 'kava was not chewed as in Western Polynesia, but was pounded' (ibid.: 449).

Marquesas: Kava (Handy 1923: 202).

New Zealand: The climate was too cold for *Piper methysticum* (Marshall 1987: 22). But the Maoris must have had some familiarity with the plant, as they called *Macropiper excelsum*, a related, and physically rather similar shrub, *kawa* or *kawakawa* and used it extensively in religious ceremonies. Furthermore *kawa* was also the word used for a class of ceremonies performed in connection with important social events involving a change of state (Brooker, Cambie and Cooper 1981: 77; Tregear 1969: 139; Williams 1957: 109–10).

Niue: Raised coral atoll. Although very little is known about the preparation of kava, Loeb states that it is 'certain . . . that the chiefs formerly drank kava in a ceremonial manner' (1926: 28). Thomson states that priests were inspired by draughts of kava (1901: 139).

Northern Cook Islands: Flat coral atolls. There was no kava on Pukapuka (Beaglehole and Beaglehole 1938: 25, 413) or on Tongareva (Te Rangi Hiroa 1932a: 91). However in a song sung on Tongareva during the preparation of the feast drink *roro* (a liquid expressed from the grated flesh of the mature coconut), the phrase 'my kava is *roro*' occurs, and Te Rangi Hiroa states that this 'is significant, indicating that a memory of kava was retained and that *roro* was a substitute' (ibid.: 121). Tongareva did not have any of the common Polynesian cultivated root plants (ibid.: 106). On Manihiki-Rakahanga, the word *kawa* means bitter (Te Rangi Hiroa 1932b: 93). The *roro* did not assume the importance that it did on Tongareva (ibid.: 98), and there are no other possible links to kava.

Rapa: Kava was not present on Rapa, although it was a volcanic island and the climate appears to have been suitable for its growth (Stokes 1930: 244–6). Stokes reports that the people explicitly stated that their ancestors did not use or even have the plant. Nevertheless, another *Piper* species grew on Rapa. It was called *kakatua* and was used as a treatment for leprosy. This may have been *Piper latifolium*, which is found in Rarotonga, where it is called *kava kava atua*, and in the Austral Islands (Brown 1935: 17). The association with leprosy is suggestive, given the myths in Western Polynesia in which kava is said to have grown from the body of a leper (Lester 1941–2: 102; Bott 1972: 215). There is also a species of *Peperomia* (which is in the same botanical family as *Piper*) called *kavariki*.

21

Rotuma: Kava (Williamson 1939: 92–6).

Samoa: Kava (Te Rangi Hiroa 1930: 147–64).

Society Islands: Kava (Handy 1930: 20–1).

Southern Cook Islands: Volcanic islands. Kava was drunk on Raratonga, Mangaia, and Aitutaki (Savage 1962: 96; Te Rangi Hiroa 1934: 138, 177–8; Beaglehole 1957: 144). Te Rangi Hiroa states that it was grown on the other islands as well (1944: 18).

Tokelaus: Flat coral atolls. 'Kava does not grow . . . but the coconut supplants it to some extent as the cup of hospitality' (Macgregor 1937: 151). Yet kava may well have been known, as a myth refers to a child in its mother's womb singing 'make the kava', and voyages to Samoa were not uncommon (ibid.: 27, 87).

Tonga: Kava (Newell 1947).

Tuamotus: Archipelago of seventy-eight flat coral atolls (with the exception of Makatea, which is raised, and which has a rich soil and varied vegetation, Emory 1975: 2). Although Emory states that 'kava does not grow in the Tuamotus' (1947: 84), a number of chants, from different islands, refer to the leaves of kava and to the kava drink (Emory 1940: 85, 94, 103, 110; 1947: 84–5). One of these chants refers to an offering of kava to a tutelary god. Stimson, who had an extremely good knowledge of the group, indicated that *kava* was an obsolete word used for *Piper methysticum* on the islands of Vahitahi, Hao and Anaa (1964: 39–40). On the last two islands it also referred to 'an unfermented beverage; prepared from the [plant]' (ibid.: 210).

Tuvalu: Flat coral atolls. There is no evidence of kava, but Ranby, in his dictionary of Nanumea (one of the atolls), gives a gloss for *kava* as 'sour, bitter, salty; a stage in the fermentation of fresh juice from coconut palm in the production of toddy' (1980: 45).

Uvea: Kava (Burrows 1937: 139–43).

Micronesia

Micronesia is the one region where there has been no controversy in regard to the traditional distribution of kava drinking. It was confined to only two places in the eastern Carolines, Ponape and Kosrae (Marshall 1987: 22; Riesenberg 1968: 102).

Nevertheless, von Chamisso, who visited Micronesia with the Romanzov exploring expedition of 1815–18, reported that they collected *Piper methysticum* from Guam, although kava was not drunk there (1986: 261). Certainly, as we shall see in the next chapter, there have been many misidentifications of *Piper methysticum*, but von Chamisso's statements should not be dismissed too readily. He observed kava drinking in the eastern Carolines, and he distinguished *Piper methysticum* from the similar *Piper latifolium* (ibid.).

Comments on the distribution of kava drinking

Obviously, the frequency, significance, and even antiquity of kava use is not necessarily the same within a given region. This is particularly true of Melanesia, but may also apply in parts of Polynesia, such as the Society Islands, and the Marquesas (see Handy 1923: 202; 1930: 21; Williamson 1939: 88–0; and my comments about Ferdon in Chapter 3). Yet if anything, the literature is likely to have understated the degree of difference. In some cases, observations apply to specific villages, or to an area which is known to be culturally homogeneous; but in others, statements are made about social units of undetermined homogeneity. For example, when Nevermann concludes, after noting that the Kanum Irebe regularly drink kava, 'evidently [they] have become kava drinkers only in recent years, as Wirz expressly says that they do not know kava' (1938: 184), it needs to be realized that although there are only a few hundred Kanum language speakers, they are in a number of villages spread out across an area of thousands of square kilometres (see Wurm and Hattori 1981: Maps 4 and 12). Nevermann's conclusions may be correct; or he and Wirz may have taken their information from different parts of Kanum Irebe territory. Similarly, caution has to be taken with many of the general statements about the presence of kava, or the use of *Piper methysticum*, amongst rather broadly defined linguistic or cultural groups.

However, even without taking the above comments into account, what is striking about the distribution of kava drinking is that it is so patchy outside Polynesia (see Maps 1–4). Great distances separate kava-drinking regions in Melanesia and Micronesia.[1] Some of the regions have no known direct links with any of the others (southern New Guinea, San Cristobal, eastern Carolines); others have possible links to each other, but not to any outside regions (Admiralties–Madang). A similar situation may have occurred within some regions, such as southern New Guinea and possibly Madang, where, as we have seen, there could be inland pockets of kava users. There are only three possible explanations for this patchiness:

1 There were never any direct links between the widely separated regions, and in each of them the psychoactive properties of *Piper methysticum* were independently discovered.
2 At one stage there were direct links between the regions. These may have

[1] Of course, as Map 1 shows, the same is true of the distance between Hawaii and the other kava-drinking areas of Polynesia. But in this case the presence of kava is simply an aspect of the more general problem raised by the colonization of Hawaii (see e.g. Kirch 1984: 71–95).

23

been trade connections which have since disappeared, or a migration from one region to another. In either case *Piper methysticum* and/or knowledge of its properties were directly transferred.

3 The links between the regions were indirect; either trading chains or sequences of migrations. *Piper methysticum* and/or knowledge of its properties diffused through these links, but at some stage before European contact the people in these intermediary areas abandoned the use of kava.

To anticipate the discussion of the chapters which follow, I will argue that possibility 1 is highly unlikely, and that possibility 2 is likely only in the case of some regions. In other words, the thrust of my argument will be that at one time kava drinking had a much wider distribution, but a number of peoples subsequently gave it up. I should point out that the argument I will develop, which is a sociological one, is really confined to Melanesia. While the Micronesian distribution is also puzzling, it can be explained in terms of the environmental unsuitability of the atolls that lie between Ponape and Kosrae and other kava-drinking regions.[1] Consequently, in the process of the migration to, and settling of eastern Micronesia, kava is likely to have been taken to a number of islands where it was unable to survive for any length of time. (The possible links between Ponape and Kosrae and other regions in which kava is used, and the botanical vulnerability of kava, are discussed in Chapter 4.)

The final comment that needs to be made at this point is that with the important exception of the southern New Guinea region, kava is found only among speakers of Oceanic languages or people in their close vicinity. The significance of this will also be discussed in the following chapters.

Kava and betel

Perhaps the most widely circulated belief about the traditional distribution of kava is that it was almost exclusive with the distribution of betel chewing. Recently this has been expressed by Marshall (1981: 146), Bellwood (1978: 139), and Burton-Bradley (1972: 66) among others, although the belief precedes the work of Rivers, who is usually thought to have been the first to give it currency[2] (see e.g. Christian 1897: 131; Brown 1908: 100).

However, although there are specific cases where kava and betel use appear to be mutually exclusive, the situation is rather more complex than the conventional wisdom allows. The boundary between kava and betel is

---

[1] As I will explain in the following chapter, at one stage kava may have been abandoned in a part of Tahiti. Nevertheless, my general point stands. The problem of the distribution of kava is essentially a Melanesian problem.

[2] Rivers actually realized that the two substances were not as mutually exclusive as had been supposed (1914, vol. 2: 243).

most clearly drawn in the Solomon Islands–Vanuatu region, yet even there the position is not unequivocal.

The international border between the two countries was the southern-most extension of betel use at the time of contact, although the Areca palm grows wild in many parts of Vanuatu, and *Piper betle* also grows wild in the northern islands (Somerville 1894: 380; Vincent Lebot, personal communi-cation)[1] and perhaps further south (see Chapter 4). If Kirch and Yen are correct in suggesting that small clumps of burnt lime found at early stages of the archaeological sequence on Tikopia indicate that betel use there has a considerable antiquity, the absence of betel chewing in Vanuatu cannot be explained by arguing that insufficient time had elapsed for diffusion to take place (1982: 37, 358).

While these points appear to provide support for the notion that kava and betel are mutually exclusive, it must be remembered that in the south-east Solomons – in Vanikoro, Utupua, Tikopia, Taumako, and Graciosa Bay on Santa Cruz Island – the two are, or were, both used (Davenport 1968: 214; Fox 1917: 190; Kirch and Yen 1982: 37, 52; Rivers 1914, vol. 2: 250). And although Fox unhesitatingly accepts the idea that kava disappeared once betel had been adopted in San Cristobal (1924: 216–17), the evidence from Eckardt suggests that the two were contemporaneous (1881: 349).

Betel was used throughout the kava-drinking areas in the Madang region and the Admiralties (Conton 1977: 37–8; Mager 1952: 85, 127; Miklouho-Maclay 1886a: 350; Riesenfeld 1947: 164–5, 181). But in parts of southern New Guinea the distribution of betel is patchy. People who are known to have used both kava and betel are the Gogodala, Samo, Masingle, the Wiram and – to a lesser extent – the Semariji and Gambadi, the Boazi speakers around Lake Murray, the Kanum Irebe, the Je-nan, the Marind-anim, the Sohur, and the Kolopom Islanders (Crawford 1981: 97; Shaw 1975: 249; Landtman 1927: 110; Williams 1936: 35, 425; Mark Busse, personal communication; Nevermann 1939: 13; van Baal 1982: 8; 1966: 22; Nevermann 1940: 179; Serpenti 1965: 51).

On the other hand, near neighbours of some of these people used kava but not betel: the Gebusi, the Kamula, the Keraki and some of their neighbours, and the Waidoro (Bruce Knauft, personal communication; Mike Wood, personal communication; Williams 1936: 425; Laba 1974: 6). Chalmers states that the Kiwai speakers living in the Fly estuary below Doumori Island did not chew betel nut (1903: 121), although Landtman says that both the Kiwai and the Maweata had learnt the use of betel from the Masingle but had generally abandoned it (1927: 110).

A current modification of the idea that kava and betel are mutually exclusive is the suggestion that in the places where both substances occur

[1] Codrington states that betel pepper 'grows naturally' in the New Hebrides and that Solomon Islanders on their way to Norfolk Island used to obtain it there (1891: 351).

they are 'used in quite distinct and separate contexts' (Marshall 1987: 16; see also Smith 1984: 5). Yet the available evidence from New Guinea indicates that this is not necessarily the case. Thus Miklouho-Maclay describes the usual course of a feast in Bongu as follows: 'first the drinking of *keu* [kava] . . . and for dessert there followed the chewing of betel nut and, finally, smoking' (1975: 196). A comment from Haddon seems to indicate that Gogodala men used both kava and betel together (1916: 150), although Crawford states that this was rare (1981: 97). And Serpenti writes that the Kolopom Islanders finish off a session of kava drinking 'with the inevitable chewing of betel' (1969: 34). Marshall does note Serpenti's observation, but without making any attempt to retract his general comment (1987: 48).

The problem of the relation between kava and betel is a complex one, and as the above discussion of the distribution of the two customs suggests, it may not be possible to make generalizations which apply to the Pacific as a whole. I will consider the question in more detail in Chapter 4.

3

Reconsidering Rivers' argument: the evidence

In this chapter and the one that follows I want to consider the most important question raised in Rivers' work: given the strange distribution of kava drinking, are we justified in concluding that at one stage it was used by many more Melanesian societies? I will consider four types of evidence relevant to this question: archaeological, botanical, linguistic and ethnological. Although no one piece of data could be said to establish an infallible case, taken as a whole the evidence shows that there are compelling grounds for believing that, in a number of areas of Melanesia, kava was once used and then abandoned before European contact. From this conclusion a number of important ethnological and anthropological problems arise.

Archaeological evidence

The presence of kava remains in a site located in an area where kava was not known to be drunk at any time during the post-contact period would obviously provide the firmest and most desirable evidence. Unfortunately, Pacific environments are generally unsuitable for the preservation of plant remains in archaeological contexts (Yen 1974: 27). Even pollen analysis offers very little prospect of providing relevant information, as the pollen of *Piper methysticum* is very small grained and difficult to identify (Jocelyn Powell, personal communication).

To the best of my knowledge, *Piper methysticum* is not present in the archaeological record in Melanesia. However, it has been found in sites in Hawaii and the Society Islands in Polynesia, and kava implements have been found in Kosrae in Micronesia (M. S. Allen 1984: 22; Sinoto 1983: 59, Cordy 1982: 131).

Neither the Kosraen nor the Hawaiian sites are of any use for our inquiry. In all but one of the sites, dates are not available. For the remaining site, Kalahuipua'a in Hawaii, the date range of AD 1500 to 1750 (Kirch 1979: 143) can add little to what is known from the ethnological record, as the extensive use of kava was reported by European visitors in the eighteenth century (Titcomb 1948: 123, 131, 134–5).

27

But the Vaito'otia site on Huahine Island in the Society group does offer relevant evidence. This site is extremely unusual for Oceania, as the waterlogged cultural layer contained a large amount of vegetal matter.[1] However, the dates obtained from this site present some difficulties. The earliest date obtained, AD 850±70, is from a whale bone which, as it comes from an arctic marine animal, may be unreliable and up to 300 years earlier than the actual date. Also, it is possible that the French nuclear testing programme in the eastern Tuamotus may have affected radiocarbon dates. Nevertheless, the dates from the vegetal matter clustered between AD 1000 and 1200, and typological comparisons of artefacts with those from other sites, indicate that it could not be more recent than 1350, although it is likely to have been considerably earlier (Sinoto 1983: 59).

The importance of this find is that it strongly indicates that the process of adopting kava could not have been a simple matter of knowledge diffusion, even in Polynesia. Ferdon suggests that kava may have been the last plant introduced into the Society Islands before European contact, and that it was 'certainly the last [introduced] into Tahiti . . . The active diffusion eastward to Tahiti was still going on as late as 1774–5' (1981: 184). He refers to the chief of one district on Tahiti as not having a single plant, whereas two years later there were large kava fields and a number of 'problem' drinkers among Tahitian chiefs. Even if the age of the Vaito'otia site is taken at the latest possible date, AD 1350, which is most unlikely, we are forced to accept that kava was used only 200 km from the main island of Tahiti at least 400 years before European contact (see also Emory 1979: 204, who thinks that even a date of 1270 is too late). Given what is known about inter-island voyaging and processes of diffusion in general, it is inconceivable that kava would ordinarily have taken so long to get from Huahine to Tahiti. The large post-contact plantations on Tahiti rule out any environmental impediments to growing *Piper methysticum*. We can only conclude either that kava was abandoned at one stage and later reintroduced just before the time of European contact, or else that there was a time when drastic steps were taken to restrict access to kava on Tahiti, possibly even to the extent of preventing it from being planted in certain regions.

Botanical evidence

One of the many criticisms that has been levelled at Rivers is that he ignored the botany of kava (Sterly 1967: 118). Yet when one looks at the confusion surrounding the topic, even at present, it is difficult to believe that Rivers would have been able to advance his argument had he tried to examine the

---

[1] Kirch has excavated a waterlogged Lapita site in the Mussau Islands which has yielded vegetal material, although analysis is not complete (Holly McEldowney, personal communication).

28

botanical evidence. There is uncertainty about the origin of the plant, about whether any genuinely wild specimens have ever been found, its relationship to other *Piper* species and the possibility of readily distinguishing it from these species, and even whether kava is everywhere made from only a single species. Most of these questions are interrelated.

Piper methysticum is a dioecious plant, i.e. the male and female reproductive organs are separated on different individuals. This means that isolated plants are unable to reproduce. Yet female plants are very rare, and none of those that have been found appear to be fertile.

Enquiries to the Botany Division of the New Zealand Department of Scientific and Industrial Research, the Rijksherbarium in Leiden, and the Lae Herbarium (PNG) uncovered the following female specimens: Conton 1 (from Madang Province, PNG), Forbes 495 MO (from Hawaii), Grant 4195 (from Tahiti), Schiefenhovel 39 (from Purari River, PNG), Schiefenhovel 155B (from Fly Province, PNG), CHR 169822 Sykes 623 (from Niue). But none of these specimens had fruits. Vincent Lebot, an agronomist formerly based in Vanuatu, who has been studying the botany of kava, has examined the collections in the Bishop Museum (Honolulu), the Kew Herbarium, the Muséum d'Histoire Naturelle (Paris), and the Singapore Botanical Garden, and was not able to find a single specimen with fruiting material. Furthermore, after a four-year investigation of *Piper methysticum* throughout Vanuatu, he found only one female specimen, and it too was sterile (personal communication).

Only four writers have described the fruit of *Piper methysticum* in the literature: Barrau (1957: 270), Cuzent (1860, cited in Lebot, Cabalion and Levesque n.d.: 2), Baker and Baker (1936) and Guillaumin (1938). The first two did not provide any herbarium identification numbers. The latter two reports are based on misidentifications, as Lebot, in collaboration with P. S. Green from the Kew Botanical Gardens, has been able to establish that the fruits were *Macropiper latifolium* and not *Piper methysticum* (Lebot, Cabalion and Levesque n.d.: 2).

Thus there are very strong grounds for believing that contemporary *Piper methysticum* can reproduce only vegetatively (Lebot, Cabalion and Levesque state that this is a certainty, ibid.). Given this, its presence over a wide area could be explained only in terms of two possibilities: it is a naturally occurring sterile hybrid of two other *Piper* species, or it is a sub-species which has become sterile as a result of the processes of human selection and development of specific mutations from a parent species.

I will consider the latter possibility first, as it is more straightforward. Both Vincent Lebot (personal communication) and Wee-Lek Chew (personal communication) believe that the most likely parent species is *Piper wichmannii* (see also Lebot, Cabalion and Levesque n.d.: 5). Its chemical composition is similar to that of *Piper methysticum*, and it is difficult to

29

distinguish between the physical form of the two plants (Sauer and Hansel 1967: 457; Lebot and Levesque n.d.).

If this really is the correct explanation, then the distribution of *Piper methysticum* could have come about only through human transport of the cuttings. But, at the very least, three of the kava-drinking regions, north New Guinea, south New Guinea, and south-east Solomons–Vanuatu, are too distantly separated – culturally and linguistically, as well as geographically – ever to have made direct contacts likely. Consequently, we would be justified in concluding that a number of people in the intervening areas would once have used kava and later abandoned it. In this case Rivers would have been correct.

But if *Piper methysticum* is a naturally occurring hybrid, the situation is far more complicated.

Although accounts from kava-drinking areas almost invariably state that *Piper methysticum* is a cultivated plant (e.g. Eisler 1979: 19; Knauft 1987: 82; Landtman 1927: 106; Miklouho-Maclay 1886a: 351; Nevermann 1938; Serpenti 1969: 32; Setchell 1924: 102; Smith 1943; Sterly 1967a: 100),[1] it has been reported as growing wild in many places where it is not drunk: New Ireland, New Britain, north-east New Guinea, south Papua and the Louisade Archipelago, Solomon Islands, and New Caledonia (Miklouho-Maclay 1886b: 694; Schumann and Lauterbach 1976, vol. 2: 238; Warburg 1890: 283; Miklouho-Maclay 1886a: 351; 1886b: 694; Bourgarel 1865: 403; Leenhardt 1946: 193). And about twenty years ago, a Tannese youth from the area in which I worked – who was studying at the Technical School in Honiara – found kava growing wild on Guadalcanal, and the drink he was able to prepare from it was indistinguishable from Tannese kava.

To the extent that they are accurate, these reports would be consistent with a situation where the natural hybridization of two closely related *Piper* species produced *Piper methysticum*. *Piper wichmannii* is an extremely strong contender as one of these species (Lebot, Cabalion and Levesque n.d.: 5). Other possible contenders are *Piper torricellense* which, according to Burkill, is said to be a possible substitute for *Piper methysticum* (1966: 1776, although he does not specify where; cf. Schumann and Lauterbach 1976, vol. 2: 240–1), and *Piper grandispicum*, which is the closest relative to *Piper wichmannii* (Chew 1972: 22). However, in a personal communication Wee-Lek Chew has stated he suspects that *Piper grandispicum*, which differs from *Piper wichmannii* only in the length of its inflorescence, may not be a separate species at all. This suspicion gains added support from Lebot's observations that the lengths of the inflorescences of *Piper wichmannii* and *Piper methysticum* vary considerably (n.d.: 7).

If natural hybridization occurred readily and frequently, *Piper methysti-*

---

[1] Hagen (1899: 199) stated that it was not cultivated in the Bogadjim area. Yet he is the only writer to make such a claim about a kava-using people.

cum could have been distributed over at least a substantial area of Melanesia without any human intervention, as *Piper wichmannii* is 'perhaps the commonest species of *Piper* in New Guinea and the Solomon Islands' (Chew 1972: 22). Yet there are two considerations which go against the possibility of easy and frequent hybridization. The first is that, if such hybridization is seriously proposed as a possibility, there must be field evidence to support it. But this does not exist, as hybridization has never been observed (Wee-Lek Chew, personal communication). The other is the unusual pattern of distribution of *Piper methysticum* in Melanesia. Other Melanesian *Pipers* are either localized or very widespread, and if those in the latter category are found in Papua New Guinea, they are also found throughout the western half of the island (Chew 1972; van Royen 1982: 1268–87). Yet, with the exception of the small kava-drinking area in the extreme south-east where *Piper methysticum* is known only as a cultivated plant, and one which does not grow easily (Nevermann 1938; van Baal 1982: 8), there are no reports of the plant being found in Irian Jaya.

Consequently, if *Piper methysticum* was produced as a result of natural hybridization, it is most likely to have been a process which would occur very infrequently and in a restricted range of environments. In this case, given that reports of *Piper methysticum* growing wild encompass a very wide area, many of these would refer to instances where it had either escaped from cultivation or persisted after previous cultivation, so it would seem justified to think that human intervention would have had to play a significant role in its present distribution. Thus, the fact that *Piper methysticum* was reported from many places where people are not known to have made any use of it would again provide grounds for believing that Rivers was right in suggesting that kava drinking disappeared from many Melanesian societies.

Yet unfortunately the matter is not so straightforward, and two crucial questions must be addressed: whether the reports of *Piper methysticum* growing wild are based on accurate identifications, and whether it is even possible for the plant to grow without cultivation.

How accurate are identifications of Piper methysticum?

An indication of the difficulty of relying even on expert identifications of *Piper methysticum* can be obtained from the experience Kirch and Yen had with specimens from Tikopia. The Tikopians stated that kava had become extinct, and only a wild type called *kavakava atua* remained, but that it was unsuitable for making kava. Yet botanists from both the Bishop Museum and the Solomon Islands Herbarium identified this plant as *Piper methysticum* (1982: 36). However, Doug Yen is not convinced that this identification is correct, and points out that the specimens originally had crinkles in

31

the leaves, but that these had been pressed out in the process of preparing them (personal communication). From his description, it is quite likely that the specimens were really *Piper wichmannii*, as crinkling of the leaves is common for this species (Vincent Lebot, personal communication). An even stronger case comes from Lebot's re-examination of purported specimens of *Piper methysticum* in the Kew Herbarium and the Muséum d'Histoire Naturelle. He found that a substantial number of specimens were either *Piper wichmannii* or *Micropiper latifolium* (personal communication).

Thus, reports by botanists of *Piper methysticum* growing wild in the distribution area of either *Piper wichmannii* or *Macropiper latifolium* have to be treated with extreme suspicion. It is only in New Caledonia that there would appear to be no danger of misidentification, as none of the *Piper* species which might be confused with *Piper methysticum* are to be found there. The only endemic *Piper* species there are either trees or vines, never shrubs (Lebot, personal communication). As Bourgarel's report of *Piper methysticum* growing wild in a number of places in New Caledonia is an early one, it is very unlikely to have been a post-contact introduction by other Pacific islanders (1865: 403).

Nevertheless, some of the early reports of wild kava in Melanesia were based on the identifications of mission assistants from kava-drinking islands (Miklouho-Maclay 1886a: 351; 1886b: 694). Yet even in such cases it is necessary to proceed with caution. In February 1986 I took a large branch of *Piper wichmannii* to Tanna, to test whether or not it would be identified as kava. I was able to show it to two groups of men before the specimen deteriorated; a group of three from the Bethel area of the west coast, and a group of eight from the Lomtihekel area of the central plateau. After examining the stem and the leaves, all the men, without exception, identified the specimen as kava. However, the men on the coast stated that it was a variety they did not know, while the inland group identified it as a 'two-day'[1] kava which, while not indigenous to Tanna, had been brought there from the north, and cultivated by a few men in other parts of the island.

Had I brought roots of *Piper wichmannii* to Tanna and a drink been prepared from them, it is very likely that the drinkers would have distinguished it from 'two-day' kava, as the roots are more fibrous, the taste is very bitter and unpleasant, and the effect is one of pronounced nausea. Nevertheless, in some parts of Pentecost, when there is insufficient kava for a large feast, people may fetch some *Piper wichmannii*, which is known as 'wild kava', from the bush and mix it in as a stretcher (Lebot, personal communication).

As early reports of wild kava in Melanesia are based on folk classifications

---

[1] So called because of its strength – the effects persist into the following day.

which will vary as to whether *Piper wichmannii* will be regarded as a variety of kava or as a separate species, and as there is no indication of the islands of origin of the mission assistants who claimed that kava was growing wild, we cannot place much faith on these native identifications either. We do not know whether any of them actually tried making a drink from the plant. Miklouho-Maclay quotes a letter from Revd Brown in relation to New Britain, New Ireland, and the Solomons: 'I got large roots of it, and natives from other islands said it was the true "Kava", but not being cultivated it was coarse, and as they soon began to use the Betel nut as the other natives, they did not use it' (1886b: 694). The coarseness of these roots increases the likelihood that they were *Piper wichmannii*.

Finally, it should be noted that *Piper methysticum* may not be the only species from which kava is made. Pierre Cabalion has told me that, according to the botanist David Frodin, the people in the Nomad area of Papua make kava from *Piper wichmannii*. This report may gain additional support from the fact that people in this area mix the ash of a palm with the kava to make it less bitter and more palatable, a practice which has not been reported from any other part of the Pacific (Knauft 1987: 83; Shaw 1981: 6).[1] Attention also needs to be drawn to Miklouho-Maclay's statement that the kava samples from the Maclay Coast had been identified as containing two separate species of *Piper*, neither of which was *Piper methysticum* (1886b: 688), although the circumstances under which this identification was made seem to leave some room for doubt.

Consequently, the only reports of *Piper methysticum* growing wild which can be treated with any degree of confidence are that of the youth who prepared a kava indistinguishable from the Tannese drink from the plant he found growing wild on Guadalcanal,[2] and the one from New Caledonia. But Vincent Lebot and Pierre Cabalion (personal communications) have warned that even the latter case should not be treated as being beyond question, as *Piper methysticum* is not mentioned in Guillaumin's synoptic flora of New Caledonia (1948).

Can Piper methysticum *survive without cultivation?*

There are a number of conflicting reports about the ability of *Piper methysticum* to grow without cultivation. If it can't, then we would have to reject even the two reports of wild *Piper methysticum* which I have suggested could be authentic.

[1] I should note that for at least two of the Nomad people, the Gebusi and the Samo, the plant from which kava is made is cultivated and not wild (Knauft 1987: 82; Shaw 1981: 6). It is not clear whether this is true also of other Nomad peoples.
[2] Another piece of evidence in favour of accepting this as a report of *Piper methysticum* is that the root of *Piper wichmannii* is a very deep yellow. While some of the 'two-day' varieties of northern Vanuatu have a similar colour, this is not true of any of the varieties of *Piper methysticum* indigenous to Tanna (Vincent Lebot, personal communication).

Degener wrote that although it was not common, in all the Hawaiian islands it 'persist[ed] after aboriginal cultivation in rich, wet forests and clearings' (1940). This has also been confirmed by Doug Yen (personal communication). Loeb states that although kava was no longer drunk by the people of Niue, the plant was apparently endemic, and was used to prepare the drink for those Europeans who desired it (1926: 172). In a personal communication Jack Keitade, the Aneityumese Assistant Curator of the Vila Cultural Centre, has described observing the process of self-propagation of *Piper methysticum* first planted in the early 1950s. Branches would fall over and a few would take root, so that thirty years later eleven plants had grown up around the original one. This can be compared to the process of cultivating kava in Rarotonga, where 'branches of the plant were bent over to root afresh' (Te Rangi Hiroa 1944: 18).

Although these accounts confirm that it is possible for *Piper methysticum* to survive and propagate without human intervention, this may be true only under certain conditions. Thus for the Tannese, the significance of the find of wild kava on Guadalcanal is that it was growing by itself, something that is said to be unknown on Tanna. I have already noted that in kava-using areas *Piper methysticum* is always a cultivated plant, rather than one taken from the wild. The people on Baluan say that unless kava is cultivated, it dies, a claim that is also made on Tikopia, with the added justification that kava has actually become extinct there (Wal Ambrose, personal communication; Doug Yen, personal communication: see also Kirch and Yen 1982: 36). But on the basis of available information, it is not possible to specify the kind of environments in which *Piper methysticum* can survive without cultivation, nor how frequently this can occur.

The above discussion indicates that, despite the unknowns, it is possible to make some reasonably confident suggestions. The question marks over the majority of the reports of wild *Piper methysticum*, the absence of any field evidence indicating the possibility of hybridization, and the admittedly weaker argument that its Melanesian distribution is unusual for a *Piper*, make it unlikely that *Piper methysticum* has been generated by the ready hybridization of two wide-ranging *Piper* species. It is true that the point about the unusual distribution could be rejected if one of the parent species occurred only in a narrowly circumscribed region, such as a small area of New Guinea or the Solomons. Both *Piper grandispicum* and *Piper torricellense* have a limited range, in the northern part of the island of New Guinea, and both are known by only a very small number of specimens (Wee-Lek Chew, personal communication; Queensland Herbarium, 1986; Schumann and Lauterbach 1976, vol. 2: 240–1). However, as I have already argued, if this were the case, human intervention would have been essential to account for the distribution of kava in the other parts of Melanesia.

34

On the other hand, there is the possibility, though very slight, that *Piper methysticum* might be a species which is produced only through very occasional hybridizations. Such rare hybridizations might be sufficient to account for its presence, without having to postulate human intervention, in the regions in which direct contacts between kava-using groups are extremely unlikely. Nevertheless, such an explanation could not account for the presence of *Piper methysticum* in New Caledonia, as none of the possible ancestors of the plant grow wild there. If Bourgarel and Leenhardt were correct in their reports, *Piper methysticum* could have been present there only as a consequence of human activity at some time in the past.

At this stage I believe that the botanical evidence does not enable us to specify the area of origin of *Piper methysticum* in other than broad terms. Insofar as the likelihood is very high that *Piper wichmannii* was an ancestor, the most we can say is that the area of origin would have been within the area of distribution of *Piper wichmannii*. This covers the whole Melanesian region to the north-west of central Vanuatu (Chew 1972: 22; Vincent Lebot, personal communication).

I must add, however, that this is not Lebot's view. After a trip in 1987 to Papua New Guinea to collect specimens he wrote to me, stating that he had visited the Trans-Fly area, the Maclay Coast, and Manus Province, and seen kava in all these places. He said that he had found four varieties, 'very degenerated dwarf plants which have to be tended, if not, they die'. Consequently he concluded that the plant had been introduced, and that the only possibility was Vanuatu. But while I would not quarrel with the statement that kava did not originate in any of the areas in Papua New Guinea where it is known at present, it does not follow that Vanuatu is the only alternative. It could also have originated in other parts of Papua New Guinea, or in the Solomons. There are no necessary reasons for thinking that kava would still have to be used at the time of European contact in the area where it was first domesticated; indeed, in terms of the argument I am developing, such a situation would be unlikely. I should also point out that Lebot may be wrong in thinking that only dwarf varieties of *Piper methysticum* exist in Papua New Guinea. Holly McEldowney has shown me a photo from Baluan Island in Manus Province of a kava plant well over two metres high.

Linguistic evidence

Linguistic data appear to offer some of the most striking support for Rivers' suggestions, although, as lexical items are more unstable and less resistant than other data, it is necessary to exercise caution. In order to facilitate the presentation of the relevant linguistic evidence, I have listed sets of apparent cognates[1] for the words used for kava in Tables 1–7. However, the underlying assumptions and the methods used to construct these tables require some comment.

It became clear, very early in my investigations, that terms used for kava were often applied to items which were seen as being similar in some ways. The precise boundaries of the semantic field thus defined are blurred. But the major items which are included appear to be *Piper betle* and other *Piper* species, areca nut, ginger and turmeric.[2] Alcohol is also included, although as it is a European introduction in all the Pacific islands, this fact is not relevant to our present task (Marshall 1976: 103). Some obvious examples occur in Samoan: kava = *'ava*, ginger (*Zingiber zerumbet* as well as other *Zingiberaceae*) = *'ava pui* (Parham 1972: 19–21); in Kamula: kava = *kawata*, *Piper betle* = *kawata ok oroma* ('chewing kava', Mike Wood, personal communication), and in the Lenakel language of Tanna: kava = *nikava*, alcohol = *nikava ituga* ('foreign kava', Lynch 1977: 75).

Such extensions and fluctuations in meaning are not surprising, and parallel Dutton's findings in a study of the words for garden items and garden food crops in Papua. Terms for crops which may be in competition with each other as a staple, or items associated with fostering or protecting the crops, are unstable. Terms for yams, taro, sweet potato, garden and fence may fluctuate between one item and another. Words for banana participate in this semantic field only in the few areas where bananas approach the position of a staple, and words for sugarcane never participate (1973).

The tables and the accompanying maps were prepared from a data base of 460 languages from Melanesia, Polynesia, and Micronesia. As these languages come from a number of Papuan phyla, as well as the Oceanic subgroup of the Austronesian family, and as I am interested in both direct and indirect inheritance, I used an inspection method to determine possible cognates (Sanders 1977: 33–4).

In a study of this kind, there are no easy solutions to the problem of determining whether two forms are possible cognates. Faced with a comparable problem in his study of Papuan word lists, Dutton treated two

(text continues p. 55)

[1] Strictly speaking, as David Walsh pointed out to me in his comments on an early version of this section, I should use the phrase 'form-plus-meaning resemblances' rather than 'cognates', as current practice among comparative linguists is to confine the latter to resemblances resulting from direct inheritance. Nevertheless, as 'form-plus-meaning resemblances' is awkward, I will continue to use the word 'cognates'. There is sufficient precedent for this use (see e.g. Dutton 1973). My usage is also consistent with Crystal's definition of cognate: 'a linguistic form which is historically derived from the same source as another . . . form' (1985: 53).

[2] There are a number of cases where the word for lime also appears to be cognate to words for betel pepper and/or areca nut, either in the same language or in nearby languages, particularly in the Madang region. However, I have not considered words for lime when selecting apparent cognates. In a study of this sort it is far wiser to err on the side of caution, and so I have limited the semantic field to narrower boundaries than the data might seem to allow.

Table 1   *Kava cognates, Set 1 (see Maps 5 and 6)*

Word/plant/people[a]	Reference	Justification/notes[b]
kava K, Mangareva	Te Rangi Hiroa 1938: 439	Expected reflex of PPN **kawa*, Pawley and Green 1971: 9; B: 709.
'awa K, Hawaii	Titcomb 1948: 105	Expected reflex of PPN **kawa*, B: 709.
'ava K, Samoa	Te Rangi Hiroa 1930: 147	Expected reflex of PPN **kawa*, B: 708.
kava K, Tonga	Churchward 1959: 257	Expected reflex of PPN **kawa*, B: 709.
nikava K, Lenakel	Lynch 1977: 75	'ni' an accretion, Lynch 1978a: 757. However, '*kava*' is not an expected reflex of POC **kawa*, Pawley and Green 1973: 32; POC **w → w*, 0 in Lenakel, T: 34. This suggests that the word has been borrowed.
nagave K, Sie	Capell and Lynch 1983: 88	k/g, Lynch 1978a: 742; T: 17, 489, -a/-e, T: 224, 359, 374.
gea K, Mota	Codrington and Palmer 1896: 23	Possible reflex of POC **kawa* in Volow dialect from adjacent island of Motlav, Pawley 1972: 27–9. 'g' almost certainly a voiced velar fricative (see Lester 1941–2: 105–6).
gi K, Torres Islands	Durrad 1940–1: 107	Possible reflex of POC **kawa* (if 'i' really 'ə'). T: 11, 27, 35.
hai K, Malo	Bob Rubinstein p.c.	Possible reflex of POC **kawa*, T: 13, 29, 37, although the final vowel is unexplained.
'awa'awa K, Arosi	Fox 1978: 19	Expected reflex of POC **kawa*, T&H: 83, 103, 107.
kakawa K, 'Are'are	Geerts 1970: 47	*kawa* possible reflex of POC **kawa*, T&H: 83, 103, 107. CV-/CVCV- (e.g. ka-/kaka-), T&H: 104, 197, 205.
ba'enakakawa K, Arosi	Fox 1978: 86	A different variety of *P. methysticum*, also drunk.
kava-qwua O, Maringe	Altschul 1973: 43	The phonetic value of the second part is uncertain.
kua B, Vaturanga (Ndi)	Ivens 1940: 14	POC **w → u* common in Guadalcanal.
kukukua O, Bausa	Hoogland 4445 (Specimen label, National Herbarium of Victoria)	*P. wichmannii*, Chew 1972: 23. Bausa is the name of a group of Miniafia speakers near Tufi, Dutton 1971: 30.
kalava O, Tubetube	M. Macintyre p.c.	Macintyre thinks this could be *P. methysticum*, but is not certain. It is common throughout the area, and could be *P. wichmannii*. 'al' could be an infix. It is also possible that the form is related to Set 2, and was created by the fusion of two forms in order to distinguish a particular variety.
kalva A, Santa Cruz	T&H: 206	Also see Set 2.
kilawa O, Sinasina	Hide *et al.* 1979: 60	v/w common, e.g. C: 866; DB: 164; S: 166; DC: 426, 433. Also see Set 2.
arava B, Mailu	Saville 1959: 6	Leaf of *Piper betle*. k-/0 common, e.g. DB: 162–5, 173. Also see Set 2.
hava A, Koiari	Dutton 1969: 125	k-/h-, DB: 165; DT: 75, 86.
haga A, Koita	Dutton 1975: 373	v/g, DC: 428, 433, and T. Dutton p.c.

Table 1 (*cont.*)

Word/plant/people[a]	Reference	Justification/notes[b]
ha A, Aomie	Dutton 1969: 125	
awaka B, Bush Mekeo	Mosko 1985: 253	Expected reflex of POC *kawa*, with final CV a probable affix, A. Jones p.c.
awaha B, Roro	A. Jones p.c.	As above.
afa'a B, Mekeo	M. Stephen p.c.	As above.
kawata K, Kamula	M. Wood p.c.	-t-/-h-, Bluhme 1970: 867; DT: 88; R: 20. t/k, W: 36; F&V: 158, 161. See also set 1C.
wakoto B, Gogodala	Baldwin n.d.	Possible metathesis. o/a, R: 16, 20, 26.
Kewato K, Lake Kutubu	Williams 1976: 285	One of the names of the man from whose body *Piper methysticum* grew. Plant used in ritual, but kava not drunk. e/a, F&V: 170, 171, 172.
gowi K, Gebusi	Knauft 1987: 82	k-/g-, R: 13, 16, 25. i/a, R: 12, 23; F&V: 169, 179. -a-/-o-, R: 16, 20; DC: 440, 472.
ikawati K, Bamol, Kolopom Is.	Serpenti 1965: 49	Variety of kava.
ka K, Kanum Irebe	N: 184	
kavavar G, Tolai	Beaumont 1979: 29	
kamavar G, Mioko	ibid.	m/v (or w) does not appear to be very common in Oceanic languages. In Tolai *kavavar* [*kawawara*] and *kamavar* [*kamawara*] are two different species of ginger. This may explain the Mioko word. v ~ w, Beaumont 1972: 28.
kavurua A, Lemeris	Riesenfeld 1947: 183	a/u, Lithgow and Claassen 1968: Chart 3.
kau K, Baluan	H. McEldowney p.c.	aw/au, S&Z: 131, 182, 192.
kuwa K, Baluan	H. McEldowney p.c.	This is a variety of kava. a/u, S&Z: 135, 211, 214.
ka K, Lou	Parkinson 1907: 303	
sakau K, Ponape	McGrath 1973: 64	
saka K, Kosrae	Cordy 1982: 131	
kau K, Bilbil	M-M: 175	
kau A, Bongu	Za: 52	
kaw A, Male	Za: 52	-au/-aw, Za: 36, 59, 93.
aw A, Kambot	L	
ʌwʌs A, Angaua	Zd: 26	s/0, Zc: 48/Zd: 24; Zc: 24, 45, 84. ʌ/a common, e.g. Zd: 12, 13, 29.
keuva K, Yangulam	M-M: 182	'eu' seems to occur infrequently in Rai Coast languages, aV/eV, Za: 14, 49, 81, 150.
keu K, Bongu	M: 5	-va/0 or -wa/0, Za: 15, 55; Zc: 24.
ka A, Danaru	Za: 52	-au/-a, Za: 42, 61, 111.
kaur B, Kamba	Zc: 53	-r/0, Za/Zc: 90; Zc: 77, 116.
aur̄ B, Garuh	Zc: 53	k-/0 common, e.g. Zc: 61, 66, 134. r/r̄, Zc: 90, 99, 124.
ɛur B, Gal	Zc: 53	ɛu/au, Za: 150, 152; Zc: 68, 122.
uwi B, Pay	Zb: 53	aw-uw, Za/Zb: 55; Zb: 107, 153. -a/-i, Zb: 71, 75; Zc: 24, 58.
ku:wiza B, Amaimon	Zb: 53	k-/0 common, e.g. Zb: 51, 59, 62. Possibly also related to Set 3.
kawaŋ A, Bungain	L	
uwaken A, Muniwara	L	a/u, Wilson 1976: 57, 70.

uwawo O, One	Darbyshire and Hoogland 8254 (specimen label, Australian National Herbarium)	*Piper gibbilimbum*, Chew 1972: 23.

Abbreviations:

Plants: K; kava or *Piper methysticum*; B, *Piper betle*; O, other or unspecified *Piper* species; A, areca palm or fruit; G, ginger.

References: B, Biggs 1978; C, Cochran 1978; DB, Dutton 1982b; DC Dutton 1973; DT, Dutton 1982a; F&V, Franklin and Voorhoeve 1973; L, Laycock 1984; M, Mager 1952; M-M, Miklouho-Maclay 1951; N, Nevermann 1938; p.c., personal communication; R, Reesink 1976; S, Scott 1978; S&Z, Smythe and Z'graggen 1975; T, Tryon 1976; T&H, Tryon and Hackman 1983; W, Wurm 1982; Za . . . Zd, Z'graggen 1980a, 1980b, 1980c, 1980d.

Linguistic conventions: C, consonant; V, vowel; *, reconstructed form; ~, allophones of a single phoneme; /, probable or known corresponding phonemes in different languages; POC, Proto-Oceanic; PPN, Proto-Polynesian.

[a] Underlining identifies those parts of possible multi-morphemic words – perhaps created initially in order to distinguish perceived varieties or subspecies – which could be cognate with other words in the set.

[b] Reference to the evidence used to justify inclusion of specific items.

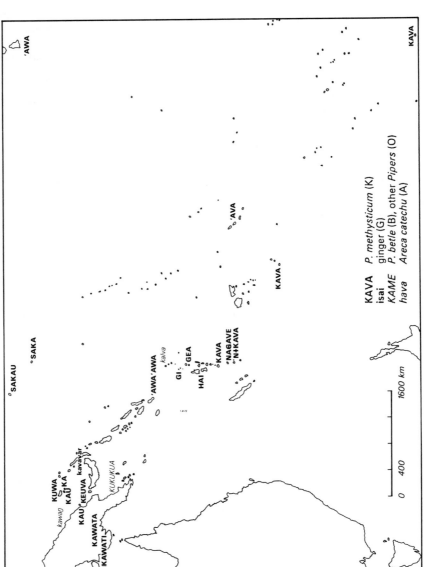

Map 5 *Kava cognates, Set 1: Pacific. See Table 1*

KAVA *P. methysticum* (K)
isai   ginger (G)
KAME *P. betle* (B), other *Pipers* (O)
hava   *Areca catechu* (A)

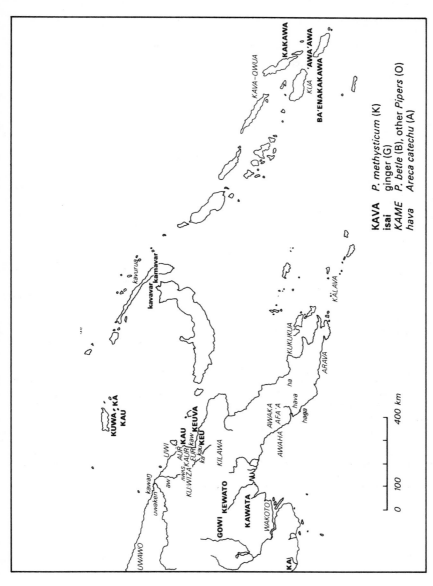

Map 6 *Kava cognates, Set 1: Papua New Guinea and Solomon Islands. See Table 1*

Table 2   *Kava cognates, Set 1a (see Map 7)*

This set may well be related to Set 1 (Table 1) through *keuva* as k-/0 is common, e.g. Za: 20, 54; Zc: 38, 85; eu/ei, Za: 23, 43. However, I have kept this set separate as some elements outside the Madang area appear problematical.

Word/plant/people[a]	Reference	Justification/notes[b]
eiv K, Amele	M: 5	
eti K, Garuh	M: 5	-v/0, Zc: 42, 89, 94.
gei A, Erima	Za: 52	k-/g-, Za: 21, 23, 58. g-/0, Za: 57; Zc: 70, 112.
ai K, Ham	M: 5	ei/ai, Za: 38, 81; Zc: 68.
aio K, Suroi	M-M: 175	-o/0, Za: 45, 58, 73.
aiu K, Gedaged	M: 5	-0/-u, Za: 42, 45; Zc: 46.
kaiyu K, Kolom	M-M: 183	
kaj K, Ganglau	M: 5	-u/0, Za: 75, 84, 90. i/j, M: 4, 5, 342. Cf. M: 115.
haia G, Kove	Counts 1969: 40	k-/h- common, e.g. Za: 48, 71; Zc: 109, 112. -u/-a, Z1: 71; Za: 1, 75.
aju K, Bilbil	M: 5	
ju B, Rerau	Za: 52	a-/0, Za: 29, 49, 61.
yo B, Male	Za: 52	j-/y-, Za: 34, 108. Male j~y, Za: viii.
yau B, Bongu	Za: 52	-o/-au, Za: 22, 28, 56.
yai B, Faita	Zd: 27	au/ai, Zc: 18, 61, 100.
kayawali B, Angoram	L	j~y common, see e.g. Zb: viii–ix; Zc: ix. i/y, Za: 70; Zb: 55; Zc: 41. See also Set 1c.
ay A, Autu	L	
oyo K, Samo	Shaw 1981: 4	o/a, C&D: 30, 32; D&T&T: 151, 152.

Abbreviations:

Plants: K, kava or *Piper methysticum*; B, *Piper betle*; A, areca palm or fruit; G, ginger.

References: C&D, Conrad and Dye 1975; D&T&T, Dye, Townsend and Townsend 1968; L, Laycock 1984; M, Mager 1952; M-M, Miklouho-Maclay 1951; Z1, Z'graggen 1971; Za . . . Zd, Z'graggen 1980a, 1980b, 1980c, 1980d.

Linguistic conventions: V, vowel; ~, allophones of a single phoneme; /, probable or known corresponding phonemes in different languages.

[a] Underlining identifies those parts of possibly multi-morphemic words – perhaps created initially in order to distinguish perceived varieties or subspecies – which could be cognate with other words in the set.

[b] Reference to the evidence used to justify inclusion of specific items.

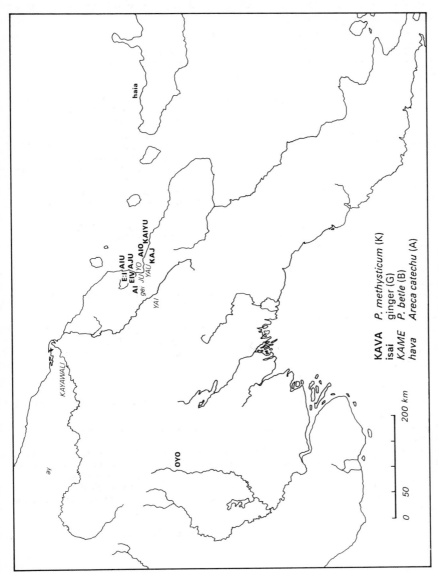

haia

KAYAWALI

ay

OVO

E:IˈAIU
EIVˈAJU
AI gei JUˈYO AIO KAIYU
YAUˈ   KAJ

YAI

KAVA	P. methysticum (K)
isai	ginger (G)
KAME	P. betle (B)
hava	Areca catechu (A)

0   50   200 km

Map 7   *Kava cognates, Set 1a: New Guinea. See Table 2*

Table 3   *Kava cognates, Set 1b (see Map 8)*
The acceptance of this set as belonging to set 1 (Table 1) depends on the likelihood of m/w. This does occur occasionally in Madang area languages, e.g. Za: 29, 67; Zb: 58, 67; Zc: 19, 32; and in the Kiwai languages, e.g. F: 566–7, Items 10, 27, 46.

Word/plant/people	Reference	Justification/notes[a]
gamada, gamoda K, Kiwai	Landtman 1927: 106; Haddon 1916: 147–9	
komata K, Mawata	Beardmore 1890: 460	k-/g-, DC: 431; R: 25; Ray 1923: 350. t/d, DC: 431, 445; R: 23, F: 570 (Item 9). -a-/-o-, R: 16, 20; DC: 441, 472.
komeda T, Gogodala	Baldwin n.d.	e/a, VO: 1256; R: 16, 23.
gemina G, Kasua	Freund 1977: 296	-t-/-n-, F: 566–8 (Item 19); F&V: 170, 177, 180. d/n, R: 14; W: 90. o/e, R: 20, 22, 23. -e-/-i-, F&T: 47; VO: 1256; R: 12; DC: 445.
kameŋ G, Mid-Waghi	Ramsey 1975: 101	n/ŋ, W: 36; CA: 199.
komiŋ T, Boiken	Gerstner 1954: 463	Gerstner says this is ginger, but it is more probably turmeric. See Sterly 1967b: 239.
kame B, Masingle	Landtman 1927: 110	
kumokɔ A, Kamula	M. Wood p.c.	-u-/-a-, R: 16; F&V: 171, 177, 178. -t-/-k-, W: 36. F&V: 158, 161.
kamak, G, Asmat	Voorhoeve 1965: 329	
kumak G, Telefolmin	Healey and Healey 1977: 112	
kamuk G, Mianmin	D. Gardner p.c.	
kamura B, Sileibi	Zd: 27	n/r, F&V: 169; D&T&T: 149. k/r, W: 88; DC: 437; CA: 199.
gamura B, Paynamar	Zd: 27	k-/g-, Zd: 8, 12, 30.
amurʌpʌ B, Ikundun	Zd: 27	k-/0, Zd: 25, 40, 52. 0/pV, Zd: 29, 42, 43. a/ʌ common, e.g. Zd: 24, 39, 40.
kamʌrʌb B, Pila	Zb: 53	-p/-b common, e.g. Zb: 18, 87, 92.
kʌmoːr B, Musak	Zd: 27	
kamor B, Usino	Za: 53	
kamo A, Langam	L	

Abbreviations:
Plants: K, kava or *Piper methysticum*; B, *Piper betle*; A, areca palm or fruit; G, ginger; T, turmeric.
References: CA, Capell 1951–2; DC, Dutton 1973; D&T&T, Dye, Townsend and Townsend 1968; F, Franklin 1973; F&T, Fleischmann and Turpeinen 1976; F&V, Franklin and Voorhoeve 1973; L, Laycock 1984; p.c., personal communication; R, Reesink 1976; VO, Voorhoeve 1970; W, Wurm 1982; Za . . . Zd: Z'graggen 1980a, 1980b, 1980c, 1980d.
Linguistic conventions: V, vowel; /, probable or known corresponding phonemes in different languages.

[a] Reference to the evidence used to justify inclusion of specific items.

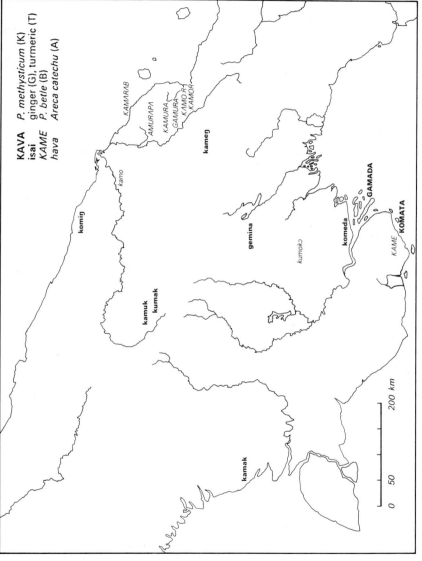

Map 8 *Kava cognates, Set 1b: New Guinea. See Table 3*

KAVA   *P. methysticum* (K)
isai   ginger (G), turmeric (T)
KAME   *P. betle* (B)
hava   *Areca catechu* (A)

komig

kamuk
kumak

kamak

KAMARAB

kamo

AMURAPA
KAMURA
GAMURA
KAMORI
KAMOR

kameg

gemina

kumoko

komeda

GAMADA

KAME
KOMATA

0   50   200 km

Table 4   *Kava cognates, Set 1c (see Map 9)*

This set could be related to Set 1 through the transformation of the final CV of the forms of the westernmost Oceanic languages in Papua from *ka* to *ta* (see Table 1 above). Alternatively, it could have come about through the fusion of a *kawa* form with a *wat*V form, possibly to distinguish a variety.

Word/plant/people[a]	Reference	Justification/notes[b]
ikawati K, Bamol, Kolopom Is.	Serpenti 1965: 49	Variety of kava.
wati K, Marind-Anim	van Baal 1966: 20	
tigwa K, Bamol, Kolopom Is.	Serpenti 1965: 49	Possible metathesis of *wati*.
tiguar A, Dorro	Ray 1923: 347	
wariki K, Kiwai	Landtman 1927: 106	-t-/-r-, DC: 461, 464, 471.
kawata K, Kamula	M. Wood p.c.	a/i, R: 12, 20, 23; DC: 453.
Kewato K, Lake Kutubu	Williams 1976: 285	This and the following word are the names of the man from whose body *Piper methysticum* grew.
Waki K, Lake Kutubu	ibid.	a/o, R: 8, 9, 12. -t-/-k-, W: 36. F&V: 158, 161.
wati K, Boazi	M. Busse p.c.	
woti O, Pare	Skingle 1970: 224	-a-/-o-, R: 16, 20; DC: 440, 472.
wet O, Telefolmin	Healey and Healey 1977: 195	-e-/-a-, DC: 449, 461; W: 90.
wɛr B, Chenapien	L	t/r, FO: 216; W: 90; V1: 68, 99.
wari B, Namie	L	
wariŋ A, Urim	L	
weti A, Daonda	L	a/e, C&D: 30; V1: 98, 99, 100.
wuti A, Simog	L	e/u, C&D: 32; V1: 98, 99, 104.
watei A, Imonda	L	
wairi B, Simog	L	
wa're'na A, Armatti	Stokhof 1983: 82	
oe'war're A, Sewan	ibid.: 100	
wasim A, Sawe (Uria)	ibid.: 119	
wəsi A, Puare	L	t/s, C&D: 30; D&T&T: 149; FO: 216. r/s, FO: 216.
wasip B, Aiku	L	
wasəm B, Kayik	L	
wasɔ B, Alu	L	
wɔsup B, Kombio	L	
wasow A, One	L	
kwas B, Kwanga	L	'k' a possible accretion. w-/kw-, Zd: 35.
kwasi A, Boiken	L	
ŋgaŋakwasi B, Abelam	L	
kwosh B, Kwoma	Bowden 1983: 160	
wɔra B, Kalou	L	a/ɔ, C&D: 30
kayawali B, Angoram	L	r/l, FO: 216; D&T&T: 149; W: 36.
watyip B, Mt Arapesh	L	
warak B, Kis	L	
arakʌy B, Ukuriguma	Zb: 53	w/0, Zb: 1, 22, 76, 111.

b∧ri A, Moere	Zb: 52	w~b, Zb: ix; Zc: ix; w-/b-, Zb/Zc: 51; Zc: 37. -a-/-∧- common, e.g. Zb: 41, 56, 98.
p∧ri A, Bepour	Zb: 52	b-/p-, Zb: 73, 100, 106.

Abbreviations:

Plants: K, kava or *Piper methysticum*; B, *Piper betle*; O, other or unspecified *Piper* species; A, areca palm or fruit.

References: C&D, Conrad and Dye 1975; DC, Dutton 1973; D&T&T, Dye, Townsend and Townsend 1968; FO, Foley 1986; F&V, Franklin and Voorhoeve 1973; L, Laycock 1984; p.c., personal communication; R, Reeskink 1976; V1, Voorhoeve 1971; W, Wurm 1982; Zb . . . Zd: Z'graggen 1980b, 1980c, 1980d.

Linguistic conventions: C, consonant; V, vowel; ~, allophones of a single phoneme; /, probable or known corresponding phonemes in different languages.

[a] Underlining identifies those parts of possibly multi-morphemic words – perhaps created initially in order to distinguish perceived varieties or subspecies – which could be cognate with other words in the set.

[b] Reference to the evidence used to justify inclusion of specific items.

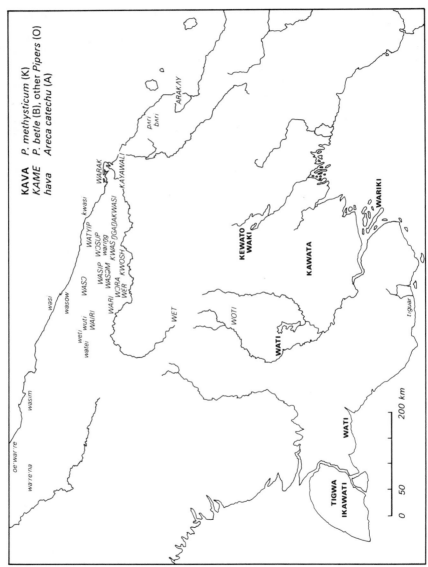

KAVA *P. methysticum* (K)
KAME *P. betle* (B), other *Pipers* (O)
hava *Areca catechu* (A)

oe·wa·re
wa·re·na
wasim
wasi
wasow
weti
watei wuti
WAIRI
WASƆ
WASIP WƆSUP
WASƆM waring
WARI KWAS ŊGAƊAKWASI
WƆRA KWOSH
WER KWOSH
WATYIP
kwasi
WARAK
KAYAWALI
pari
bari
ARAKAY
WET
WOTI
KEWATO
WAKI
KAWATA
WARIKI
WATI
TIGWA
IKAWATI
WATI
t·guar

0   50   200 km

Map 9   *Kava cognates, Set 1c: New Guinea. See Table 4*

Table 5 *Kava cognates, Set 2 (see Map 10)*

Word/plant/people[a]	Reference	Justification/notes[b]
kial K, Male	M-M: 182–3	
kial' K, Bom	ibid.	
bala u'kili' K, Jabem	Zahn 1982: 27	ia/a, Za: 44; Zb/Zc: 62, 85.
kalimu A, Bwaidoga	Jenness and Ballantyne 1928: 395	
kalava O, Tubetube	M. Macintyre p.c.	-ai-/-a-, Zb: 29, 44, 81, 138.
kala B, Halia	Allen *et al.* 1982: 140	
kalva A, Santa Cruz	T&H: 206	
kaula A, Tikopia	ibid.	
kilawa O, Sinasina	Hide *et al.* 1979: 60	
arava B, Mailu	Saville 1959: 6	Leaf of *P. betle*. k/0 common, DB: 162–5, 173. l/r common, C: 866; DB: 161–2.
gila B, Mailu	ibid.	Catkin of *P. betle*. k-/g-, DB: 163–4; C: 866.

Abbreviations:
Plants: K, kava or *Piper methysticum*; C, *Piper betle*; O, other or unspecified *Piper* species; A, areca palm or fruit.
References: C, Cochran 1978; DB, Dutton 1982b; M-M, Miklouho-Maclay 1951; p.c., personal communication; T&H, Tryon and Hackman 1983; Za . . . Zc, Z'graggen 1980a, 1980b, 1980c.
Linguistic convention: /, probable or known corresponding phonemes in different languages.

[a] Underlining identifies those parts of possibly multi-morphemic words – perhaps created initially in order to distinguish perceived varieties or subspecies – which could be cognate with other words in the set.
[b] Reference to the evidence used to justify inclusion of specific items.

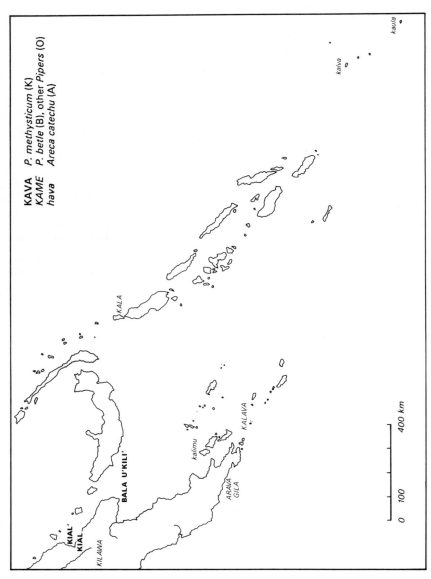

KAVA *P. methysticum* (K)
KAME *P. betle* (B), other *Pipers* (O)
hava *Areca catechu* (A)

KILAWA
KIAL'
KIAL'

BALA U'KILI'

ARAVA
GILA
kalimu

KALAWA

KALA

kaiva

kaula

0   100   400 km

Map 10 *Kava cognates, Set 2: Papua New Guinea and Solomon Islands. See Table 5*

Table 6   *Kava cognates, Set 3 (see Map 11)*

Word/plant/people[a]	Reference	Justification/notes[b]
kisa K, Usino	E. Henty p.c.	
isa K, Sumau (Garia)	Lawrence 1984: 224	k-/0 common, e.g. Za: 20, 54, 68.
hasabi G, Boiken	Gerstner 1954: 463	k-/h- common, e.g. Za: 37, 48; Zb: 59. a/i, Zb: 38, 90; Zd: 15, 20.
kʌːza A, Kare	Zc: 52	s~z, Zc: viii, ix; -s-/-z-, Zc: 35, 67. ʌ/a common, e.g. Zc: 38, 41, 42.
kuːwiza B, Amaimon	Zb: 53	
asa A, Murupi	Zc: 52	i-/a-, Za/Zc: 45; Zc: 22, 59, 73.
ise K, Erima	M-M: 182–3	-e/-a, Za: 40, 48, 49, 78.
kase A, Samosa	Zc: 52	
gwa asa G, Jabem	Zahn 1982: 171	Variety of ginger, used for divination.
isai G, Waffa	Stringer and Hotz 1979: 463	A wild ginger. -a/-ai, Za/Zc: 67; Zc: 50, 68, 100.
asama G, Waffa	ibid.	A variety of ginger.
kasa kasam G, Wantoat	Davis 1968: 47	A small, hot variety of ginger.
isat A, Wantoat	ibid.: 42	
asiva A, Rotokas	Firchow *et al.* 1973: 8	
kasi A, Kunabena	Lanyon-Orgill 1950: 61	
kasu A, Varisi	ibid.	

Abbreviations:
Plants: K, kava or *Piper methysticum*; B, *Piper betle*; A, areca palm or fruit; G, ginger.
References: M-M, Miklouho-Maclay 1951; p.c., personal communication; Za . . . Zc, Z'graggen 1980a, 1980b, 1980c.
Linguistic conventions: ~, allophones of a single phoneme; /, probable or known corresponding phonemes in different languages.

[a] Underlining identifies those parts of possibly multi-morphemic words – perhaps created initially in order to distinguish perceived varieties or subspecies – which could be cognate with other words in the set.
[b] Reference to the evidence used to justify inclusion of specific items.

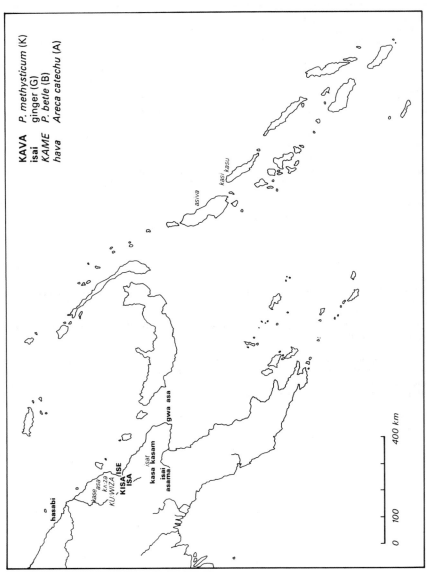

KAVA   *P. methysticum* (K)
isai   ginger (G)
KAME   *P. betle* (B)
hava   *Areca catechu* (A)

kasu

kasi

asiva

hasabi

kasa asa

KUWIZA

kasa

KISA

ISE

ISA

isai

isat

kasa kasam

isai/
asama

gwa asa

400 km

0   100

Map 11   *Kava cognates, Set 3: Papua New Guinea and Solomon Islands. See Table 6*

Table 7   *Kava cognates, Set 4 (see Map 12)*

Word/plant/people[a]	Reference	Justification/notes[b]
kurar K, Keraki	Williams 1936: 427	
koriar K, Ngowugar	N: 182	-u-/-o-, DC: 440, 464; Ray 1923: 350, 351.
kerear K, Mani	N: 184	-o-/-e-, F&T: 50, 51, 52. ia/ea, DC: 448, 472; F: 569/70 (Item 56).
kerakerar G, Miriam	J. Beckett p.c.	
kerəkerə G, Mabuiag	J. Beckett p.c.	
kuraka K, Bamol, Kolopom Is.	Serpenti 1965: 49	Variety of kava. -e-/-u-, Ray 1923: 347, 350: DC: 457.
kurua A, Bamu Kiwai	Ray 1913–14: 30	a/ua, DC: 426; F: 566/71 (Item 72), 566/7 (Item 92).
gore A, Island Kiwai	Ray 1923: 351	k-/g-, DC: 427, 431, 518; R: 25.
keroaro O, Waragu	Schiefenhovel 1970: 80	
kerare K, Daribi	Wagner 1972: 153	Used ritually, not drunk.
ankə̆rə A, Angaathiha	Huisman and Lloyd 1981: 67	
kurukiira A, Waffa	Stringer and Hotz 1979: 317	Wild areca palm.
kere kere O, Maring	Rappaport 1984: 272	
ɛrɛ A, Anaberg	CA: 201	k-/0, CA: 200, 204, 205. e/ɛ, CA: 199, 200.
karaŋimi K, Gende	Aufenanger and Höltker 1940: 101	Plant used medicinally, not drunk. -e-/-a-, W: 86, 89; Za: 75; Zd: 39.
karia A, Faita	Zd: 26	
kʌːre A, Musak	Zd: 26	a/ʌ common, e.g. Zd: 8, 24, 25.
hare sibi B, Bun	L	k-/h- common, e.g. Za: 37, 48; Zb: 59, 63. See also Z1: 91.
mpaŋkare A, Iatmul	Staalsen 1962: 78	
kora-uru B, Namau	Ray 1913–14: 59	
heheri A, Orokolo	Ray 1913–14: 30	k-/h-, DT: 75, 86.
haga kare B, Koita	Dutton 1975: 373	-o-/-a-, F: 581 (Items 11, 25, 80), 582/3 (Item 78).

Abbreviations:

Plants: K, kava or *Piper methysticum*; B, *Piper betle*; O, other or unspecified *Piper* species; A, areca palm or fruit; G, ginger.

References: CA, Capell 1951–2; DC, Dutton 1973; DT, Dutton 1982a; F, Franklin 1973; F&T, Fleischmann and Turpeinen 1976; L, Laycock 1984; N, Nevermann 1938; p.c. personal communication; R, Reesink 1976; W, Wurm 1982; Z1, Z'graggen 1971; Za, Zb, Zd, Z'graggen 1980a, 1980b, 1980d.

Linguistic convention: /, probable or known corresponding phonemes in different languages.

[a] Underlining identifies those parts of possibly multi-morphemic words – perhaps created initially in order to distinguish perceived varieties or subspecies – which could be cognate with other words in the set.

[b] Reference to the evidence used to justify inclusion of specific items.

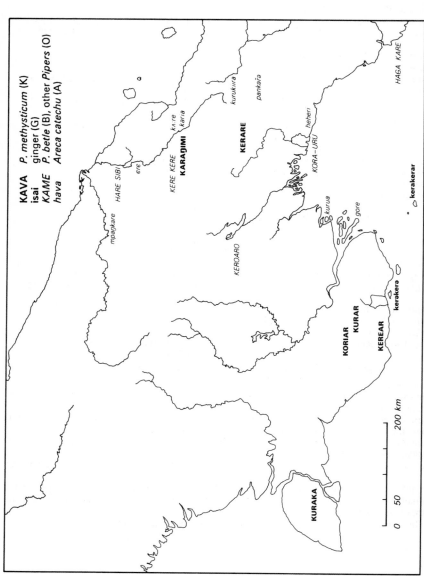

KAVA P. methysticum (K)
isai ginger (G)
KAME P. betle (B), other Pipers (O)
hava Areca catechu (A)

mpaŋkare

HARE SIBI

ere

KEROARO

KERE KERE   kꭤre
             karia

KARADJIMI

kurukirra

pankarã

KERARE

heheri

KORA-URU

kurua

kerakerar

gore

KORIAR

KURAR

KEREAR

kerakera

KURAKA

HAGA KARE

0   50   200 km

Map 12 *Kava cognates, Set 4: New Guinea. See Table 7*

forms as apparently cognate 'if corresponding sounds in forms with the same meaning differed from one another in no more than one of the following respects: (a) for consonants: point and manner of articulation; (b) for vowels: tongue height and forward or back position' (1973: 420). Minor modifications of sounds such as devoicing were ignored and absence of a sound was counted as only one difference. In words of more than two syllables the rules were relaxed for the last syllable.

Yet, although Dutton's work served as a stimulus to my own attempt to use lexical data, his method, while rigorous, is extremely liberal (Saunders 1977: 35). For this study it was necessary to adopt far stricter criteria for acceptance. Dutton was dealing with a narrower geographical range of occurrence and a larger number of items, as well as with items that are generally more likely to appear on word lists than the ones I was dealing with. (The word for areca nut is a possible exception.) Furthermore, he was dealing with a different kind of question from that with which I am concerned, and the effect on his conclusions of wrongly accepting two forms as cognate would not have been as damaging as would be the case in my work.

I was concerned only with finding apparent cognates for terms used for kava. I started by examining the word lists for kava, and then I proceeded to the lists for areca nut, *Piper betle* and other *Piper* species, ginger and turmeric, using the same criteria as those used by Dutton to establish initial sets of possible cognates. However, once these had been established, I examined available word lists for dialects, closely related languages, or geographically close languages to look for possible sound correspondences, choosing as evidence only those cases where there appeared to be no doubt that the forms were cognates. Where possible, I used examples from both basic and cultural vocabulary, in order to make it more likely that correspondences arising out of both direct inheritance and borrowing would be included. I also referred to sound correspondences which had already been established by linguists. Items from the initial cognate sets were retained if there was strong evidence that appropriate correspondences existed in groups of languages which either were related to the one from which an item under consideration was taken, or could have been feasible sources of borrowing. In those cases where information from relevant languages was not available, evidence that the appropriate correspondences occurred in a reasonable number of languages in the general region was regarded as sufficient. In a few cases, however, it was possible to show that a word was an expected reflex of the reconstructed Proto-Oceanic word for kava. Once I had established an apparent set, I re-examined the lists to see if any other words, initially omitted, should be included.

Given our present state of knowledge, and the fact that for most of the languages considered borrowing could have taken place from a large number of other languages, a more reliable approach was not possible. But if there was any doubt, words were discarded from the lists, as I was more concerned to exclude non-cognates than with failing to include possible cognates.

Because of space considerations, sets of apparent cognates which come from the languages of only a single kava-drinking region have not been included: such sets would add no information relevant to the evaluation of Rivers' argument. Also, where a number of words of obviously very similar form occur in geographically close languages I have usually included only one or two of them.

Before proceeding with a discussion of the material presented in the tables, it is necessary to point out an unavoidable geographical bias in the data. Although words for areca are quite frequently – though by no means invariably – given in word lists, this is not the case with any of the other species considered. Both Laycock and Z'graggen included words for areca and *Piper betle* in their word lists of the Sepik and Madang regions respectively, and as a consequence both areas are heavily over-represented. Out of the 258 languages from which I obtained a word for *Piper betle* 179, or 69 per cent, came from one of these researchers. For areca the figure is 180 out of a total of 380 languages, or 47 per cent. Neither Laycock nor Z'graggen collected words for ginger, and as the information for the seventy-two languages from which I could obtain the relevant word(s) came from dictionaries and ethnographies, there is far less of a problem in this case.

It is possible to distinguish three main bases on which the semantic field demarcated by the pattern of cognates represented in the tables could be created: perceived similarity in physical form, consistent association in a particular activity, or similarity of use or effects. Unfortunately, in the case of areca nut and other *Piper* species it is not possible to distinguish between the three. Thus the presence of a word for, say, areca nut which appears cognate to the word for *Piper methysticum* could be due to a similarity of use and possible competition between the two substances. But alternatively, it could be the result of an initial perceived similarity in form between *Piper betle* and *Piper methysticum*, with a later transfer of the word to areca nut because of its association with *Piper betle*.

The case of ginger and turmeric is a little different, as there is no similarity in above-ground physical form between them and any of the *Piper* species. The only visual connections would be the roots, and these would most probably be made by people who used the roots of *Piper methysticum*. But fluctuations between words for gingers and kava could also come about because the two were used in similar contexts, or for similar effects. Thus, ginger does appear to be used as a means of intoxication by a number of Pacific people. Examples are the Bimin-Kuskusmin, the Mount Hagen people, the Elema, the Motu, and the Boiken speakers near Wewak (Poole

1987; Vicedom and Tischner 1983: 230; Williams 1940: 107; Kwapena 1974: 251; Gerstner 1954: 463). Of course, such use also raises the possibility of a perceived similarity between ginger and the betel mixture.[1]

Yet despite our inability to distinguish between the different possible causes of the transfer of meaning, the fact that the fluctuations clearly demonstrated in the tables actually occur is informative in two ways. Firstly, they may point to possible past familiarity with kava among people who have no contemporary familiarity with it, as well as suggesting routes whereby the plant and/or knowledge of its properties were transmitted. In other words, they enable us to broaden the range of evidence we may legitimately consider as relevant to our problem. The extent of the fluctuations, particularly in Papua New Guinea, and their occasional congruity with expected reflexes of the Proto-Oceanic *kawa*, strongly suggests that the processes to which they bear witness are of some antiquity.

Secondly, if we accept Chowning's suggestion that 'names other than those for the starch staple tend to be stable as long as the plant itself is regarded and used in the same way by speakers' (1963: 42), the fluctuations point to changing patterns of priority and use of items. If Rivers was correct in believing that betel displaced kava, we would expect to find exchanges of meaning between words for kava and elements of the betel mixture, although as other explanations are also possible, these exchanges cannot be used as conclusive proof. But they do contradict one of the arguments Riesenfeld used against Rivers, that 'among the words used in Melanesia for betel pepper . . . there is not a single word resembling the word *kava* or its derivatives' (1947: 205).

Each of the cognate sets isolated includes areca nut and betel pepper and, with the exception of Sets 1c and 2, they all include ginger. The absence of ginger from these two sets may well be an artefact of the relatively small number of words I was able to find for the plant. But paucity of information is not an explanation for the presence of turmeric in only one set, 1b, as Tryon and Hackman include the word for turmeric for 105 of the 111 Solomon Islands locations they surveyed. The most likely reason for the absence of turmeric from the other sets is that its connection with kava is more tenuous than is the case with the other items, and exists at all only because of its relation to ginger.

The most striking point to emerge from the data I have presented can be seen from Map 5: apparent cognates of the word *kava* are used for *Piper methysticum* at all the extremities of the plant's distribution: Hawaii, Mangareva, Ponape, the Madang area, the Admiralties, and Kolopom

---

[1] There are other possible links between ginger and betel. There are occasional reports of ginger being added to the betel mixture, and although, as a basis for a transfer of meaning, this would not seem to be as strong as in the cases of items which are invariably associated, it cannot be completely ignored (Healey and Healey 1977: 195; Marshall 1987: 49).

Island. With the exception of the two last-named areas, there can be no doubts about the authenticity of the relevant words, as they were first noted very soon after contact. Thus it is extremely unlikely that they could have come about as a result of post-contact travels by islanders from other kava-using areas. And although the word from Kolopom Island – from the village of Bamol – appears to have been collected first in the 1950s after two decades of European contact (Serpenti 1965: 8–9), it clearly looks as though it is cognate to the Lake Kutubu name of the man from whose body the *Piper methysticum* plant grew. Williams obtained this word very soon after the people were first discovered by Europeans (Williams 1976: 285).

Furthermore, words which certainly appear to be cognate to *kava* are used for the plant in every one of the distinct kava-drinking areas identified on Map 1. In a number of additional areas apparent cognates occur for other items in the semantic field. With the exception of the southern New Guinea region and Sinasina, all the relevant languages are either Oceanic, or spoken by people who live in close proximity to Oceanic speakers. This suggests that these words are of Oceanic origin, and this is consistent with Pawley and Green's reconstruction of a Proto-Oceanic form of kava (**kawa*, 1973: 32).

The presence of apparent cognates in the southern New Guinea region, hundreds of kilometres from the nearest speakers of an Oceanic language, parallels the findings of Dutton's study of the words for 'garden', 'fence' and major food plants.[1] He found that many of the cognate sets he isolated had members from the Trans-Fly stock languages and the Oceanic languages around Port Moresby. He suggests that the most likely explanations are that the words were distributed either through the network of trading links around the Gulf of Papua, or through direct contact by former trading voyages across the Gulf, which were discontinued before the arrival of Europeans (Dutton 1973: 481–2).

Set 1 is the only one which unambiguously contains words for kava distributed in more than one kava-drinking area. Although Set 1a contains apparent cognates for kava from both the southern New Guinea and Madang regions, it would be unwise to place too much emphasis on the Samo word *oyo*. Despite the large amount of data available for the Sepik region, plausible forms in the intervening area between the Samo and Madang are rare (cf. Sets 1c and 4), and the similarity may be due to coincidence. Set 4 contains words for kava from southern New Guinea and a possible word for kava from a people who are close to the Madang kava-drinking region, but not from the actual region itself.

[1] There is another piece of possible evidence that is worth noting: one of the Foi words for *Piper methysticum* is *ta'ano* (James Weiner, personal communication). This looks very similar to the Proto-Oceanic form for kava bowl **taanoa* or the Proto-Polynesian **taano'a* (Wurm and Wilson 1975: 23; cf. Tonga *tano'a*, Churchward 1959: 453; Hawaiian *kanoa*, Titcomb 1948: 158).

Ethnological evidence

Ethnological materials, which Rivers used almost exclusively in developing his account of the history of Melanesia, are the final kind of data that must be examined in a reconsideration of his argument. But the range of evidence which we can legitimately use is far more restricted than that considered by Rivers. Our primary problem is not to examine underlying cultural patterns in Melanesia and disentangle the migrations of the different peoples which produced them. Rather, it is to consider whether the strange distribution of kava is more satisfactorily explained as a consequence of independent discovery in a number of places, or as a once-only discovery transmitted throughout the Pacific by migrations and trading links involving at least some people who subsequently abandoned the drink. While the outcome of this enquiry will certainly have a bearing on the broader question of the peopling of the Pacific, the links between kava-using areas relevant to our task have to be established independently, and for this only information directly relating to kava preparation and consumption can be used.

Yet, although it is a relatively straightforward task to delimit the range of relevant data, the problem of interpreting it is another matter entirely. It is a problem which takes us to the heart of long-standing controversies between diffusionists and their opponents. Both sides tend to agree that the case for diffusion between specified areas depends on the sharing of arbitrary traits, i.e. traits which do not appear to be necessitated or facilitated by functional considerations, widespread or universal psychological, cultural or social characteristics, or environmental constraints. The difficulty lies in deciding whether a particular trait is arbitrary, or one of a limited number of equally likely possibilities (cf. Jett 1971: 34–5; 1984: 474; Marshall 1984: 617–19; Meggers 1975: 20–2). For a number of cultural domains – mythology and religious symbolism for example – there are well-developed theoretical positions, such as structuralism or Freudianism, which obviate any need to resort to diffusion to explain the duplication even of complex series of traits.[1]

An attempt to use similarities in the cultural elements associated with a psychoactive substance such as kava as evidence for a single origin is particularly subject to the risk of treating 'natural' traits as arbitrary. Although in the case of alcohol it has been convincingly demonstrated that there is considerable intercultural and intracultural variation in drinking practices and people's responses, there are also some general similarities (MacAndrew and Edgerton 1969; Marshall 1979; cf. Mandelbaum 1979: 17–19). Marshall, developing a suggestion of MacAndrew and Edgerton, has argued that similarities in both drunken behaviours and beliefs about

---

[1] For a sophisticated examination of common elements in collective representations which makes no attempt even to consider diffusion as a possible explanation, see Needham 1978.

the disinhibiting effects of alcohol in Oceania, North America and Mesoamerica are a consequence of the diffusion of European beliefs and drinking patterns (1983: 197–8, 209–10). Nevertheless, one cannot dismiss the possibility that the pharmacological action of alcohol has a tendency to produce a particular range of behavioural responses, and ideational elaborations on these responses, among most humans – even though this range may be broadened by certain, as yet unknown, cultural factors. Mandelbaum points out that 'the chemical and physiological properties of alcohol obviously provide a necessary base for drinking behaviour' (1979: 17), and even Marshall agrees that it is necessary to assess 'the proportion between social learning and biophysiological effects' (1983: 221), while admitting that this may not be possible given the present state of knowledge.

What applies to alcohol applies with even greater force to kava. As we have already seen, although there have been many pharmacological studies of kava, there are still disagreements as to the exact number of psychoactive constituents, their precise effects, and differences between kava prepared by chewing and grating. The systematic study of variations in chemical constituents among different cultivars has only just commenced, and so far has been confined to samples from Vanuatu and Fiji (Duve 1981; Lebot 1986; Lebot, Cabalion and Levesque n.d.). The situation is further complicated by the possibility, mentioned earlier, that kava can be prepared from more than one species. Consequently, while some of the physiological effects generally ascribed to kava – such as its properties as a soporific and muscle relaxant (Marshall 1987: 24; Lewis and Elvin-Lewis 1977: 439) – would seem to lead to a limited range of cultural elaborations, the problem of deciding whether similarities in central elements of the kava complex are due to independent development or diffusion is fraught with difficulty.

Thus we have to proceed with great caution, considering the cultural context of any elements which might appear to offer relevant evidence, and disallowing the applicability of those elements which might conceivably be a product of the physiological properties of kava, and hence more likely to have come about through independent development.

The other major problem in using ethnological evidence is substantive rather than theoretical. Data about kava use and customs for some of the areas in western Melanesia most crucial for evaluating the likelihood of a single source are very sparse. We know very little about kava ritual and associated beliefs in the Admiralty Islands, Madang and San Cristobal regions, especially about the incidental details least likely to have been produced by the inherent properties of the substance and regularities in the human response to it (cf. Jett 1984: 474). In the case of the southern New Guinea region the situation is a little better, but the material still falls considerably short of the detail available for Ponape, Fiji and western Polynesia, and parts of Vanuatu.

In the presentation that follows I will continue the practice of the previous section, and consider only elements that are shared by people in more than one kava-drinking area. Elements which appear common to only a single area, such as Polynesia – within which, for these purposes, Fiji can legitimately be included – or Vanuatu, will be ignored as they can add nothing to the argument. I have divided the material into three sections: apparently arbitrary characteristics which are either widely distributed or which occur in widely separated regions; widely distributed characteristics which may be the result of properties of kava or the expression of underlying cultural patterns common to many areas of the Pacific; and apparently arbitrary characteristics with a more restricted distribution and which may suggest connections between specific areas. There are some borderline cases where it is very difficult to decide whether a characteristic is arbitrary or not, or where it seems justified to identify particular, more localized sub-sets of broader, widely distributed characteristics, and these difficulties are identified where appropriate.

Widely distributed or separated arbitrary characteristics

One of the strongest pieces of cultural evidence in favour of a single origin for kava use is perhaps the most obvious, although no one seems to have remarked on it before: the fact that a *drink* is prepared from *Piper methysticum*. There is no special reason why kava could not be consumed in a manner similar to the way sugar cane is consumed in the Pacific. The psychoactive constituents would be as easily absorbed by the body if kava were chewed, the resulting juices swallowed, and the fibrous residue spat out.[1] Indeed, in the literature dealing with kava-drinking areas there are a few references to people also consuming the plant by simply chewing the root; usually, however, in special circumstances (Capell 1960: 49; Fox 1919: 167; Landtman 1927: 107; Schwartz and Romanucci-Ross 1979: 257; Williamson 1939: 90).

The other psychoactive substances used in the Pacific provide no models for the preparation of a drink; betel, and the various gingers, fruits, barks, etc. always appear to be chewed (Gerstner 1954: 463; Kwapena 1974: 251; Poole 1982: 193; 1987; Vicedom and Tischner 1983: 230; Williams 1936: 426–7). And as the tables presented in Powell's discussion of plant utili-

---

[1] In a personal communication Michael Young has suggested that perhaps some water may be necessary in order to release psychoactive properties of the root. If this were the case, the fact that a drink is prepared could not be cited as an arbitrary characteristic. However, in parts of southern New Guinea, the kava drink consists solely of saliva and the natural juice of the plant, without the addition of any water. Serpenti describes how kava is prepared on Kolopom Island. The stalks are chewed 'and the juice, mixed with saliva, is spat into a mug or a coconut-shell' (1969: 33). He specifically compares this with the practice in Polynesia where the kava 'is diluted with water' (ibid.: 34). Van Baal describes a similar practice among the Marind-anim (1966: 21). See also Haddon (1916: 149).

zation in New Guinea show, it is rather rare for a plant of any kind to be prepared for consumption by masticating or grinding the root or stalk and then drinking the extracted or diluted juice. Of the 326 examples of plants which appear to be ingested in some form, either as a food or for medicinal purposes, only seven are consumed after a process which could be seen as similar to that used for kava, and all involve the crushing of the stem or root, not its mastication (1976: Tables 3.1, 3.8, 3.10, 3.12, 3.13).

In a number of places people believe that it is necessary to keep water away from the kava paraphernalia or the unprepared root. Riesenberg states that in Ponape 'the earth is knocked off the roots but there is no washing' (1968: 103; see also Christian 1899: 190–1), and Schwartz and Romanucci-Ross refer to 'bowls of muddy kava . . . [because] the soil in which it grew was not to be washed from the roots' in the Admiralty Islands (1979: 257). On Tanna, men believe that if water falls on kava roots they will become 'cold' (i.e. without power, cf. Lindstrom 1981b: 382). Thus, roots which have accidentally been left in the rain will be drunk only after they have been dried out, either by leaving them in the sun, or in rafters over a fire. Haddon, presenting a summary translation of an article in Russian by Miklouho-Maclay, states that in Astrolabe Bay the insides of the coconut shell kava bowls are 'covered with a dark green deposit, the remains of long service, as custom does not allow the washing or cleaning out of a bowl in which *keu* [kava] is drunk' (1916: 145). For Mbau in Fiji, Lester reports that kava cups, bowls and the hibiscus strainers are not washed (1941–2: 234). Similar restrictions appear to have been in force in western Polynesia. Although such restrictions are not explicitly recorded, there are a number of references to the incrustations of kava which form on the insides of the kava cups (e.g. Samoa, Te Rangi Hiroa 1930: 151; East Futuna, Burrows 1936: 201; Uvea, Burrows 1937: 140).

A further arbitrary practice is the spinning of the empty kava cup after drinking. This is reported, sometimes as a prerogative of chiefs, from Fiji, East Futuna, Uvea, and Samoa (Ford 1967: 169; Lester 1941–2: 234; Hocart 1929: 61; Burrows 1936: 203; 1937: 143; Williamson 1939: 63). A similar practice was also found in New Guinea, among the Yabob of Madang Province, but there it was the weather magician who, in the course of performing his rituals, would spin the kava cup out of which he had just drunk (Aufinger 1939: 281, 284, 288).

The association that the Yabob make between kava and weather magic is also made by a number of people in Vanuatu. Layard reports that the people of Atchin, who did not drink kava, nevertheless used the plant in wind magic (1942: 376). A similar association, again among a people who did not drink kava, occurred in south-east Ambrym (Bob Tonkinson, personal communication). In both Maevo and Aoba, kava was regarded as having great power to control the weather (Codrington 1891: 201–2; Michael

Allen, personal communication). In southern New Guinea, the Kiwai used the *karea* rite, which incorporated the sprinkling of kava as its central act, for weather magic. In this case, however, the significance is much less than in the previous examples, as the *karea* rite was used in many other forms of magic as well (Landtman 1927: 107–8). Kava was also used in Niue as an essential component of the *kavauha* rite, which was performed to bring rain (Loeb 1926: 171–2).

In many parts of Polynesia, because of concern about their possible defilement, kava bowls, and sometimes cups, were provided with suspension lugs and/or cords so that they could be hung up when not in use (Burrows 1970: 51–3). Examples are to be found in Fiji, Hawaii, Marquesas, Samoa, Tonga, and Uvea (Lester 1941–2: 121; Titcomb 1948: 157–8, 160, 163; Linton 1923: Plates 60, 61; Mead 1930: 103; Te Rangi Hiroa 1930: 148; Gifford 1929: 62; Burrows 1937: 121). In Ponape, kava cups had to be kept in the spread upper end of a stick of hibiscus wood which had been driven into the ground, and split in four down to its middle (Riesenberg 1968: 105). In parts of Vanuatu, observers have recorded an explicit prohibition on certain kava paraphernalia making contact with the earth. Rivers reported that in the Banks Islands there is a rule that the coconut or wooden vessels used for making kava should never touch the ground (1914: vol. 1: 84). A similar rule exists in the neighbouring Torres Islands, and in Vanikolo (ibid.: 186; 227; Durrad 1940–1: 108). Gerard Haberkorn states that in North Pentecost a man must never allow his kava cup to touch the ground after drinking (personal communication). Michael Young has informed me that in Epi there is a prohibition against spilling kava on the ground (cf. Deane's statement that in Fiji, kava 'when being poured from one cup to another, must on no account be spilled on the ground', 1921: 158). While all these cases are confined to Polynesia, Micronesia and Vanuatu, and thus may properly belong in the last section, there appears to be a corresponding practice in Papua: the Gebusi keep kava roots which have been empowered by special yells from touching the ground, lest their strength drain away (Knauft 1987: 82–3). Finally, in an inversion of the normal pattern, yet quite probably related to it, the Tannese say that if a man passes his kava cup directly to a second man (so that it can be refilled for other drinkers) without touching the ground with it first, the second man will obtain the 'power' of the drinker's kava for himself.[1]

---

[1] The notion that the effects of kava can be transferred is also reported from Epi, where it is said to occur if someone passes in front of a man while he is drinking (Michael Young, personal communication), and Hawaii. Titcomb states that there were two situations in which this might occur in Hawaii: a kava chewer who had been treated rudely might appeal to her personal god to transfer the effect away from the offending person; and a noble who wished to drink for ceremonial or other reasons, but who felt that if he was to get drunk he might be in danger from enemies, might ask a priest to pray to have someone else obtain the effects (Titcomb 1948: 124).

The final characteristic I wish to present in this section appears to be arbitrary, although this may simply be due to a dearth of information about drinking utensils in Melanesia. The men of Kolopom Island drink their kava through a straw made of unspecified materials (Nevermann 1938: 190; Serpenti 1969: 34). Schwartz and Romanucci-Ross state that in the Admiralty Islands kava is drunk through cane straws (1979: 257). In the past, straws were also used for drinking kava on Tanna (Gray 1892: 661), and in Fiji they were used by priests (Clunie 1986: 169–70). Rivers refers to the distinctive way in which kava was drunk in the Banks Islands. Men did not put their lips to the edge of the kava cup, but sucked up the liquid instead, although they did not use a straw (1914: vol. 1: 84–5).

Widely distributed characteristics whose arbitrariness is open to question

In virtually all the societies in which kava is drunk, its use is restricted to specific categories of people, usually adult men. While there are reports of women drinking kava, these appear to be confined to four types of cases:

1 Women of high rank in stratified societies, as in Ponape, Samoa, Tonga (Riesenberg 1968: 109; Holmes 1967: 112; Collocott 1927: 22).
2 Old women, or those past the age of child-bearing, as among the Kanum Irebe, Marind-anim, Usino, and in Aoba (Nevermann 1938: 184, 1985; Conton 1977: 156; Michael Allen, personal communication).
3 The relaxing of restrictions consequent to European contact, as in Kiwai, Tahiti, Tongariki, Fiji, and Aneityum (Landtman 1927: 107; Oliver 1974: 602; Gajdusek 1967: 120; Thomson 1908: 346; Matthew Spriggs, personal communication).
4 Illicit drinking by women, as in Astrolabe Bay, Banks Islands, Torres Islands (Haddon 1916: 146; Rivers 1914, vol. 1: 82–3, 187).

While there are a few accounts suggesting that in some areas there was a more relaxed attitude towards women drinking kava, none of these appear to be firmly grounded, and are most probably either instances of one – or more – of the four situations described, or of inaccurate information. Thus Titcomb states that Hawaiian women were permitted to drink, though under some restrictions (1948: 128–9). But she later cites evidence suggesting that, in the case of women of common rank, this may have been only after the abolition of the taboo system (ibid.: 137). Williams states that he had been told that the women of Waya, on the west coast of Viti Levu, drank kava amongst themselves, although it was not something that he had seen for himself (Williams and Calvert 1859: 114). Nevermann stated that Makleuga women drank kava, but it is not clear whether this was a recent innovation, and whether it applied only to those over child-bearing age (1938: 188). Aufinger states that married Yabob women were able to drink kava, but, again, this may well have been only a modern development (1939: 280, cf. 277).

Restrictions on drinking in terms of age were even more severe. There are very few cases in which boys or youths were traditionally allowed to take any kava whatsoever, and none where it was generally available. On Tanna, boys might be given small amounts for medicinal purposes, although ordinarily they could not drink kava until they were adults. Cook reported that a young Hawaiian boy who was only about twelve years old was permitted to drink, but it is quite clear that this was an exception, due to the fact that he was the son of a chief (cited in Titcomb 1948: 136). Similarly, while visiting the Big Nambas village of Amok in Malekula in 1970, I noted that the chief's son, who was only about twelve or thirteen, drank kava. He had, however, already been named as the successor to his father.

The significance of these restrictions is highlighted when we consider betel which, as Marshall has pointed out, is typically 'used by nearly *everyone* in a Pacific society' (original emphasis; 1987: 28; for further evidence see e.g. Burton-Bradley 1979: 484; Guppy 1887: 95). There are some exceptions to this generalization, but they appear to be few. Ivens states that 'Lau women and children did not eat the betel-mixture in old days' (1930: 240). Similarly, Oram states that in the past Motu youths and adolescent girls were not allowed to chew at all, and young men and women were allowed it only sparingly, although this restriction no longer exists (n.d.: 2). Peter Lawrence told me that Garia women were not allowed betel at all until the 1960s, and Lewis writes that among the Gnau pre-menopausal women and young men were not allowed to include lime in the betel mixture and had to use ash (1980: 3). Landtman states that among the Kiwai 'only grown men indulged' in betel, although even they did not use it to any great extent (1927: 110).

But the exceptions do not really negate the general pattern in which kava drinking is subject to strong restrictions whereas betel chewing is unrestricted. The obvious question is, why should there be such a difference?

A possible answer might be couched in terms of the ritual or psychoactive powers of kava *vis-à-vis* betel. But this is not easy to assess. While there is rarely any ritual surrounding the actual consumption of betel, in many areas areca nuts, betel spit, or the state of intoxication brought about by betel have important religious or ritual significance (see e.g. Crawford 1981: 97; Ivens 1927: 288–9; Keesing 1982a: 131, 188; Schwimmer 1973: 165–6). Betel can also have a powerful psychoactive effect on the user; one which may be as intense as that of kava. Yet, on the other hand, my impression is that the effects of a normal dose of betel are of shorter duration, and are of less hindrance to ordinary activities and interaction than is the case with kava (see e.g. Burton-Bradley 1979: 482, 484; Firth 1967: 299; Lepowsky 1982: 335–7; Marshall 1987: 16–21; Raghavan and Baruah 1958: 339–40; Young

1971: 249–52). The situation is further complicated by the fact that betel, like kava, exhibits considerable species and regional variation in alkaloid content (Lebot 1986; Raghavan and Baruah 1958: 335–6). Thus the kava normally used in some societies may have considerably less psychoactive effect than the betel normally used in others.

Some anthropologists have attempted to explain the difference in the restrictions surrounding kava and betel in terms of differences in scarcity and ease of preparation (Rivers 1914, vol. 2: 254; Marshall 1987: 24). But there are difficulties with such an argument. In many parts of the Pacific, one or more of the constituents of the betel-mixture are in short supply (see e.g. Dornstreich 1973: 132, 223; Gewertz 1983: 109; Ivens 1927: 286; Lepowsky 1982: 334; Oliver 1955: 297–8; Watson 1987: 127). While this scarcity may have been used as the rationale for restrictions on betel chewing in a few areas (e.g. Motu, Oram n.d.: 2; Lau, Ivens 1930: 240), it did not lead to any restrictions elsewhere. And although the need to pound, grate or chew the kava means that the preparation of the drink takes longer,[1] and involves more effort than combining the ingredients of the betel chew, it should be realized that the preparation of the partially slaked lime – an essential component of the betel mixture – also involves a significant amount of time and effort. (See, for instance, Williams' description of lime manufacture in the Purari Delta, 1924: 24, or Iamo's description for the Keakalo, 1987: 140–1.)

I referred earlier to Marshall's argument that the aboriginal peoples of Oceania and elsewhere who were introduced to alcohol by Europeans did not just adopt the drink, but also adopted the associated beliefs and behaviours. This provides some circumstantial grounds for thinking that the universality of restrictions on the consumption of kava might be a consequence of its diffusion from a single area, and that the notion of kava as a restricted substance was transmitted along with the knowledge of its preparation. In other words, for both kava and betel, the effect of local patterns of age and gender relations in determining usage would have been less important than the 'package' of beliefs and behaviours associated with the substances themselves. Additional support for this suggestion is provided by the fact that, although a number of Papua New Guinea people make some kind of conceptual identification between alcohol and betel, this does not mean that the same categories of people can use them (see e.g. Lepowsky 1982: 331, 335; Schwartz and Romanucci-Ross 1979: 256–62). As Marshall notes, women rarely, and children hardly ever, take alcohol in Papua New Guinea (1982: 4).

Although the above discussion suggests that it may be possible to argue for a single origin of kava in terms of the common patterns of age and sex

---

[1] But my earlier references to the fact that kava need not be made into a drink at all should be borne in mind.

restrictions on its use, it would be foolhardy to give these prohibitions the same status as the common characteristics discussed in the previous section. At this stage the argument can be based only on circumstantial evidence and the – uncertain – elimination of alternatives. It is possible that future research on the physiological and psychological response to kava under specific social or cultural conditions may help explain the restrictions. Yet whatever the explanations may be, I also think that the restrictions on kava use have a wider relevance in understanding the strange geographical distribution of kava. This is a point I will return to later in this book.

Occasionally, a people will justify the taboo on women drinking kava by claiming that it causes sterility. Humphreys states that this is the case in Erromanga, where it is also believed that men who drink in excess become impotent (1926: 180). On Epi people say that kava is bad for a woman's reproductive system (Michael Young, personal communication). In Fiji it is said that the excessive use of kava causes sterility, but there is disagreement as to whether this is permanent or temporary. The taboo on women drinking kava was lifted in post-contact Fiji, although pregnant women are discouraged from drinking (Lester 1941–2: 98). A Kiwai man with a pregnant wife cannot drink kava, as it could enter her through intercourse and utterly destroy the embryo (Landtman 1917: 330; 1927: 107). Kava was used as an abortifacient by the Marind-anim, Samoans, and Hawaiians (Nevermann 1938: 185; Holmes 1967: 110; Titcomb 1948: 127). Riesenberg states that Hambruch claimed that it was similarly used on Ponape, although his own informants denied this (1968: 103).

The existing literature on the physiological effects of kava does not appear to provide an empirical basis for these beliefs. Concern with depopulation among the Marind-anim and their neighbours led the Dutch to initiate various research projects to investigate the causes, but they were unable to obtain any evidence that kava had any harmful effects on fertility (van Baal 1966: 21–2; Serpenti 1969: 34). However, given the incomplete state of knowledge about the pharmacologically active constituents of kava and their effects, it would be foolish to dismiss such a possibility. Furthermore, the known soporific and local anaesthetic effects of kava mean that the development of associations of impotence and hence sterility is unlikely to be adventitious (Meyer 1967; Marshall 1976: 113; 1987: 24). Gajdusek states that in the Vanuatu island of Tongariki 'it is quite evident that kava drinkers rarely engage in sexual activity on the nights when they are drunk. Interviews with the women substantiate this' (1967: 121: see also Lindstrom 1987: 117–18). Alternatively, the associations might simply be seen as nothing more than rather obvious ways in which different Pacific people would rationalize – and in some cases subsequently elaborate – any prior restriction on women drinking kava.

Earlier, I discussed the singularity of preparing a drink from the roots of

67

the kava plant. This is perhaps further highlighted by a widely distributed story explaining how the effects of kava were discovered. An animal, nearly always a rat, is seen nibbling kava roots, then falling down in a stupor. The persons observing this, who may be of either sex, then try the root for themselves, but the step from chewing at the root to making a drink is left undescribed. This theme is widespread in northern Vanuatu (Michael Allen, personal communication). It also occurs in Tonga and Samoa, Tikopia, and Ponape (Gifford 1924: 71–3; Lester 1941–2: 103; Firth 1970: 216; Riesenberg 1968: 102). A similar theme is found among the Bilbil of Madang Province, although there the drunken animal is a pig, not a rat (Dempwolff 1911: 100–1). But caution needs to be exercised in explaining the wide distribution of this story. Contemporary observers frequently have seen rats chewing growing kava plants, and there are occasional reports of pigs doing the same (Vincent Lebot, personal communication). Consequently, independent development is as likely as not to have been responsible.[1]

Another common element in myths of the origin of kava is that it grew from a grave or the body of a dead person. In a Lake Kutubu myth the kava plant grows out of the place where the earth was filled in to entomb Waki, an underground man, and Williams' informants appeared to believe that the plant was Waki himself (1976: 285). A number of myths from Vanuatu state that kava grew from the body of a dead woman, usually her vagina or breasts, although in a Tannese variant it grew from a living woman's vagina (Allen, n.d.; Kirk Huffman, personal communication; Sizai 1982; Michael Young, personal communication). In Tonga and Taveuni (Fiji) kava is said to have grown from the body of a leper (Gifford 1924: 73; Lester 1941–2: 102). Other variations on the theme of kava's origin from a human body are found in Rotuma, the Marquesas, and Vanua Levu (Churchward 1939: 465–6; von den Steinen 1934–5: 196, 227–8; Hocart 1952: 127). In Tikopia, one myth states that it grew from the body of the Female Deity (Firth 1970: 217). Although it may be tempting to link the Lake Kutubu version to those in eastern Melanesia and Polynesia, once more it is necessary to exercise caution. Tales of plants growing out of the bodies of people, gods or monsters are very widespread in the Pacific (e.g. Hogbin 1970: 31–2; Kirtley 1971: 106; Landtman 1917: 119; Riesenfeld 1950: 94, 96, 184, 193, 220, 299; Serpenti 1972–3: 176).

Haddon, again presenting Miklouho-Maclay's Astrolabe Bay observations, states that drinkers separate to the margins of the cleared feasting area and turn their backs to the others (1916: 145–6). Young reports that on Epi men should turn their backs or go into a corner when drinking (personal communication; this is possibly connected to the belief about transferring

[1] See also Dobkin de Rios 1984: 194–7, and Furst 1976: 169–71, for reference to hallucinogens in other parts of the world whose properties are said to have been revealed by animals.

the effects of kava referred to earlier), and on Tanna drinkers move off to the edge of the kava-drinking ground (*yimwayim*) and also turn their backs to the other men.[1] The difficulty here lies in deciding whether or not this is simply an appropriate way of symbolically representing an individuating or liminal aspect of the altered state of consciousness produced by, or sought from, kava (cf. Dobkin de Rios 1984: 210, 213).

Other elements which are extremely widespread, but which could well be a result of underlying Pacific, or even pan-human, cultural themes are the general association between kava and funerals, mourning and the dead, and the use of kava in libations or other kinds of offerings to ancestors or gods. Examples of the strong nexus between kava and funerals and mourning rites are to be found among most of the peoples in the Madang region, Baluan and Lou Islanders, the Gogodala, the Bedamini, the Arosi, and the people of Pentecost (Aufinger 1950: 786; Conton 1977: 156; Hannemann 1944: 7; Schwartz and Romanucci-Ross 1979: 257; Crawford 1981: 98; Sørum 1982: 54; Fox 1924: 216; Rivers 1914, vol. 1: 187). The connection was evident even among some people who did not actually drink kava. On Vao men bite off, then spit out, a piece of kava root during the rite celebrated on the anniversary of a man's death (Layard 1942: 557). Among the Foi, kava leaves are rubbed on the jaw bone of a dead man at his final mortuary feast and are used to wrap his skull (Weiner 1988: 112, and personal communication). The Nukuria word for cemetery was *kawa*, and in Ontong Java it was *'ava* (Ray 1916: 45; Ian Hogbin, personal communication). But there are other, equally plausible, explanations than diffusion for these associations. Physiologically powerful substances are commonly believed to have supernatural qualities, and given the powers widely ascribed to spirits of the dead in Melanesia, the tendencies for an association to develop independently would be strong (see e.g. Keesing 1982a: 188; Lowman-Vayda 1971: 339; Poole 1982: 205 for Melanesia; for cross-cultural evidence on the association between psychoactive substances and death, see Furst 1976).

Among the people who made libations with kava were Fijians, Samoans, Hawaiians, East Futunans, Mangaians, Banks Islanders, Torres Islanders, Big Nambas, Tikopians, Ponapeans, and the Masingara (Lester 1941–2: 253–4; Te Rangi Hiroa 1930: 155; Titcomb 1948: 142; Burrows 1936: 203; Te Rangi Hiroa 1944: 19; Rivers 1914, vol. 1: 84; Durrad 1940–1: 86, 88; Deacon 1934: 584; Firth 1970: 220–3; Christian 1899: 191; Haddon 1916: 149). Kava was offered to the spirits of the ancestors by being scattered in a spray of spit or some other means by the Tannese, the Yabob, the Kiwaim, and the Gogodala (Brunton 1979: 95; Aufinger 1939: 280; Landtman 1927:

[1] Gregory, Gregory and Peck state, 'to drink, one walks a few steps into the *nakamal*' [Bislama: drinking ground] and that *after* drinking 'a man may walk to the edge of the *nakamal*' (1981: 301). My own observations are at variance with this (as are those of Lindstrom, see 1981a: 61; 1982: 428). I made a point of discussing the matter with informants during my visit to Tanna in 1986, and they stated that the correct procedure is as I have described it.

107–8; Crawford 1981: 98). But as Codrington noted nearly a century ago, offerings to the dead, such as small pieces of food or areca nut, are extremely common in the Pacific (1891: 128). And the spitting or blowing of magically potent substances is also very widespread (e.g. Bogesi 1948: 329; Johannes 1975: 270; Lewis 1980: 76, 182; Young 1983: 58).[1]

Finally, for the sake of completeness, I should mention two other characteristics of kava use which are extremely widespread, although it would be unwise to see them as anything other than rather compelling consequences of the physiological action of the drink. The first is the abstention from food before drinking, which obviously facilitates the absorption of the psychoactive ingredients by the body (e.g. Astrolabe Bay, Miklouho-Maclay 1886: 692; Kolopom Island, Serpenti 1969: 34; Ponape, Riesenberg 1968: 102; Samoa, Williamson 1939: 51; Hawaii, Titcomb 1948: 144; Tanna). The second is the association between kava and peaceful relations (e.g. Kiwai, Landtman 1927: 107, 133; Usino, Conton 1977: 157; Ponape, McGrath 1973: 64–5; Tonga, Williamson 1939: 71; Tanna). Given the muscle-relaxant and soporific effects of kava, this does not require diffusion as an explanation (Meyer 1967; Marshall 1976: 113; 1987: 24).[2]

Arbitrary characteristics whose distribution is relatively restricted

In this section I will describe elements which appear to occur only in Micronesia, Polynesia (including Fiji), and Vanuatu. Some of these have been reported for all three regions, the others for only two. Although evidence that is confined to these regions does not make any substantial contribution to the consideration of the validity of Rivers' argument, I am presenting it as a basis for the further discussion of the most likely transmission routes for kava in the next chapter.

[1] The frequent spitting after drinking kava that has been noted in a number of parts of the Pacific may also be a cultural construct (see e.g. Lindstrom 1980: 229; Miklouho-Maclay 1886b: 692; Riesenberg 1968: 103; Rodman 1973: 189–91; Thomson 1908: 348). Lindstrom states, on the basis of his own experience, that 'one of the effects of a strong dose of kava is a disinclination to swallow . . . and spitting neatly solves the problem of what to do with excess saliva' (1980: 229), and I must confess that I originally assumed that the spitting was a purely physiological reaction (Brunton 1988: 128). Although my personal experience was more equivocal than Lindstrom's – sometimes I felt a strong urge to spit, at other times I didn't – I simply, and unthinkingly, supposed that this was due to minor changes in my own physiological state. It was only when Michael Young, after reading my comments, said he 'found no urge to spit, even after several draughts of kava' (personal communication), that I realized my assumption may have been incorrect. The existing literature offers little guidance on the matter.

[2] Nevertheless, as both Bott (1972: 217) and Turner (1986: 209) have noted, kava occupies an ambivalent position in many cultures. In a Tongan myth of the origin of kava, the Tui Tonga tells the people 'it would be their curse or their blessing, according to the way they used it' (Gifford 1924: 75). Kava may be used for sorcery, or seen as an actual or potential poison (e.g. Deacon 1929: 463; Gardiner 1898: 517; Landtman 1927: 322; Lester 1941–2: 253; Nevermann 1938: 184; Sahlins 1981b: 125–6; Titcomb 1948: 147–9). As Turner points out, 'as a thing of power it can be used for evil as well as good' (1986: 209). I will return to this point later.

The most widely distributed trait of the ones to be discussed is an association between canoes and kava bowls. The traditional wooden Tannese kava bowls were canoe shaped, and were called *niko*, which is also the word for canoe (Brunton 1979: 94). Similarly shaped bowls were used on Aneityum and were called *neilgo*, which likewise means canoe (Jack Keitade, personal communication). Although the form of the Big Nambas kava bowl was rather different, it was called by a term which means 'boat with the kava' (Deacon 1934: Plate XXIV; Kirk Huffman, personal communication). As well as the more common round ones, the Hawaiians and Fijians also used canoe-shaped kava bowls, and similar bowls appear to have been found in Samoa (Titcomb 1948: 113; Koch 1981: 195–6; Lester 1941–2: Plate IIB; Te Rangi Hiroa 1930: 150). In Ponape the water added to the pounded kava roots was traditionally kept in the boat-shaped wooden *kasak* (Riesenberg 1968: 105).

Hand clapping during certain stages of the kava ritual is widely reported from western Polynesia – Samoa, East Futuna, Tonga, Niue – and Fiji (Holmes 1967: 109; Burrows 1936: 203; Collocott 1927: 34; Loeb 1926: 28; Lester 1941–2: 232–3; Williams and Calvert 1859: 113). Lutke, who visited Kosrae in the 1820s, recorded that the preparation of kava was preceded by clapping (Burrows 1970: 114). Deacon, reporting on the Big Nambas, stated that as soon as a visiting chief has finished drinking, the other men present begin to clap (Deacon 1934: 374; Guiart makes a similar report but with slightly different details, 1953: 444). The men of north Pentecost clap their hands before receiving their kava, although this is possibly a Fijian-inspired modern innovation (Gerard Haberkorn, personal communication).

While Riesenberg tends to emphasize the differences between the kava ceremony in Ponape and in western Polynesia, it is clear that there were also a number of probably diagnostic similarities, especially with Fiji. Thus, a master of ceremonies called out specific stages of the proceedings, songs were sung during parts of the rite, and in the morning kava ceremony, regarded as the most important, there were tight restrictions on the kinds of movements allowed with the hands and the strainer when preparing the kava. The morning kava was also characterized by the server's peculiar gait as he took the filled cup to the chief (Riesenberg 1968: 104–7; Burrows 1970: 114; cf. Hocart 1929: 60–70; Thomson 1908: 344–5; Williams and Calvert 1859: 111–13; Thompson, 1940: 71, describes the odd gait of the server in the southern Lau Islands).

On Tanna, men make *timavha*[1] with their last mouthful of kava, spitting a broad spray into the air, then uttering a statement or invocation to the spirits (Brunton 1979: 95; Lindstrom 1980: 228–32). Williams describes a very similar practice in Fiji, although there it is called by a non-cognate term

---

[1] I have used the Lenakel form of the word; in Kwamera it is *tamafa*, and in the language of south-west Tanna it is *tamahua* (Lindstrom 1980: 228; Gregory, Gregory and Peck 1981: 302).

(Williams and Calvert 1859: 115). There can be little doubt that the word *timavha* is Polynesian: Capell states that libations of kava, termed *taumafa*, were made at the commencement of drinking on West Futuna; as on Tanna, men spat out a mouthful and called out to the spirits. He translates *taumafa* as 'sacrifice' (1960: 44, 57). In the Tongan language *taumafa* is the regal term for *kai* 'to eat', and *inu* 'to drink', and *taumafa kava* is the monarch's kava (Churchward 1959: 465; Urbanowicz 1975: 34). In Samoa *taumafa*, which means food, was the term used for the kava of some chiefs; *taumafa* was the word for food offerings in Tikopia; and in Raratonga, *tauma'a* is the word for curse or citation (Te Rangi Hiroa 1930: 158; Firth 1970: 228; Savage 1962: 364).

There are three other elements of kava practice in southern Vanuatu which have parallels to those found further east, but which do not appear to be present elsewhere in Melanesia. Firstly, although Tannese men now drink kava from coconut-shell cups, traditionally they drank out of cups made from a folded banana leaf (Gray 1892: 661). In Tonga a similar method was used, but only for the most ceremonious occasions (Collocott 1921: 157). There are also references to kava cups fashioned out of folded leaves in Tahiti (Williamson 1939: 90).

Secondly, the Tannese have two techniques for growing kava that alter the natural form of the roots, and the plants thus produced were allowed only to the occupants of certain titles, as well as being subject to other restrictions. One of these techniques, used for making the type of kava called *nousumiriang*, involves growing the plant over a wide piece of wood laid horizontally in the ground, so that the bulk of the root system grew parallel to the surface.[1] Hocart describes a very similar technique in the Lau Islands of eastern Fiji, although there a flat stone was used, rather than wood (1929: 108).

Finally, while the normal procedure for making kava in Erromanga involved the use of a wooden bowl, an alternative method was to prepare it in a hole dug in the ground and lined with taro leaves (Humphreys 1926: 180). A south Tannese myth refers to the god Kalpapen making his kava in a bowl dug into the earth (Guiart 1956a: 250). In the upper reaches of the Rewa River on Viti Levu, kava was similarly made in a hole in the ground, lined with alocasia leaves (Lester 1941–2: 111).

The final characteristic that I need to discuss is the process of macerating the kava root. Although there are only a limited number of ways in which this can be done, the distribution of the processes traditionally used provides evidence which must also be taken into account when considering possible

---

[1] See also Guiart 1956a: 86, who incorrectly uses the term *topunga* to refer to both of the altered types. The *topunga* type has a long straight root created by placing a vertical cylinder made from tree fern around the base of the root and packing earth into it.

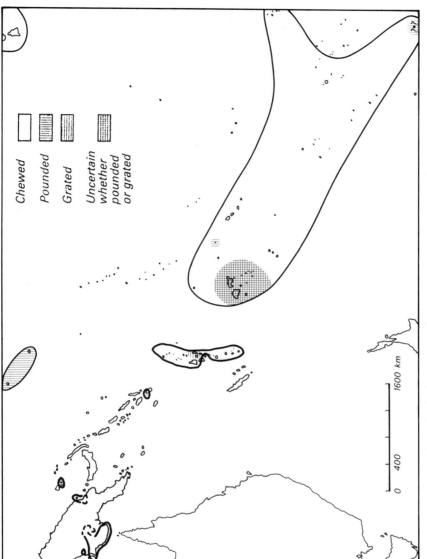

Map 13   *Traditional method of preparing kava*

transmission routes for kava. The relevant information has been presented in Map 13. But, while it is generally a straightforward matter to determine the traditional way of preparing the root, there are some equivocal cases.

Early European observers in Fiji reported that kava was chewed, although old men stated that this was a Tongan innovation (Williams and Calvert 1859: 111; Brewster 1922: 18; Lester 1941–2: 226–7). But it is not so easy to ascertain whether the old method of preparing kava in Fiji was grating or pounding, whether there were regional variations, or indeed, whether there was any culturally marked distinction made between the two. Both Williams and Lester refer to grating, whereas Brewster states that the ancient Fijian way of making kava was 'to pound up the roots with stones' (1922: 18), and Hocart's statements, while phrased in somewhat ambiguous terms, suggest that pounding was the traditional method in Lau (1929: 51, 59–60).

It also seems that pounding was the traditional method of preparing kava in Uvea. Burrows explicitly compares it with (East) Futuna, where kava was originally chewed; and although he states that some Futunans had abandoned the practice, there is no indication that the Uvean method he describes was anything but traditional (1936: 210; 1937: 140). A more puzzling case is that of Mangareva. According to Te Rangi Hiroa, there the kava was pounded, although the basis for his statement is an inference from a chant, and not any specific observations (1938: 449).

The only other problem is the precise distribution of chewing and grating in Vanuatu. There is no doubt that it was grated – using a piece of coral – in Pentecost, Aoba and Maewo, and chewed in most of the other islands (Rivers vol. 1: 211; Speiser 1923: 163–4; Michael Allen, personal communication). But in Santo the situation is confused. Speiser states that it was grated (1923: 162), while Harrisson (1936b: 333) and Guiart (1958: 49) state that it was chewed. Regional variation cannot explain this contradiction, as the two latter authors were writing about some of the same regions as Speiser. The situation on Malo is also unclear: Speiser says that in North Malo the method of preparation was the same as on Santo (1923: 162).

Yet, irritating though these differences may be, they do not really compromise the overall picture. With the exception of San Cristobal, the Admiralties, Ponape and Kosrae, where it was pounded, in all places other than those already mentioned kava was chewed (Fox 1924: 216; Parkinson 1907: 373–4; Burrows 1970: 114). In the next chapter I will combine this fact with the other evidence I have presented in order to suggest the most likely routes of diffusion for kava.

4

Reconsidering Rivers' argument: assessment and implications

Although I drew some inferences from the evidence presented in the last chapter, a proper assessment of Rivers' argument requires a systematic examination of the three possible explanations for the patchy distribution of kava drinking. This will also enable us to consider various routes through which the custom may have been transmitted.

Possibility 1: independent discovery of kava in a number of regions

The arguments against the independent discovery and development of the psychoactive properties of *Piper methysticum* in a number of different regions are compelling. The botanical evidence, despite its gaps, strongly suggests that *Piper methysticum* is a sterile plant which has been produced and dispersed by a process involving human selection and propagation. The presence of words for the plant or drink which certainly seem to be cognates of *kava* in all of the kava-drinking regions, including the non-Austronesian language areas of southern New Guinea, provides additional support for believing that kava originated in a single location. There is also the fact that every people who utilize the psychoactive properties of *Piper methysticum* prepare a drink from the plant, even though there do not appear to be any pharmacological reasons or widespread cultural models for doing so. Finally, there is the occurrence in Melanesia, Polynesia and Micronesia of similar, apparently arbitrary, cultural associations of kava.

Possibility 2: direct links between kava-drinking regions

The above discussion shows that there can be little doubt that kava drinking had a single point of origin. But its puzzling distribution might simply be a reflection of some earlier pattern of direct trade or migration in which communities located in the areas between the kava-drinking regions were either bypassed, or else rejected kava when the people responsible for its diffusion made it available to them (as the Bai villagers of the Rai Coast in Madang did when their neighbours offered it, Miklouho-Maclay 1975: 271).

If this were the case, there would be no grounds for arguing that the patchy distribution of kava drinking is a consequence of its abandonment by a number of peoples before Europeans were in a position to record its presence. While the arguments against this possibility are not as decisive as those against independent development, they are still powerful. The most appropriate way to present them is to consider the possibilities of pre-contact transference and post-contact transference separately.

Pre-contact transference of kava

Obviously, in the region east of Vanuatu kava must have been transferred by direct voyages over very considerable distances: the human settlement of Fiji and Polynesia required a number of open sea crossings of around 1000 kilometres or more (Finney 1985; Kirch 1984: 71–9). The question is whether or not it is reasonable to think that similar voyages could have been responsible for the distribution elsewhere.

Kava drinking in Micronesia does not necessarily represent a problem. As is evident from the material presented in the last section of the previous chapter, the cultural elements associated with kava in Ponape and Kosrae indicate affinities with Vanuatu and Fiji. This is in line with the linguistic evidence which suggests that the nuclear Micronesian languages are most closely linked to those spoken in the northern/central Vanuatu region (Tyron 1984: 155; Marshall 1984: 614), as well as some archaeological evidence relating to early pottery forms from Ponape (see Ayers and Mauricio 1987: 27). Although the process of colonization may well have been more complex than the linguistic evidence suggests (Craib 1983: 924), the presence of kava in Ponape and Kosrae could be explained by arguing that it was taken there by people, perhaps the original colonizers, travelling from anywhere in the Vanuatu–south-east Solomons–Fiji region. In other words, despite the distances involved, the possibility of such voyages is at least consistent with evidence from other sources. Even if the voyages were not direct, and landfall or settlement was first made on one of the nearer atolls, their environmental unsuitability for kava (Holmes 1973: 3; Marshall 1987: 22) while offering a technical instance of the disappearance of kava, could hardly be said to provide an example of any significance for the evaluation of Rivers' argument.

The situation is not dissimilar for the Admiralties. Although less information exists for kava use there than for any other region except San Cristobal, the data that we do have suggests a close relationship with Micronesia. Kava was pounded in both regions; indeed, Parkinson stated that the process of preparing the drink in Lou was exactly the same as in Ponape (1907: 374). And the more widespread taboo relating to water and kava was expressed in exactly the same way in both regions, in that the soil was not washed away from the roots. Again, despite the distances involved, evidence of contact – which, given the geography, would either have to be direct, or mediated through atolls which were environmentally unsuitable for kava – comes from other sources. The languages of Manus and the nearby islands have many affinities to those spoken in Micronesia (Smythe 1970: 1209). Ambrose refers to the find of an obsidian spear head, normally known only within the Admiralty Islands region, in a grave on Ponape (1978: 330), and Marshall notes the belief held by a number of scholars who have worked in the Admiralty Islands that the region has had a substantial cultural input from Micronesia (1984: 615). While it might still be legitimate to suspect that kava may also have been introduced to locations in the Admiralties other than Baluan and Lou, only to disappear subsequently, it could also be countered that the people on Baluan and Lou might have been the only ones to accept it.

Whether or not kava actually was transferred directly from the region around Vanuatu to Ponape and Kosrae and from there directly to Baluan and Lou, it is not an unreasonable route to suggest. Consequently, the presence of kava in Micronesia and the Admiralties cannot be used in support of the abandonment hypothesis, other than in the trivial sense that some atoll dwellers would have been unable to cultivate it successfully. However, the crucial test of the likelihood of pre-contact transference of kava through direct links centres on its presence on the island of New Guinea. Firstly, we can examine the possibilities with a postulated origin for kava in the south-east Solomons–Vanuatu regions.[1] Then the obvious direct route for the transfer of kava to the Madang region would be through the Admiralties. The Manus people made voyages to the mainland of New Guinea (Ambrose 1978: 329–30), so it is not implausible to suggest that the people of Baluan or Lou could have made similar voyages some time in the past. The linguistic evidence, though equivocal, is at least consistent with such a connection: the Bilbil word for kava is *kau*, which is the same as the Baluan word.[2] However, the process of preparing kava is very different in the two regions. In Madang kava was chewed, and the overall procedure was similar to that used in southern New Guinea (Miklouho-Maclay 1886b: 689–91; Haddon 1916: 147–50; Crawford 1981: 142–3). To the best of my knowledge, there are no distinctive localized cultural elements which might link kava drinking in the Admiralties with Madang. Nevertheless, the difference in techniques of preparation is not a sufficient reason to reject

[1] As I argued in the previous chapter, all the botanical evidence indicates that *Piper methysticum* originated somewhere in the Melanesian region to the north-west of central Vanuatu. But even in the highly unlikely event that this is incorrect, and the origin were in Fiji or Polynesia, this would not affect the present discussion.
[2] Other explanations are also possible. For example, they may both directly reflect the Proto-Oceanic *kawa*; or the Bilbil word could reflect *kawa*, while the Baluan word could be derived from the Ponape *sakau*.

confidently the possibility of a direct Admiralties–Madang transmission route.

It is when we turn to southern New Guinea that a direct link – or series of direct links – from a south-east Solomons–Vanuatu origin becomes totally implausible. We would either have to accept that the Madang people traded directly with, or migrated directly to, southern New Guinea, or that the people from the south-east Somomons–Vanuatu region – or beyond – did. There are simply no grounds for thinking that this ever occurred.

If we postulate a New Guinea origin for kava, the likelihood of direct connections is even more remote. A Madang origin and a direct Lapita, or Proto-Oceanic, transfer of kava to the south-east Solomons might be thought feasible, given the probable voyaging abilities of the Lapita people (cf. Kirch 1984: 46; Pawley and Green 1984: 141–3; Terrell 1986: 78). But by raising the prospect of a Lapita use of kava this would cause greater difficulties for the direct links hypothesis than it would solve, given the presence of Lapita sites in many places in Melanesia where kava drinking has not been recorded. Furthermore, it would still be necessary to find a plausible explanation for the presence of kava in southern New Guinea. And with a southern New Guinea origin, even the Lapita connection would need to be disallowed, unless indirect links, and the subsequent abandonment of kava, were accepted.

Post-contact transference of kava by Pacific islanders

European voyages in the Pacific brought about a dramatic increase in the mobility of Pacific islanders. By the early decades of the nineteenth century substantial numbers of Polynesians were travelling on ships, as crew, and as passengers (see e.g. Bennett 1987: 39; Dening 1980: 99, 120–1; Shineberg 1967: 17–22; Strauss 1963: 9–18), and it is possible that some of them may have carried kava. Obviously, it is necessary to consider whether kava could have been introduced in this way to New Guinea. Yet at the same time it should be realized that the rather involved process of preparing the drink makes it extremely unlikely that it could have been diffused through contacts as transitory as those between ships anchored at sea and visiting canoes, or brief shore visits by apprehensive landing parties.

Although the north-east coast of New Guninea had been known to European explorers since the seventeenth century, it was not until Miklouho-Maclay's visit in 1871 that any contact of a kind that could have led to the adoption of kava was established (Hughes 1977: 13–33; Lawrence 1964: 34–5). Yet Miklouho-Maclay found that kava was widely used. Certainly, noting its patchy distribution, he inferred that the custom had been introduced 'not very long ago . . . and is still in the progressing state' (1886a: 351). The alternative explanations of an earlier abandonment of kava drinking, or unwillingness to adopt the custom in the first place, did not seem to occur to him, just as it did not occur to Codrington, contemplating the absence of kava drinking on Gaua (see Chapter 2). But Miklouho-Maclay did state 'the natives however have no tradition about its introduction' (ibid.), and this can be compared with the accounts he was given about the introduction of tobacco during the youth of the fathers of his older informants, i.e. perhaps seventy to eighty years previously (ibid.: 352). It is also instructive to compare the considerable similarity of the words used for tobacco throughout the Madang area (Hays 1984; Riesenfeld 1951: 85) with the diversity of words used for kava (see Maps 5–12; Miklouho-Maclay 1886b: 687; 1951: 182–3). Consequently, there is no difficulty in rejecting post-contact transmission as the explanation for the presence of kava drinking in the Madang area.

At first glance, the case of the southern New Guinea kava-drinking region might appear to be somewhat different, as a growing number of ships began to pass through the Torres Straits from the early years of the nineteenth century. Nevertheless, it is highly unlikely that the conditions under which kava could have been transferred – on-shore visits by Pacific islanders for other than brief periods of time – were met at least until the middle of the century, if not later. Commercial fishing, mainly for trepang, began on a small scale in the Torres Straits in the mid 1840s, and pearling began two decades later (Beckett 1987: 5, 32–3; Hughes 1977: 13–33). Pacific islanders were certainly working in both industries, at least from the 1860s, and Beckett notes that in 1871, when the London Missionary Society (LMS) missionaries first landed at Darnley Island, they encountered 'a European trepanger and a score of so of his Pacific Island workers, who made free with [the Darnley Islanders'] gardens and women' (1987: 24).

However, as we have seen in Chapter 2, the only Torres Straits islands in which kava was drunk were those immediately adjacent to the New Guinea coast, such as Boigu and Dauan. There is no indication of its use in any of the other islands – indeed Haddon claimed that it was unknown (1912: 141) – and the word used for kava, *gamada*, suggests that kava was introduced from New Guinea, rather than by Pacific islanders. Observations of kava use in British New Guinea date back to the earliest explorers, starting from D'Albertis who was in the Fly River region in the mid 1870s, with a number of other reports from the 1880s (D'Albertis 1880, vol. 2: 197; for the other early reports see Haddon 1916: 147–9). The first accounts of kava drinking in Dutch New Guinea come later, from the early 1890s (ibid.: 147), but it was only at this time that contacts other than the most fleeting ones appear to have been established (Serpenti 1965: 6–9; van der Veur 1966a: 9–13, 61–72; 1966b: 86–106; Wirz 1922: 5–11). Furthermore, while some of the people in southern New Guinea, such as the Mawata and the Kiwai, stated that they had adopted kava from their neighbours, the direction of the introductions was *not* from the areas where contacts with the outside world were taking place (Crawford 1981: 97; Landtman 1927: 106; Wirz 1934: 453). Neither is there anything to suggest that these introductions were recent.

There are other good reasons for thinking that kava was of some antiquity in southern New Guinea. In common with Madang, the words used for kava in the region show considerable diversity (see Maps 5, 6, 8, 9, 12; Nevermann 1938) compared to the words used for tobacco, which had been introduced into most places within the period a generation or two before first contact (Haddon 1947: 246–7; Hays 1984: 89, 103; Riesenfeld 1951: 79–80). Also, words for kava which suggest a connection with other parts of the Pacific tend to occur in places away from the coast. Finally, it would be extremely difficult to explain the distribution of cognates in Papua depicted in Map 6 in terms of a post-contact introduction of kava.

Possibility 3: indirect links between regions, loss from the intermediary areas

The preceding discussion demonstrates that there are very strong grounds for accepting that the overall distribution of kava drinking can be explained only if the links between at least some of the known kava-using regions were indirect. In other words, there were people in intermediary areas between the kava-using regions in Melanesia who once drank kava as well, but they abandoned it some time before European contact. Therefore, a central insight of Rivers' work can now be vindicated. However crude and fanciful his notions of 'kava-people' and 'betel-people' may have appeared to his critics, Rivers was wrestling with the explanation of an important and fascinating anthropological problem that he had identified.

While I do not think it will ever be possible to specify the precise location of the intermediary areas which abandoned kava drinking, a general impression can be obtained by considering the likely transmission routes for the custom. Nevertheless, it needs to be recognized that these routes are tentative, and the arguments in their favour are not as strong as the arguments in favour of the abandonment hypothesis itself.

The transmission routes for kava

Some archaeologists have speculated that kava drinking may have been part of the Lapita complex: Kirch reports that R. C. Green thinks it possible that the elaborately decorated, flat-bottomed Lapita ceramic bowls with out-turned rims were used for kava (1984: 67). Geoff Irwin has made a similar conjecture to me, arguing that the high degree of decoration, combined with their local use, suggested that the bowls had a ritual function.

This is hardly a surprising inclusion, given the widespread conviction that the Lapita culture was the precursor to the ancestral Polynesian culture (e.g. Bellwood 1978: 254–5; Kirch 1984: 44–69; Spriggs 1984; Terrell 1986: 254–5). Although it is more controversial, there is a substantial amount of current thinking and research which links the Lapita people and the speakers of Proto-Oceanic, and locates their homeland in the Bismarck Archipelago region (J. Allen 1984; Anson 1986; Pawley and Green 1984; Ross 1987; Tryon 1984: 155; but cf. Kirch *et al.* 1987; Terrell 1986: 252–4). But even if the Lapita–Proto-Oceanic connection is questioned, the linguistic evidence presented in the last chapter does suggest that it is reasonable to propose a link between kava and the speakers of Proto-Oceanic. And whatever the ultimate origin point of the Lapita culture, there are strong reasons for thinking that the Bismarck Archipelago was the Proto-Oceanic homeland (Ross 1987: 11, and personal communication).

The pattern of Set 1 of the kava cognates (Maps 5 and 6) is definitely consistent with a Bismarck Archipelago origin for kava, with its subsequent distribution a consequence of the dispersion of the Oceanic-speaking peoples. In this scenario, the presence of kava in southern New Guinea would have been the result of trade, either direct or indirect, with people of the region around Port Moresby. Certainly, it seems more probable that kava was transmitted along a coastal route from Madang to southern New Guinea rather than via one of the more direct overland routes. Sets 1b (Map 8) and 1c (Map 9) – if they are indeed separate sets – and Set 4 (Map 12), which might seem to point to an overland route, do not contain words for kava which occur in both regions, and thus the more likely explanation is that a word used for one of the other items in the semantic field transferred its meaning to kava in parts of southern New Guinea. Even if Sets 1b and 1c are related to Set 1, the link with a form for kava appears in only a single kava-drinking area. (This is perhaps less certain in the case of Set 1b, but even so, the links between a form similar to the Usino *kamor* and any of the forms for kava in the Madang area do appear rather tenuous.) With just one exception – Kis in Set 1c – these sets contain words only from non-Oceanic languages, though always from more than one phylum.

Athough the arguments in favour of a Bismarck Archipelago origin are not beyond question, they are not inconsiderable. Thus, had kava originated in southern New Guinea and been transmitted 'back' along the New Guinea coast to the Madang region, as well as eastward to the Solomons, we could expect to find much less of a bias in Set 1 to Oceanic languages or languages in close proximity to Oceanic. (Similar considerations would apply had kava originated in the Vanuatu–south-east Solomons region.) Furthermore, the archaeological evidence suggests that a settlement of the southern coast of Papua, sufficiently intensive to support exchange networks which could have transmitted kava and/or knowledge of its manufacture across the Gulf of Papua, did not occur until around 2000 years ago (Allen 1977: 391–3; Rhoads 1982: 132–42; White and O'Connell 1982: 197–204). This is later than the most probable date at which Proto-Polynesian broke up, around the middle of the first millennium BC (Green 1981: 153). Yet the widespread distribution of kava in Polynesia, and the reconstruction of a Proto-Polynesian term not only for kava, but for associated items as well, suggest that the ancestral Polynesians were already familiar with the drink (Pawley and Green 1971: 6, 10; Wurm and Wilson 1975: 114; see also Kirch 1984: 67).[1]

Given the importance of establishing the arguments for the abandonment of kava on as firm a footing as possible, it would have been unwise to use the distribution of techniques of preparing the drink, and other elements of cultural similarity, as the basis for *ruling out* one of the other possibilities. But there can be no objection to using these data for the more tentative, and less crucial, task of examining probable transmission routes. Consequently, I will rely on my earlier discussion in which I suggested that the kava complex was transmitted to Micronesia from somewhere in the south-east Solomons–Vanuatu–Fiji region, and from Micronesia to the Admiralties.

Finally, I want to consider southern Vanuatu, which, while rather peripheral to the overall scheme, may exemplify a process that I will be discussing later. The earliest plausible archaeological evidence for human occupation in southern Vanuatu is 2940±80 BP in Aneityum, and there are a few sites on other islands with dates around 2300 BP. Sherds from one of these latter sites, on Erromanga, suggest that there was an earlier Lapita settlement in the region (Spriggs 1984: 208–9). There are authenticated Lapita sites on neighbouring Efate to the north, and New Caledonia to the south-east (Green 1979: 52–5). If the proposition that kava was an element of the Lapita complex is accepted, we could legitimately assume that the occupants of these sites were using kava.

Yet there are both linguistic and cultural grounds that suggest a later introduction. The words used for kava would appear to have been borrowed, as they are not expected reflexes of Proto-Oceanic *$kawa$ (Tyron 1976: 33–4; Lynch 1978a: 746). There is a Tannese myth which states that kava was brought to the island from the east, and this is used to justify the practice – which, however, is by no means always followed – of facing in this direction when drinking. The *timavha* and the traditional use of banana leaf cups on Tanna, referred to in the previous chapter, indicate the possibility of a source in the chiefly kava ceremonies of Tonga. However, a Tongan

---

[1] Of course, evidence about trade networks among hunting and gathering peoples (see e.g. McCarthy 1939) shows that transmission could have taken place in a series of step-wise movements long before 2000 BP, when the Papuan coast was very thinly populated. The earliest evidence of human presence on the Papuan coast dates from 4000 BP (White and O'Connell 1982: 196–7). If kava was transmitted to the rest of the Pacific in this manner, it must have been subsequently abandoned by an even larger number of communities than would be the case had its origin been among an Oceanic-language-speaking community.

origin is difficult to reconcile with the linguistic evidence: the most likely agents of transmission, the Polynesians of Aniwa and Futuna, speak a language which is believed to be more closely related to Samoan than Tongan (Clark 1979: 258–9). But the precise source is not so important and, in any case, specific cultural and lexical elements of the kava ceremony are likely to have been borrowed from neighbouring communities; as we have already seen, the Fijians adopted the custom of chewing the root as a result of Tongan influence in the pre-contact period.

The significance of southern Vanuatu is that it may offer a pre-contact instance of kava being used, then abandoned, then re-adopted at a later stage. Obviously, this is highly speculative; as I have just pointed to the likelihood of the borrowing of items associated with kava, it would be foolish to deny its possibility in this case. Yet, as I will show in Chapter 6, the abandonment and re-adoption of kava, sometimes more than once, has taken place in a number of Tannese communities in the post-contact period.

Map 14 shows the transmission routes discussed in this section.[1] However from my point of view, the question of the transmission routes for kava is a secondary one. I am a social anthropologist, not a culture historian. Having demonstrated that there are very good reasons for thinking that kava was once drunk by many peoples in Melanesia who subsequently abandoned it, the interesting issues that arise as a consequence are not so much those relating to possible migrations, or other links between cultures. Instead, they are the question of why kava was abandoned, and the possible implications this has for our understanding of cultural and social processes in particular kinds of societies.

Explaining the loss of kava

Competition between kava and betel

As I explained in Chapter 1, Rivers believed that in the places where the betel-people came into contact with the kava-people, such as in the Solomons,[2] the use of kava was gradually abandoned in favour of betel (1914, vol. 2: 252–5). Thus was created the puzzling contemporary distribution of kava drinking.

Rivers cited Christian as another author who believed that kava drinking had its ultimate origin in betel chewing (ibid.: 257). But Christian, who had

---

[1] Of course, in a situation such as this Ockham's razor need not be the most appropriate tool. The actual process of transmission could have been far more complex, involving earlier or later travellers and traders as well. But even if later peoples were involved, the fact that Polynesian words for kava are invariably expected reflexes of Proto-Polynesian *kawa* is an indication that the process is of some antiquity.

[2] Rivers' belief that the Solomons had been populated by the kava-people was an outcome of circular reasoning: he inferred their presence from the existence of the cultural traits he associated with them, such as ghost cult, totemism and the practice of taboo (1914, vol. 2: 252–3).

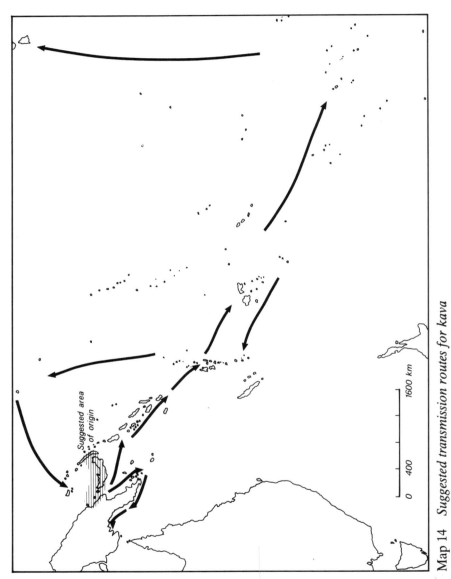

Map 14   Suggested transmission routes for kava

earlier drawn attention to the general non-overlap between the areas of kava use and betel use (1897: 131), drew a different conclusion. He suggested that kava would have been the more attractive substance, and hence more likely to be the displacer rather than the one displaced (1899: 189–90).

Insofar as authors have taken the question of the distribution of kava seriously, they have tended to accept the explanation that Rivers gave (e.g. Fox 1924: 216–17; cf. Riesenfeld 1950: 650). The appeal of this explanation would seem to lie in the belief that kava and betel are mutually exclusive. As I have shown in Chapter 2, this belief is largely mistaken, although there are a few instances, such as the distribution of kava and betel use in the south-east Solomons–northern Vanuatu area, and in a few parts of southern New Guinea, which provide it with some credence. It is a belief which also appears to have entered into folk explanations: David Kausimae – the 'Are'are politician to whom I wrote requesting information about the possible use of kava in Malaita – replied, 'we 'Are'are people do not use it because we do have the betel nut'.

There is both linguistic and botanical evidence which is consistent with the notion that there may have been competition between the two substances, with one eventually displacing the other. The evidence presented in the last chapter, indicating that the words for kava, areca nut, and *Piper betle* participate in a single semantic field, is exactly what we would expect to find had such competition taken place (Chowning 1963: 42; Dutton 1973). Yet, as already noted, this evidence cannot decide the issue, as there are other, equally plausible factors that may underlie the creation of this semantic field. Further relevant evidence is that the term for areca palm in a number of Tannese languages, *napwok*, is an expected reflex of the Proto-Oceanic *mpua* (Lynch 1978a: 730).[1] This raises the possibility that betel may have been used there at some time in the past. Although other explanations are also possible (cf. Chowning on the widespread distribution of cognates for the non-utilized and non-cultivated nettle tree in Melanesia, 1963: 43), it appears that *Piper betle* also grows wild in Tanna. During my visit to Tanna in 1986, a Tannese who had travelled to Papua New Guinea to participate in an arts festival assured me that the betel pepper he saw everywhere in the country was exactly the same plant as that which grew in a number of relatively inaccessible places around the base of Mt Tukosmere on Tanna. In the past this man has always been careful to provide what he believes to be the correct information, and his description of the plant was completely consistent with *Piper betle*. Unfortunately, owing to the brevity of my stay, I was unable to obtain a specimen for verification. Nevertheless,

[1] In a personal communication Malcolm Ross has stated that the Proto-Oceanic word should be *mpuaq* or, using his preferred orthography, *buaq*. This does not affect my argument, however.

there are accounts of *Piper betle* growing wild in other parts of Vanuatu (Vincent Lebot, personal communication; Codrington 1891: 35). But insofar as this may point to the displacement of the one narcotic by the other, it is along the lines proposed by Christian, not Rivers.

There is some additional, circumstantial information which also needs to be borne in mind when considering the relation between kava and betel. Both have spread to new areas in the post-contact period. Betel use has spread into the Highlands of Papua New Guinea (Burton-Bradley 1966: 744; Farnworth 1976: 85; Marshall 1987: 16, 19). Kava has been adopted by Aborigines in northern Australia, and by the people of south Malekula and Ambrym who are not known to have used it traditionally (Alexander 1985; Cawte 1986, 1988; Kirk Huffman, personal communication; Bob Tonkinson, personal communication). But although the post-War years have seen a growing amount of inter-country travel among Pacific islanders, neither substance has had any success in penetrating the other's traditional geographical region. Fox states that betel was rapidly displacing kava in Motlav in the Banks Islands (1924: 67). However, while contemporary Banks Islands people remember betel being used about forty years ago (possibly brought in through church contacts with the south-east Solomons), it is not used now and kava is still drunk (Kirk Huffman, personal communication). A few authors have cited a statement made by Rannie in 1889 that betel chewing was growing rapidly among Fijians, but to the best of my knowledge no other observers have described such a process, and there is no evidence of it today (Riesenfeld 1947: 157; Theodoratus 1953: 100).

If we were to accept the argument that betel did displace kava before European contact in parts of Papua New Guinea and the Solomons, a more satisfactory explanation of why this should occur than the explanation proposed by Rivers would be necessary. It is not at all clear *why* we should expect competition to occur between kava and betel. As we saw in Chapter 2, in both the north and south of New Guinea, kava and betel are used in conjunction with each other.

The introduction of tobacco into the Pacific, which has occurred over the past four hundred years, does not appear to have had any effect on the consumption of either betel or kava, at least in Melanesia (Riesenfeld 1951: 69; Hays 1984; Marshall 1987: 29–32). However, the historian Anthony Reid has argued that although the use of tobacco coexisted with betel chewing in Indonesia from the early seventeenth century, in this century cigarette smoking has tended to displace betel, which is now used only by the elderly in a number of areas. Yet the material he presents can be subjected to a different interpretation, one in which the relative position of the two substances is a consequence, not of any internal relation of competition between them, but of their individual connections with other social processes.

Reid's argument is phrased in status terms. Although various forms of smoking had been adopted by Indonesians in the period to the nineteenth century, the most popular way of taking tobacco was by chewing; either adding it to the betel mix, or else holding a wad of it in the mouth. The cigarette-like *bungkus*, made from shredded tobacco wrapped in a dried banana or maize leaf, was also widely used, but its popularity among ordinary Indonesians made it unattractive to the upper status groups. The situation changed with the increasing commitment to smoking cigars and cigarettes among European males during the course of the nineteenth century, and Reid suggests that this made it inevitable that it would be 'only a matter of time before the whole society adopted the habit' (1985: 538). Furthermore, betel chewing and modernity came to be seen as antithetical. It is these associations, *separately established*, which are important. For although men generally abandoned it earlier than women, large numbers of women have given up betel chewing also. But they have not taken up smoking which is 'almost entirely restricted to men' (ibid.: 542).

I have come across only one plausible reason why the use of kava and betel might tend to be incompatible and, even then, it would not seem to be a particularly powerful factor. Crawford says that when the Gogodala consume kava and betel together 'the effect, apparently, is quite drastic' (1981: 97), and Landtman, writing about the Kiwai, states that if kava and betel were taken together men became heavily drunk (1927: 110). Crawford says that joint consumption by the Gogodala is only very occasional (although this would appear to be negated by the observations of Butcher and Landtman; see Haddon 1916: 150), yet both kava and betel were culturally important. Observers in other areas of New Guinea who have witnessed kava and betel being taken one after the other make no reference to intensification of effects, and it may be that these were a product of characteristics specific to local varieties of one or both substances (see e.g. Serpenti 1969: 34). Yet even if intensification of effects was a problem, it could explain only why kava and betel might not be used together, leaving unanswered the question of why they might not be used in different contexts.

In summary, the above discussion suggests that while the possibility of competition between kava and betel in some areas cannot be ruled out, neither are there any strong grounds for thinking that the reason behind the loss of kava in so many Melanesian societies was its displacement by betel. Certainly, displacement may have occurred in some cases; but if we wish to understand the disappearance of kava, we must consider other, more compelling reasons.

Actual or perceived negative qualities of kava

A number of authors have observed that, along with its beneficial qualities, kava also has associations with poison (Bott 1972: 216; Sahlins 1981b:

125–6; Turner 1986: 210–12). Turner briefly refers to the use of kava in sorcery in Fiji, although his argument is mainly based on some of the semantic extensions of words for kava and related items in Fiji and Polynesia, and on interpretations of themes in Tongan myths of the origin of kava (ibid.: 209). As his own comments imply,[1] the case he makes is not as strong as might be desired. Thus he refers to the fact that an additional meaning of the word *kava* or its cognates in a number of Polynesian languages is 'bitter', and Lester's speculation that the Fijian word for kava derives from a word which means bitter (1941–2: 105). Turner then notes that in the Bauan dialect of Fijian 'the term meaning bitter (*gaga*) also means poisonous and this lumping of the two meanings is a feature of the semantic structure of Polynesian languages as well' (1986: 210). Bott's argument also depends on the interpretation of kava origin myths in Tonga, and the use of the morpheme *kava* in various compound words for fish poison and nausea (1972: 216; see also Knauft 1987: 86, for a metaphorical association between kava and fish poison among the Gebusi of Papua). Sahlins similarly uses Tongan myths, pointing out that they are widely known in eastern Fiji. As well, he infers that as the Fijian chief is ritually reborn during his installation ceremony he must have been 'killed' by something, and concludes that he is 'poisoned' by the kava he is given (1981b: 125). Although the analyses of these authors can be said to show only that the negative associations of kava, while certainly present, are relatively muted, they nevertheless highlight an aspect of kava that needs to be considered. There are some other areas of the Pacific where these negative associations seem to be both prominent and quite consciously articulated.

Nevermann states that occasionally young Kanum Irebe men were poisoned by the kava they were first given after their initiation (1938: 184). In the Marquesas, there were also instances of men dying from excessive kava drinking (Dening 1974: 252; 1980: 240, 258). The dangers associated with kava were expressed in accounts the men of Karkar Island gave to Romola McSwain. People boasted of the strength of their ancestors, who 'had been able to drink [kava] without turning a hair, but how later men, when they tried it, used to lose their senses because they were less strong' (personal communication).

In Vanuatu, there are also references to a link between kava and death. In the Hog Harbour area of Santo, widows of men who had achieved high rank in the graded society were given kava before they were strangled (Deacon 1929: 463). Kirk Huffman has informed me that many of the people of north-east Malekula are frightened of kava because it was formerly used to perform a particularly dangerous kind of sorcery –

---

[1] Kava 'is simultaneously regarded as life-enhancing yet tainted, *however tenuously* [my emphasis], by death and disease' (Turner 1986: 212).

although it was also used to make peace – and unlike most of their fellow countrymen, have generally not participated in the post-Independence upsurge in kava drinking. The utilization of kava in sorcery is found in a number of places in Vanuatu and elsewhere (e.g. Aoba, Michael Allen, personal communication; Tanna; Fiji, Lester 1941–2: 253; Hawaii, Titcomb 1948: 147–9; Kiwai, Landtman 1927: 322). This is hardly surprising given the supernatural powers generally ascribed to kava, and the difficulty of confining the use of such powers solely to good ends. In this sense Turner is quite correct to point to the ambivalence with which kava is regarded (1986: 209).

Nevermann mentions a further danger associated with kava drinking in pre-contact times: its soporific power made drinkers vulnerable to surprise attack. He explains the infrequency of kava drinking among the Sohur as being due to their fear of headhunters, and states that he was repeatedly told by old Marind-anim that in the past, because of similar fears, they drank much less than they did after the Dutch pacified their region (1938: 185–6; see also Haddon 1916: 149). Informants on Tanna told me that during the time of intense fighting in the last century, triggered by the introduction of firearms, men faced a continual threat of being attacked while intoxicated on kava (see also Paton 1965: 92). Consequently, only the older men were allowed to drink, while the men of fighting age kept guard. These examples show that the perceived dangers of kava drinking might result, not in outright abandonment, but in its limitation to a narrower range of men or occasions. It is not unreasonable to think that in many cases such restrictions would have served to increase the ritual potency and value of kava. Yet, as I will suggest in the concluding section and in later chapters, in the long term these restrictions could operate to make kava just as vulnerable to disappearance.

Two widely reported side-effects of kava are vomiting, and the development of characteristic skin lesions or scales among heavy drinkers (e.g. Bott: 1972: 230; Frater 1952; Handy 1923: 203; Landtman 1927: 107; Lemert 1967: 192; Serpenti 1969: 34). Obviously, the undesirability or otherwise of these effects is a matter of cultural interpretation: Emerson states that Hawaiians would deliberately drink large amounts of kava in order to bring about the skin condition, because when the scales fell off, the skin was left 'soft and smooth – a kind of snake experience' (1903: 137; see also Titcomb 1948: 121). Tannese men regard the vomiting which may follow kava as a beneficial purgative, and their only concern is that a man who is vomiting should go into the bushes surrounding the kava drinking ground so that he will not be in the full view of others.

As was the case when considering the question of competition between betel and kava, concerns about harmful effects of kava such as those noted above cannot be ruled out as possible explanations for the abandonment of kava amongst particular people. Thus, it would appear that the men of north-east Malekula, long believed not to have been kava users (Deacon 1934: 373; Layard 1942: 376), did in fact drink kava, and that its association with sorcery was at least part of the reason for its abandonment, before early European observers had the opportunity to record the practice (Kirk Huffmann, personal communication). Furthermore, no doubt some people perceived damaging consequences of drinking which we are unlikely to anticipate: people in south-east Santo told Guiart that they gave up kava because it caused lumps in their limbs (1958: 49).

However, as the last example suggests, once we have noted the possibility that fear of its effects may have induced some people to abandon kava, further analysis could proceed only if a sizeable corpus of highly specific material relating to a people's concepts of health and disease, etc. were available. But given the time frame we are considering – up to 3,500 or more years if the Lapita–Proto-Oceanic connection is accepted – and the variability and volatility of the cultural elements involved, the processes that may have occurred are simply irrecoverable.

Such a realization might be thought to compromise the whole point of this study. Obviously, any attempts to explain the loss of kava will be speculative. Nevertheless, as I will suggest later, by taking a case study of the abandonment of kava in the known post-contact period it is possible to uncover the operation of social processes which must have been present in many Pacific societies with poorly developed and unstable political hierarchies. Although the argument will still be dependent on many conjectural elements, it will be more firmly grounded and generalizable than could be the case with an argument based on cultural processes of the kind we have been considering so far. I think that it is also potentially more productive in an anthropological sense, in that it can encompass and illuminate other problems of interest to Pacific scholars. Before I begin to develop this argument, however, I intend to note one further possibility.

The vulnerability of kava to botanical extinction

Kava appears to grow satisfactorily only under a rather limited range of conditions. It requires high rainfall, particularly in the first six months of growth, and is unlikely to survive in areas with a long and marked dry season. It also requires a soil which is well drained and rich in organic matter, and it needs to be sheltered from the sun and wind (Gatty 1956: 244; Lebot 1983: 85–9).

These requirements may help explain the variations in the ability of kava to survive and propagate without human intervention that I discussed in the previous chapter. (Yet, they are not the whole story; the above conditions are met over most of Tanna, where kava is known only as a cultivated plant.) They also explain another point I mentioned in Chapter 3: the great difficulty that people in some areas have in growing kava. Thus van Baal states that the Marind-anim find kava a 'notoriously risky crop' (1966: 921). Serpenti writes that 'it is not easy to grow *wati* [kava] on Kolepom. Only the older and abler cultivators can boast of having *wati*-gardens of any significance. The others are totally dependent on these few for their supply of the liquor' (1969: 32). Nevermann was told by people on the south coast of Kolopom that all their kava plants were destroyed in storms some years previously, and that they had not attempted to cultivate the plant again, but relied on neighbouring people for their supply (1938: 189).

Obviously, as I have already suggested, in the course of human migrations in the Pacific kava would have been carried to places where it could not survive, such as flat atolls. In other areas, it may have survived for a time, and then been wiped out by particularly adverse conditions, such as noted in the example above. Of course, these situations may not be peculiar to kava: extreme weather conditions may eliminate a number of cultivars within a given region. However, as kava is a species which is, or at least has become, totally dependent on vegetative reproduction, its range of variability is far more restricted than species in which sexual reproduction can take place, and it is therefore more vulnerable (Darlington 1973: 59; Raven, Evert and Curtis 1981: 154–5).

But there is an additional reason why kava may have been more vulnerable to botanical extinction than other cultivated plants: the likelihood that it could also be lost as a result of social and cultural factors of the kind being discussed in this chapter. The point can perhaps best be made by considering the effects of a catastrophic climatic event, such as a severe cyclone. Although gardens and future planting stock of particular cultivars might be wiped out over quite large areas, reintroduction of the lost varieties or species could take place as a result of contacts with unaffected, or less severely affected areas. In the case of widely distributed staples such reintroductions would not present a problem, at least in a historical sense; new planting material would in principle be obtainable from the closest unaffected areas. (See for example Waddell's discussion of the traditional response of New Guinea Highlanders to the destruction of gardens by frost, 1974: 41.) At a later point in time there might be no indication that localized extinctions had ever occurred. But if the distribution of a species was already restricted as a result of other factors, the ability to obtain replanting material would be correspondingly reduced, thus increasing the possibility that the extinction would be permanent.

In other words, I am suggesting that once the process of abandoning kava had commenced within a given region, it could reach a stage at which a climatic catastrophe of sufficient impact could make it irreversible. I think that this is the most likely explanation for a feature of the geographical distribution of kava which, although so far unremarked, may already have struck the reader: while its distribution outside Polynesia is patchy, it does tend to occur in regional clumps. Yet, if I am correct in my suggestion that kava originated in the Bismarck Archipelago region, from where it was taken into the Pacific by Oceanic language speakers, it might be expected that small areas of kava drinking would be found scattered over more parts of seaboard Melanesia. The point of this section has been to suggest that this is not a necessary expectation.

The sanctity and religious significance of kava

I have left what I believe to be the most important, as well as the most anthropologically interesting, explanation until last. As a primary factor, perhaps it should have been discussed before botanical vulnerability which, as I indicated, would more commonly depend on the prior operation of the other factors to be effective. However, the issues to be raised under the present heading are an introduction to the material I will be considering in the second half of this book.

It is possible to distinguish two quite separate explanations for the disappearance of kava in *The History of Melanesian Society*, although Rivers made no attempt to distinguish them himself. He thought that in the matrilineal area of the central Solomons the most important cultural characteristics of the kava-people were present: a religion based on the cult of ghosts, the institution of totemism, and the protection of property through the use of taboo signs associated with the ghosts. Furthermore, this was the one area of the Solomons which possessed any evidence of secret societies (1914, vol. 2: 252). Consequently, he had to argue that this culture was 'relatively little influenced by the betel-people' (ibid.: 253). Nevertheless, the people did use betel and there was no contemporary evidence of kava drinking. As well as explaining this absence by recourse to the familiar argument that betel had displaced kava, Rivers suggested, albeit in a somewhat muddled way, that kava could also disappear as a result of internal social processes. The association between kava and secret societies made kava vulnerable. If the secret societies disappeared, so would kava. Alternatively, kava might become progressively more restricted, either to limited social contexts, or to specific categories of people, so that finally it might be lost. Noting that until he discovered it, kava drinking in Vanikolo had been overlooked because its sanctity made it so infrequent, Rivers suggested that in other parts of the Solomons 'its disappearance would have been merely the result of a further progress of the [same] changes' (ibid.: 254). And whereas Codrington had thought that the absence of kava on Santa Maria Island (Gaua) in the Banks group indicated that it had only recently been introduced to the other islands (1891: 351), Rivers stated that he was told that kava had been 'given up by the people, only the chiefs having been allowed to drink it' (1914, vol. 1: 86). In other words, kava disappeared because of its cultural and religious significance.[1] The same idea has been used by Kirch and Yen to explain the recent extinction of the kava plant in Tikopia, and they suggest that this extinction 'may be symbolic of its former cultural and religious importance compared with the surviving betel' (1982: 37; see also Firth 1970: 201). Phrased in these terms, the problem of kava's disappearance is simply one aspect of the much broader problem of the high degree of religious instability in Melanesia.

In the second part of this book I will consider the relationship between the fortunes of kava and the processes of post-contact religious change on Tanna. While the concentration on Tanna is obviously a consequence of the fact that it has been the site of my fieldwork, as well as the fact that it has been the subject of a very substantial corpus of ethnographic and historical material, it should not be thought that it is an otherwise adventitious choice. Many observers have noted the Tannese preoccupation with kava, and it was my own experience of this preoccupation which provided the initial stimulus for my interest. Yet the expression of this preoccupation has not been constant. Although, considering the island as a whole, kava has always been drunk on Tanna since the pre-contact period – and no doubt always will be – at different times and places the use of kava has been both abandoned and intensified in response to the vicissitudes of religious affiliation; Tanna affords an excellent example of a religious volatility found in many parts of Melanesia.

Ultimately, my argument will be based on two straightforward assumptions, both of which have informed my earlier work on cargo cults and religion in Melanesia (Brunton 1971, 1980). The first is that there is an essential continuity between the nature of pre-contact and post-contact religious change. In the present context this means I am assuming that radical religious changes of the kind that occurred in the period following European contact and control also occurred previously, and that any differences are those of degree rather than kind. As well as mercurial shifts in religious affiliation, these changes include the abandonment of key rituals after what appears to be only minimal pressure, and the ready adoption of new religious movements and rituals (see e.g. ibid.; Larcom 1982: 330, 336–7; Schwartz 1973: 159; Wagner 1979: 163–4). While some Melanesians

[1] In an earlier paper dealing with the disappearance of the canoe, pottery and the bow and arrow from parts of Oceania, Rivers also suggested the importance of religious factors, and was more careful about disentangling these from other factors. He pointed out that 'in many parts of Oceania an art practised by a special group of craftsmen is not a mere technical performance, but has a definitely religious character and may be regarded as a long series of religious rites' (1978 [1912]: 204). He went on to make a comment which – as we will see in later chapters – is probably even more applicable to kava. 'The quenching of [craftsmen's] spiritual power, the *mana* of Oceania, may have been another and most potent factor . . . [in] the disappearance of useful arts' (ibid.: 205).

may make assertions about the changeless traditions of the past, these are often ideological statements, forged either in internal power conflicts between different categories or classes of people, or in attempts to preserve autonomy in the face of external interference by missionaries or Government officials (Brunton 1980; Keesing 1982b; 1987).

The second assumption is that these radical changes can be explained in sociological terms, rather than by reference to an apparently irreducible enjoyment of 'novelty for its own sake' (Tuzin 1984: 4; cited in Harrison 1987: 493), or something similar. As such, it should be possible, at least in principle, to explain variations in the degree to which these changes occur, although I shall only be touching on this possibility in the present work.

By considering the Tannese material in a comparative context I hope to identify those characteristics of Melanesian social organization that may be responsible for this cultural instability. I will be proceeding on the supposition that the prestige which can be gained by those who successfully introduce radical changes to a community provides a sufficient – though in any given case not necessarily sole – motivation for attempts by individuals to bring about such changes (see e.g. Allen 1981b; Lindstrom 1984). The focus of my analysis will be on the reasons why, at certain times, *others* are willing to go along with these radical changes. This is particularly important in the present context: what might make men agree to abandon customs, such as kava drinking, from which they appear to derive a great deal of pleasure and satisfaction? I will argue that this willingness was both the outcome of identifiable weaknesses in institutions of co-ordination and control, as well as a significant contributor to the perpetuation of these weaknesses.

5

Kava on Tanna: traditional ritual and contemporary modifications

An indication of the importance of kava on Tanna can be seen in the number of articles it has occasioned (Brunton 1979; Gregory, Gregory and Peck 1981; Lindstrom 1980, 1981b, 1982, 1987). There are many other indices that can also be cited: the inevitable presence of roots of kava in every form of prestation, the amount of time men spend on cultivating the plant and preparing, consuming and enjoying the effects of the drink, its focus as a topic of conversation, and its role in magic and communication with the supernatural world.

Guiart has suggested that the importance of kava drinking may have been inflated by Presbyterian attempts to eradicate the custom (1956a: 246). But, while it is true that at certain times kava became a symbol of pagan resistance to the mission, all the available evidence indicates that its key role in Tannese culture was established long before the establishment of Christianity.

Although J. R. Forster noted that *Piper methysticum* grew on Tanna, none of the members of Cook's voyage seem to have observed kava drinking there (1982: 620). This is not particularly surprising, as they all appear to have returned to the ship, or at least not to have ventured beyond the beach, by sunset, the only time at which kava was traditionally drunk. Nevertheless, Forster indicates that the Tannese all left in the early evening 'to go to sleep' (ibid.: 591). Far from this being a result of concern about being exposed to the cold as he suggests, or a fear of ghosts as his editor Hoare states, the most likely reason is that the men were going to drink kava, while the women were returning to their hamlets, from where they would be unable to see men drinking (see Wawn 1973: 26).

The first actual description of kava drinking on Tanna comes from Turner, who pointed to its religious and social significance, noting that it was drunk every evening by all adult men (1942–3: 8; 1861: 85). The great importance of kava in traditional Tannese culture is confirmed by many others whose observations predate the first Tannese baptisms in 1881: the comments of Copeland (1861: 171), Markham (1873: 191), J. Paton (1965: 180) and Watt (1896: 203–4) leave no room for doubt on the matter.

The traditional kava ritual

None of the early sources for kava on Tanna provide the richness of detail of Mariner's description of the Tongan ritual (1818, vol. 2: 172–96), or even Williams' account of the Fijian ritual (Williams and Calvert 1859: 111–15). While this probably reflects differences in the character and sympathies of the respective observers, the main explanation is more likely to have been the lesser degree of formality surrounding kava on Tanna. Although there were a number of restrictions involved in the preparation of the drink, compared to western Polynesia the proceedings were relaxed, almost casual. It was only in the actual drinking of kava, and the conditions under which its effects were enjoyed, that the 'alerting quality' of ritual action (Lewis 1980: 19–20) appears to have been really evident.

Nevertheless, despite their sparseness, if the nineteenth-century accounts are used in conjunction with those of contemporary informants – who readily point out changes that have taken place[1] – it is still possible to provide a reasonably detailed description of the traditional kava ritual.

Kava was always drunk on the *yimwayim*, a circular or oval-shaped area of cleared ground up to fifty or sixty metres in diameter. In his 1956 survey, Guiart listed the names of nearly six hundred,[2] many of which belonged to extinct groups (1956a: 263–402; see also Gray 1892: 648). Every *yimwayim* was shaded by at least one banyan tree, usually several. On the periphery there was at least one sacred grove dedicated to the spirits, and around the *yimwayim* were scattered small hamlets containing not more than ten households (Turner 1861: 84). The larger *yimwayim* were also used for dances and prestations. Although women were permitted on them for much of the day,[3] at around an hour before sunset, when men began to gather for kava, they were forbidden to be in the vicinity and had to use special paths which circumvented the *yimwayim*. Women could not consume kava under any circumstances, but they were allowed to grow, own and handle kava. However, it was believed that if a woman were to see the drink being prepared or consumed her child or another relative would fall ill, or that a house in her hamlet would burn down. Should this happen accidentally, misfortune could be averted by touching her head with a branch of kava. I have been told that this was a traditional remedy, although there is no doubt that violence might also have been directed against the woman: thus

[1] Cf. Adams' claim that Turner was told by the Tannese 'that the precise format of the ritual was "sacred" and if transgressed "would be the cause of some great evil, if not death"' (1984: 8). In fact, Adams has read more into Turner's words than is justified, as is quite apparent from the original document (1842–3: 8).
[2] In my article on kava, as a result of misinterpreting a rough translation of Guiart's book, and a failure to attempt a count of the *yimwayim* listed, this figure is incorrectly given as 233 (Brunton 1979: 93).
[3] Turner states that women were never allowed on the *yimwayim* except at times of feasts and dances (1842–3: 8), but my informants deny that the restrictions were ever so severe.

towards the end of the last century a man from Irakik shot and killed one of his wives for this offence (cf. Lindstrom 1987: 100).

Unless there had been a meeting or other gathering, the number of men drinking at any one *yimwayim* was relatively small, perhaps up to twenty, consisting of the men resident in the surrounding hamlets and a few visitors (cf. Gray 1892: 662). Some informants stated that it was preferable to have no more than ten or a dozen drinkers at the one *yimwayim*, otherwise it was difficult to ensure that there would be no noise, which would 'spoil the kava'.

Kava was prepared in a *niko*, a wooden, canoe-shaped bowl about half a metre long. The root was broken up into pieces which were cleaned with a wad of coconut husk. Men and youths would then bite off portions, which they would chew for a few minutes until the kava was completely macerated, when it would be disgorged into the *niko*. The process of preparing the kava was not hurried, and was punctuated by frequent conversation, as men gossiped and discussed matters of common interest.

When there was sufficient kava in the *niko*, water from a flask (*uipil*) made from a hollowed-out coconut was poured over it.[1] A youth, who had been circumcised, but not yet initiated into sexual activity, kneaded and mixed the kava, ensuring that the chewed root was evenly dispersed. A strainer (*nivhau*), made from the stem of a banana, was then placed into the bowl. This absorbed the liquid, at the same time excluding most of the solid matter.[2] The contents of the stem were poured into a cup made by gathering up the sides of a fresh banana leaf, and the kava was drunk through a piece of wild cane from which the pith had been removed.[3] Preparations were organized so that drinking would take place 'just as the sun sinks out of sight' (Gray 1892: 661), the only time at which kava was consumed. Explaining this, as well as the reason for drinking only at *yimwayim*, men said that spirits were present only there, and only after the sun disappeared. (There is also mythical justification for drinking at this time: see Guiart 1956a: 250–1.) At each *yimwayim* there was a shrub called *kapouaitai* whose leaves curled up around the time of sunset and, when the sky was overcast,

---

[1] One of my informants stated that in the past it was forbidden to use water from any other source, although he could provide no specific rationale for this. At a number of points in the preparation of the drink, paraphernalia made from parts of the coconut palm are used. As I will describe later, while some of these items are no longer used, others, also made from the coconut palm, are now utilized elsewhere in the ritual. I know of no Tannese myths which link kava and the coconut, although there are myths which justify the use of some other paraphernalia (see Guiart 1956a: 250–1). Schutz has recorded a text from Nguna which recounts the origin of kava and explicitly links it with the coconut (1969: 78–9).

[2] Gray, who appears to have been a reasonably careful observer, states that cordage fibre was used (1892: 661). It is quite possible that there were regional variations, although in general terms Tanna does display a high degree of cultural homogeneity (Lindstrom 1981a: 14).

[3] Again, there may have been regional variations. Gray states that a tube made from a banana leaf was used (1892: 661). There is a staged picture of a man drinking through a leaf straw from a banana leaf cup in Bonnemaison (1975: 101).

men used this as the signal to begin drinking. After all the water in the *niko* was exhausted, more water was added, and a fresh bowl was made for those who had not yet partaken. Each man drank only one cup. Strictly speaking, only men who had fathered a child were permitted to drink, although informants stated that this rule was relaxed for bachelors or childless widowers who had reached middle age.

The requirements for having a virgin youth knead and mix the kava was a consequence of the more generalized belief that once a man had had sexual contact with a woman he should never directly touch anything that would be consumed either by himself or by others. As J. R. Forster first observed in 1774, Tannese men hold their food between two leaves (1982: 591). There were also a number of specific restrictions giving additional expression to the disjunction between the women's domain and kava drinking. Men from a number of areas on the island could not mention women's names while kava was being prepared, and if it was necessary to refer to them for any reason, a circumlocution was used, such as 'those who are in the hamlet'. While this taboo did not apply to men in the area around Lomtihekel in which I worked (see Map 15), they were forbidden to handle fire during the period starting from the first pouring of water to make the kava, and ending when every man had drunk. However, these taboos were not just locality specific. When a man from an area where a taboo applied was drinking at a *yimwayim* where it normally didn't apply, it still had to be observed by all the men drinking with him. Thus, for example, when men from the Enfitana area visited their relatives at Laruanu, both sets of restrictions were in force. My informants state that the two taboos are equivalent[1] and justify this claim by referring either to women's use of fire to prepare *nahunu* – food which men eat after drinking kava, and which cannot be taken back to the hamlets[2] – or to a myth of kava's origin in which, like fire, it was originally taken from a woman's vagina by men. (For further restrictions and avoidances, particularly those relating to the consumption of foods after drinking, see Lindstrom 1981b: 380–2; 1987: 106.)

Drinking order appears always to have been more flexible than in western Polynesia, a point that seems to be confirmed by the fact that the early sources make no mention of any order of precedence. Generally, the senior men drank first, the younger men last. But this would not always apply. At certain times, such as during a naming ceremony, or after the appropriate

[1] Guiart refers to a further taboo on touching certain trees in some – unspecified – areas. The sap of one of these trees is used to make babies vomit soon after they are born (1956a: 248). This may indicate that the same principle as is said to lie behind the other two restrictions is at work here. Guiart makes no mention of the restriction on uttering women's names, and sees no connection between the two restrictions he cites. My informants said that they had not heard about the taboo on trees, and thought that if it really existed it would be in distant areas of the island. No other writer mentions it.

[2] At least this is what men say. Nevertheless, occasionally I have observed youths parcel up their share of the *nahunu*, and carry it back to their hamlets.

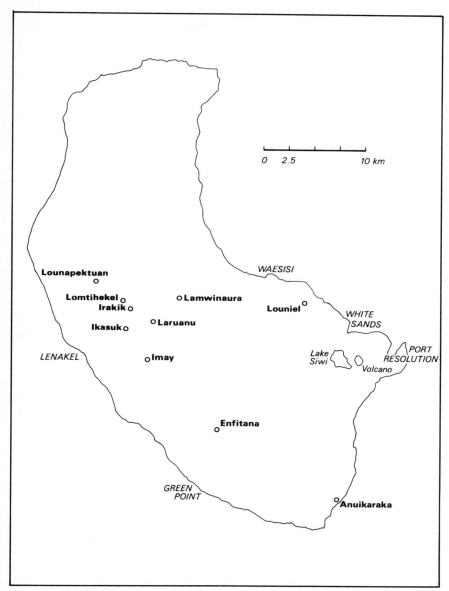

Map 15   *Tanna, showing the major places referred to in the text*

title holder had performed the magic for a particular crop, specific individuals central to the event would drink first. Also, if a visitor was present, and the other men wished to honour him for some reason, he would be offered the first cup (see also Lindstrom 1981b: 390, 392).

Turner wrote that kava was 'drunk with great ceremony' (1842–3: 8; see also Paton 1965: 180). Men moved away from the others while drinking, and spat out the last mouthful of kava in a spray to make an invocation or statement (*timavha*) to the spirits.[1] Such an invocation was an essential component of all magical ritual, serving to activate special stones that would have been manipulated earlier in the day. A *timavha* could also be in the form of a simple request, made independently of any earlier magical performance. After making his *timavha* a man would emit a long yell or yodel.[2] Each man had his own distinctive yell, and a competitive element was involved, with men boasting that theirs could be heard the furthest. An old man from Irakik, 5 km from the coast, claimed that his father's yell was so loud and penetrating that the people on the coast would know that he had drunk his kava.

The drinker then discarded his banana-leaf cup and took his share of the *nahunu*. He would not have eaten for some hours, as Tannese assert that otherwise the effect of the kava is reduced. In explaining this, one informant used the metaphor of smoke in a hut which had all its openings closed up.[3] The youths who had assisted in the preparation would also be given a share of the *nahunu*.

During the few minutes it took for the food to be distributed, conversation continued. The men would move away to choose a spot on the *yimwayim* where they would sit for an hour or more, experiencing the effects of the drink, 'listening to the kava', as the Tannese say. Alternatively, some men might sit around a common fire, but they would ignore each other's presence. There was no conversation. Were it really necessary to communicate with someone, it had to be in the form of a whisper and be concluded as quickly as possible. If there was any loud noise from one of the surrounding hamlets, on the following day the man whose family was responsible would have to present kava to all the men whose kava 'had been spoilt'. This period of quiet was perhaps the most striking aspect of the whole ritual. Gray, who provided the most detailed and sympathetic of the early accounts, described it as follows:

---

[1] In his published account, Turner stated that the chief of the village uttered a short prayer *before* kava was drunk (1861: 85), and this was repeated by Agnes Watt (1896: 108). However, this is not correct. Turner is more accurate in his journal, where he states that the prayer is uttered 'before the meal' (1842–3: 8), although he does not make it clear that men eat after drinking.
[2] Humphreys wrongly states that this was made before drinking (1926: 82).
[3] Cf. Lindstrom's comments about men being seen as 'closed', whereas women are 'open' (1987: 117).

The effect on an onlooker is peculiar. A still evening settling into the gloom of night; half a dozen privileged youths bursting with fun; a dozen or more men sitting around a fire looking at one another without seeing one another; the gulp of deglutition and the whish of expectoration that seems to come in between the chirps of innumerable crickets.

(1892: 662)

Eventually, men would retire to the men's house on the *yimwayim* to sleep, or they would return to their own hamlets. But each man would get up and leave without a word of farewell to anyone. Indeed, the kava ritual was explicitly perceived to be a farewell in itself.

Continuities and modifications

Many elements of the traditional ritual have been retained, and appear to be adhered to as strongly as they ever were in the past. But there have been a number of changes. In this section I will confine the discussion to ritual kava drinking, leaving the changes associated with the development of a secular pattern of kava consumption until the next chapter.

Every day, pagans – and most Christians belonging to denominations which do not proscribe kava – still gather at *yimwayim* in the late afternoon to drink. Men usually arrive individually, or in groups of two or three, accompanied by boys and youths. Some men carry roots of kava. Although strict accounts are not kept, there is strong criticism of men who always expect others to provide them with kava, and who never bring any in return.

Soon after they arrive, the men and the youths squat down in groups and begin the process of cutting and cleaning the roots. This is done at a leisurely pace, and is accompanied by spirited conversation. Apart from talking about daily events, men discuss matters relating to traditional rights and *kastom*. It is a time 'for straightening out the thoughts of men', they say. Conversation continues while the kava is being chewed, although men who try to talk with a mouthful of kava are not always intelligible.

After the kava has been masticated to the appropriate consistency, it is disgorged onto a leaf. The *niko* passed out of use long ago. It was still being utilized at the time of Humphreys' fieldwork in 1921, although its obsolescence seems to have been well under way (1926: 81). Guiart was able to obtain one in 1956, and he photographed another, but by then they were very rare (1956a 251, Plate VI). Informants state that they are simply too much trouble to make.

A separate heap of chewed root is prepared for each drinker, although if there is insufficient kava, heaps are shared. Each is about the size of a closed small fist, and contains two or three mouthfuls of kava, usually chewed by different men. However, if a host wishes to honour an important visitor, he may ask someone 'whose heart he knows' to chew for him alone. Also, a man may signal his displeasure with others by chewing his own kava,

101

although if he is seriously annoyed he is more likely to take one or two boys to a small *yimwayim* and drink on his own.

A few minutes before the drink is due to be made, young boys, and occasionally some of the resident men, go to the surrounding hamlets to fetch water and the *nahunu*. The Tannese are still particular about drinking at sunset, and if it is overcast they take their cue from one of the increasing number of men with watches. In places where the taboo on handling fire or mentioning women's names applies, one of the older men will shout a warning just as the first cup is about to be made.

The kava is still prepared by a virgin youth, who puts a heap in a piece of the mat-like coconut stipule which serves as a strainer. Underneath this, a bowl made from a half coconut shell is placed. A man then pours water onto the heap from a bamboo tube, a bottle, or any other convenient source. While two men or youths hold the corners of the strainer, the youth kneads the heap, forcing the liquid out into the bowl below. Although men stress the obligation of youths to help with kava, and may threaten to withhold crucial information about titles, land and other rights from those who do not, there are times when no suitable youths are around. Then men will use two sticks from certain trees, or two iron pipes, to pick up the chewed kava and knead it in the strainer.

When all the liquid has been squeezed through, the youth wrings out the strainer in a twisting movement to extract the last drops, and the desiccated heap is returned to the leaf. This enables further bowls of kava to be made for the man whose turn it is to drink, should he desire them. The drinker then takes the bowl of kava, or else it is handed to him by one of the assistants. He moves off to one side, and drinks his bowl without pausing. The straw of wild cane is no longer used.[1] After the drinker has finished, he makes his *timavha*, which might be uttered out loud or, more frequently, mumbled under his breath. Then he may let out his distinctive yodel.

Before returning his bowl to be filled for the next drinker, the man should touch it to the ground. Were he to hand it directly to someone, it is said that this person would gain the power of the drinker's kava for himself. Nevertheless, some men do not bother about this.

After they have finished drinking, men move to where the *nahunu* has been placed, and take their share. The boys and youths are also given some food, and most of them depart. Men continue to talk while the *nahunu* is

---

[1] I am uncertain why the practice of drinking through a straw was abandoned. This appears to have occurred before Humphreys' fieldwork, as he makes no mention of it. My informants were never able to shed much light on the matter, beyond stating that the new way was easier. Lindstrom was told by one informant that drinking through straws took too long and thus increased the likelihood of vomiting (1980: 229). This is quite possible although, as noted in the previous chapter, provided that a man does not vomit directly in front of others, there is no stigma attached; rather, Tannese say that vomiting has a cleansing and salutary effect on the body.

being distributed, but the conversation dies down as they begin to feel the effects of the kava. They separate to sit around the side of the *yimwayim*, under one of the banyans, or around a fire, to smoke tobacco and 'listen to the kava'.

The *yimwayim* soon becomes quiet in the growing dark, except for the intense chirping of cicadas – the immediacy of which seems to be heightened by the kava – and the sound of men spitting. It is a period of extraordinary, almost magical, tranquillity.

The restrictions on noise and social interaction during the time that men are enjoying the effects of kava have not been weakened. But now, when men get up from the spot at which they have been meditating, they rarely go to the men's house to sleep. Indeed, on some *yimwayim* there is no men's house. They return to their hamlets, and when they arrive their wives will try to prevent children from making any noise. If the effects of the kava have worn off, a man may eat and chat with his family before going to sleep.

Lindstrom states that during his visit to south-east Tanna in 1983, rumours were circulating that women in a Presbyterian village in the Middle Bush district had been told by their men to chew and maybe even to drink kava (1987: 116). When I asked about this in 1986 – having seen a version of Lindstrom's paper before it was published – men in my area said that they had not heard these rumours, and that if women had been allowed to participate in the kava ritual it must have been surrounded by considerable secrecy. However, when I first began fieldwork on Tanna in the early 1970s, I was told by some old men, now dead, that many years previously a man called Yawiok, from Ikamrei in north Tanna, had allowed unmarried girls to prepare kava because nearly all the young men in his village were away working. This innovation caused an enormous dispute with neighbouring villages, and Yawiok was forced to abandon it. As the men who told me about this said, 'to allow women to chew and prepare kava would be the same as making poison for yourself'.

Lindstrom also claims that women are permitted small sips of kava as a medicine (1987: 101; see also Ellis 1984: 27). However, my informants deny this, and say that if it really does occur in any parts of Tanna at present, it could have been introduced only by Christians completely indifferent to *kastom*.[1]

I have come across only a single contemporary instance of any weakening by Tannese of the taboo on women's access to kava. This was not in Tanna but in Vila, and in a highly secularised context. Willie Lop, the Tannese owner of a kava bar or *nakamal* in the town, allows women to buy kava, and even to drink it on the premises if they wish. But very few did so – there were none on the three occasions when I visited in February 1986 – and if

---

[1] In a personal communication Lindstrom has informed me that he was simply told that this was a 'possibility', and that he has never actually seen women take kava medicinally.

women were around, any Tannese men present would move to a part of the *nakamal* where they could not be seen drinking. In any case, most Tannese regard Willie's bar as too secularised and, apart from his relatives, I saw none among his clientele. The Tannese men whom I spoke to in Vila preferred to drink at more traditional *nakamal* from which women are excluded (and where kava is chewed, rather than ground up in a meat mincer as is the practice in Willie's bar). Tannese men who visit those islands in Vanuatu where secularization of the kava ritual has proceeded to the extent that women are allowed to participate claim that they politely refuse any bowls of kava that may be offered to them. Some say that they may request kava root, which they will take to a separate place, where they will prepare and drink it in a manner which follows the ritual forms as closely as possible. On occasions when I have visited Tannese working and living on plantations outside Vila, I have noted their concern to observe proper *kastom* in regard to their kava drinking. However, as they are not on a *yimwayim*, no spirits are present, and strictly speaking the ritual loses its significance.

While gender restrictions on kava remain intact, age restrictions have changed. Informants state that at first, during the period of intensified violence in the last century, restrictions were increased, as a favourite tactic was to ambush men drunk on kava (see also F. Paton 1903: 13; J. Paton 1965: 92, 180). Consequently, as I indicated in the previous chapter, men who were still of fighting age had to keep watch, and were not permitted to drink. In practice, this meant that men might be in their late forties before they started drinking. But now, age restrictions have been relaxed, even beyond their original bounds, and men no longer have to wait until they have fathered a child.

Lindstrom states that, in his area, a man is given his first cup of kava immediately after his marriage and utilizes this observation as evidence in his argument that kava drunkenness is the symbolic equivalent of sexual intercourse (1987: 100, 112–16).[1] My own observations differ. I saw no *formal* association between marriage and kava drinking, although some men do begin drinking around the time of their marriage. Others wait for some months. Furthermore, some young unmarried men in their late teens may also be permitted kava.[2] The reason behind this is that some young

---

[1] Lindstrom's statement that 'men achieve (legitimate) access to kava and to women simultaneously' (1987: 101) simply did not apply traditionally. This was not only because men had to wait till they were fathers before drinking, but also because they were initiated into sexual activity *before* marriage, by a woman called a *peraieuanhin*, a term that contemporary Tannese translate as 'whore'.

[2] Guiart notes that teenagers were also allowed to drink during the early years of the John Frum movement, but that the old restrictions were later reasserted (1956a: 249). From the many comments that have been made to me about the wilfulness of young men, and their ability to evade the consequences of their behaviour in an age of easy travel and numerous alternatives to *kastom*, I suspect that nowadays older men are less certain of their ability to maintain successfully the age restrictions than their fathers were.

men are suspected, usually with good reason, of drinking illicitly, and it is thought preferable to have them drink in public where their adherence to correct behaviour can be ensured. It is also a means of containing the potentially subversive effects that could follow from their disregard of the restrictions.

Understanding the Tannese kava ritual

It is always a risky undertaking to attempt an explication of the themes of a ritual and the identification of the cultural and social conflicts and dilemmas it may be addressing. But in the present case a number of factors may make the task less problematical. The Tannese kava ritual has been described by a number of observers, and although there are points of disagreement, and elements noted by one writer but not others, there is a substantial degree of concord as to its main features. The time depth of these observations, and the fact that changes are known to have occurred, offer some opportunity for testing the significance of themes by examining continuities and modifications. They also afford a degree of confidence in the internal consistency of the ritual. The actions and objects which constitute the ritual are not particularly opaque or mysterious, and my Tannese informants discussed them freely, readily offering comments and interpretations. While noting Turner's warning that informants' exegeses tend to stress the harmonious aspect of social relationships and ritual symbols (1967: 33), what applies to the Ndembu does not necessarily apply to the Tannese who, at least in some circumstances, are quite willing to admit to the conflicts and ambiguities that characterize their social life.

This is not to pretend that my analysis is unassailable, or that it necessarily would be accepted by the Tannese. Other anthropologists have also attempted interpretations of the kava ritual on Tanna and, while there is a fair degree of compatibility between their work and what I will be presenting, there are still some important differences, especially with Lindstrom, the most prolific writer on the subject. My analysis is based on the one presented in my earlier paper, but with some modifications and further argument to take into account extra data I have obtained on kava and related topics, and the additional consideration I have given to the problems of understanding Tannese culture and society in the period since that paper was written (Brunton 1979). There will also be differences of emphasis arising out of the different questions addressed. In the 1979 paper I was attempting to explain the apparent distinctiveness of the kava ritual in Tanna compared to other parts of Vanuatu. While still recognizing this distinctiveness, in this book I am using the Tannese case as a possible exemplar of the processes that led to the disappearance of kava in other parts of Melanesia, and consequently I am more concerned to draw attention to aspects of Tannese social organization that are widespread in Melanesia. These aspects will only be briefly touched on in this and the next chapter, and will be examined in more detail in Chapters 7 and 8.

The overall form of the Tannese kava ritual and the organization of its constituent elements strongly suggest that the social problems from which it departs, and the 'solution' to which its operations are directed, are problems common to competitive societies characterized by a substantial degree of egalitarianism: the inter-related problems of conflict, co-ordination and power. While other ritual forms could, of course, be developed as a response to these general problems, the characteristics of kava as a drug of tranquillity – be they derived from its physiological action or its common cultural sub-stratum – make it particularly appropriate for such development. The ritual moves from the normal sociability of everyday life to a completely asocial state, through the progressive differentiation of Tannese society. In arriving at this state Tannese men are presented with a 'model of' and a 'model for' their society (Geertz 1966: 7–40; Ortner 1978: 7–8). In its 'model of' dimension the ritual identifies the major structural categories of Tannese society as points of cleavage, and 'recognizes' that social co-ordination can be achieved only if people pay strict heed to the taboos that are placed on them. In the 'model for' dimension the ritual creates an otherwise unattainable state of harmony between men, albeit at a cost which amplifies the 'model of' dimension: all social interaction has to be abandoned.

Gender relations

As is obvious from the previous sections, the first, most thoroughgoing, and most enduring differentiation is that between male and female. Of course, given that restrictions on women's access to kava are virtually universal, there is nothing particularly remarkable in the fact that Tannese women cannot drink kava or see it being prepared. It is the precise content of the restrictions, and their relation to the ritual as a whole, that is of interest.

Lindstrom, in a paper exploring the gender associations of kava on Tanna, chooses to ignore the fact that ordinary women were excluded from kava throughout the Pacific, and starts instead from the statement that 'women can and do take drugs in various Pacific cultures' (1987: 99). He goes on to suggest a number of perspectives which might explain why kava intoxication is forbidden to Tannese women. The most important of these focus on male control. But while I would agree that the question of control is central, I think that many of Lindstrom's statements tend to be misleading. Firstly, he claims that men fear that women drunk from kava would 'become crazed' (ibid.: 108–9). Although it may be legitimate to suppose such a fear from his informants' comments, I strongly suspect that such comments are idiosyncratic; a creative response to the anthropologist's project rather than the expression of any prior justifications. Certainly, I have never heard these fears, and when, after reading a draft version of Lindstrom's paper, I suggested them directly to my informants, they denied that kava would produce such behaviour. In support of this denial, some men cited the fact that a number of women in Vila and other places in Vanuatu drank kava, and that it did not have this effect on them. This is not to say that they were in favour of these women drinking. But their *stronghed* attitudes and behaviour were the cause of their drinking, not the consequence. When pressed, the kinds of explanations my informants offer for the prohibition on women consuming kava, or watching men consume it, focus on shame: as it originally came from a woman's vagina, both men and women would feel shame in the presence of the other sex, given what is being done to the kava.

Secondly, lacking a comparative perspective, Lindstrom misses the most distinctive aspect of gender relations in the Tannese ritual, even though it is a fairly ready inference from his own data. Although women's immediate presence is completely precluded, it is important to realize that they have a crucial role, both direct and implied, in the Tannese kava ritual. It is they who cook the *nahunu*. The *nelual* (Bislama *laplap*, a pudding made from one of the starch staples), which is one of the most important components of *nahunu*, can be made only by women. Furthermore, a woman makes *timavha* to the spirits by pounding her hand on the *nelual* when she prepares it.[1] Certain kinds of magic are effective only if both men's kava *timavha* and women's *nelual timavha* are made. Apart from this direct involvement, women are the absent audience, both to men – in the taboos on touching fire or mentioning women's names, in the avoidance of 'feminine' foods after drinking, in the knowledge that they are consuming something that originally came from a woman's vagina – and to themselves (cf. Oosterwal 1976: 328–33; Barth 1975: 210). Women must obey a series of injunctions that apply only during the kava ritual – avoiding the *yimwayim*, not calling out to the men who are there, and after sunset, once the men have drunk, ensuring that the children do not cry out, and that their own conversation is too soft for the men to hear, lest it 'spoil their kava'.

In other parts of the Pacific women may be present or absent when kava is drunk; if they are absent, the ritual appears to take place with a very limited acknowledgment – if any – of their existence. But on Tanna, while male and female are kept separate, the two categories are articulated in a

[1] I was not aware of this until I read Gregory, Gregory and Peck (1981: 302). My informants confirmed it during my 1986 visit. The fact that women can make *timavha* in this manner tends to weaken the scope for seeing the kava ritual as an attempt by men to compensate themselves culturally for women's natural creativity, although it does not completely undermine such a view (cf. Brunton 1979: 97).

complementary – though admittedly unequal – and parallel relationship during the kava ritual.

Solidarity and separation amongst men

The first phase of the kava ritual, when men and boys clean and chew the kava, is a period of lively sociability. During this phase, apart from the distinction between uncircumcised boys – who do not chew – and the rest, males are relatively undifferentiated as a category. Certainly, although they usually assist with cleaning the root, as men get past middle age they tend to do less and less chewing. But this is a rather ill-defined boundary, which seems to have as much to do with the state of a man's teeth as with any social considerations, and it is not marked in any way.

During the next phase of the kava ritual,[1] which starts at the point of sunset when the drink is prepared, the differentiation of males becomes clearer. First there is the distinction amongst circumcised males between those who are virgins, who can knead the chewed heaps of kava, and those who are not. Then, amongst the men who have had sexual experience, those who are mature enough to drink are distinguished from those who are not. The movement of males between these categories is ceremonially marked. A small feast is held when the circumcised boy makes kava for the first time. When a man drinks for the first time his wife's male relatives bring the kava and place it on the *yimwayim* with the crown of a banana plant (from which the traditional cups were made) on top. In the past, when youths were sexually initiated by the *peraieuanhin* shortly before they were to be married, they were given a leaf to hold by a male relative after she had touched their hand. This signified that they could no longer make kava. It also signified, although in a more diffuse way, their future role in maintaining the complex, and theoretically unchangeable, structure of marriage alliances that bound local groups together (Brunton 1981a: 361–6; I will discuss this topic in greater detail in Chapter 7).

But superimposed on this progressive differentiation of categories, in the second phase of the ritual there is a more complex dialectic of solidarity and separation. In its overall form this has persisted despite particular changes of detail.

Thus, the identity of all the males present is expressed by the fact that, as soon as the preparation of kava commences, a taboo on touching fire or using women's names that may be incumbent on a single man becomes incumbent on everyone. Traditionally, the chewed kava was indiscrimi-

---

[1] While the Tannese themselves do not distinguish phases of the ritual as I am doing, my distinctions are more than just a matter of convenience. If sufficient kava has been chewed before sunset, men will wait until the sun goes down before making the drink.

nately mixed together in a common bowl,[1] and drunk from individually made cups which were then discarded. Now, although separate piles of kava are prepared, they contain the mastications of a number of men, except for those occasions when a visitor is marked out for particular honour. The kava is squeezed out from a communal strainer – referred to as *niko*, which identifies it with the obsolete bowl – into drinking shells, which are kept in the men's house or in the crevices of banyans, and shared indiscriminately among a group of men. The act that is equivalent to the previous discarding of the banana-leaf cup is the touching of the shell to the ground after drinking; the means whereby a man 'insulates' his kava from others, retaining the power for himself.

The drinker separates himself from the others by standing apart, with his back towards them. But this also affords the opportunity for expressing solidarity. Two men may be handed their bowls at the same time, either as an act of friendship, or because a shortage of kava has led to two bowls being squeezed from one pile. When this occurs both men move apart and synchronize their drinking, with one waiting for the other to finish before spitting and making his *timavha*.

The second phase comes to an end with a final act of solidarity, the distribution of *nahunu*, prepared by the women, and shared by all the males, even the uncircumcised boys. This is immediately followed by the most profound act of separation. All social relations come to an end, as each man moves off to 'listen to the kava'.

It is important to be very careful in specifying exactly what is involved at this stage. Lindstrom argues that the frequent spitting following kava is a form of communication among a solidary group of intoxicated men. 'Spitting defines the boundaries of a male social group . . . [and] sets forth a claim to a place within this group for each individual drinker. If you do not spit you are not drunk, and you are definitely out of it' (1980: 233). In support of this, he claims to have experimented first spitting, and then hearing 'the chain reaction of answering expectorations which travel rapidly around the edges of the clearing' (ibid.). When I first read this comment I was surprised. It was not something I had noticed myself, yet as it would bring about a tendency for spitting to occur in a pulsating ebb and flow, it would be hard to miss. Consequently, when I returned to Tanna in 1986, I experimented every evening, with very different results to those reported by Lindstrom. Sometimes I would be followed by a few men, though hardly ever all; but just as often no one else would spit.

There is another reason for questioning Lindstrom's depiction. As I

[1] A statement in my earlier article on kava is misleading on this point. I said that while a number of men might chew a single pile at present, some informants said that this was not the case in the past (1979: 94). I recorded these comments very early in my fieldwork, before I learnt that, traditionally, piles of kava were not made at all. I now realize that this was the point that my informants were trying to make.

mentioned earlier, Tannese explicitly state that by drinking kava together men have farewelled each other. Consequently, to talk in terms of 'social group' is very misleading. It would be more accurate to say that men are simply aware of the presence of others. But they are constrained not to act on this awareness, lest the harmony that has been established – both between men and the spirits, and men and each other – is threatened. I would suggest that the use of a mild drug like kava may offer a greater likelihood than would otherwise be the case that the restrictions against noise and social interaction will actually be followed. At least in normal doses, the effects of kava are perceived as relatively fragile, and this has certainly been my experience as well (see also Gajdusek 1967: 120). Thus the restrictions are maintained not only by the possibility of future sanctions from an external source – human or supernatural – but also by the expectation that if they are broken the transgressor will spoil his own kava as well as that of everyone else.

Some of the lore surrounding intoxication helps to extend our understanding of the social implications of kava. Tannese say that if a man drinks at the one *yimwayim*, night after night, he is less and less likely to get drunk. Behind this belief appears to be a notion that, unless resisted, the centripetal tendencies which might result from the difficulties of maintaining potentially refractory social relations would lead to a kind of supernatural fatigue. The spirits at the *yimwayim* get too used to the man who drinks there every night without a break. When a man finds that he is not getting drunk at his own place, he should drink at another *yimwayim* where the spirits are not so accustomed to him. This spiritual and social invigoration is said virtually to ensure that he becomes intoxicated.[1]

Nevertheless, there are limits to what kava can do. Informants say that if a man is angry with any of his drinking partners, or if he fears any of them, he will not get drunk. On a couple of occasions I saw men leave the *yimwayim* at which they were intending to drink because of incidents that occurred while the kava was being prepared. In the first case a man was angered because of an insulting reference to a long past dispute in which his people had been involved. The second was during the political troubles in 1980, when word arrived at Irakik that some Vanuaaku Party sympathizers from neighbouring villages had been held by Tanunion people in the Middle Bush area. As soon as he heard this, a man from Middle Bush who had been visiting left. Although he was in no immediate physical danger, especially as the drinking had just commenced, others explained that there was no point

[1] There is some research to suggest that there may actually be physiological reasons behind the Tannese belief. People who are accustomed to taking a drug in certain circumstances may react automatically to that environment so the drug's effects are lessened (Siegel and Macrae 1984; Fred Westbrook, personal communication).

in him waiting for his kava, as he would have been too frightened about the reactions of those present.

The ritual, and the social contradictions that must have operated to mould its form, are further illuminated by a myth which gives a different account of the origin of kava from the one already mentioned. This myth hinges on the relation between men during a time called *niproou*, a period of peace in the distant past when there were no social divisions, no ownership of land and no jealousy. Men could wander freely throughout the island. But there were no exchanges, and people ate wild foods and did not drink kava. *Niproou* came to an end with the arrival of the two brothers Numrukuen and Koiameta, who came from the east bringing pigs, the traditional cultivated foods, and kava. But they also brought sorcery and war, and since their arrival men have quarrelled. As Wilkinson recognizes, *niproou* represents a deeply desired ideal, one that has played a major role in the Tannese affinity for millenarianism (1979: 279–80). But it also expresses the painful realization that conflict is an inevitable component of the social life and relations they have created (or, as the Tannese see it, have been created for them). Harmony is possible only if social relations are set aside (cf. Bloch and Parry 1981: 27–31; Burridge 1960: 85; 1965: 227–8).

Power and the supernatural

When asked to explain why kava is so important to the Tannese, the most frequent response is that it is a source of power, and that by drinking kava and making *timavha* men ensure the continuing productivity and health of the island. Guiart (1956a: 252–4), Lindstrom (1980: 230; 1981b: 389) and Gregory, Gregory and Peck (1981: 302) all claim that *timavha* are addressed to the ancestors. While it may be hazardous to differ with the combined force of these opinions, I have never been able to get an unequivocal answer to the question of who the *timavha* are addressed to. Nor can the nineteenth-century sources be used to decide the matter. Turner talks of prayers to the gods (1861: 85), John Paton refers to an exclamation made to Kumesan (1965: 180), a traditional demiurge, while Gray says only that 'there are doubtless religious beliefs connected with its use' (1892: 662). Some of my informants specifically denied that *timavha* are made to the ancestors; others said that they could be. On more than a few occasions I was told something that completely contradicted what the same person had said during an earlier discussion (for an account of a comparable diversity among the Kwaio see Keesing 1987: 163). Some men even say that Jesus is the object of *timavha* and counter the obvious response that they have learnt this from the Christians with the claim that the Tannese have always known about Jesus. The one point on which all my informants do agree is

111

that *timavha* can be made to the agricultural deity Mwatiktik and to the spirits associated with him, and that they must be made on *yimwayim*.[1]

The claims about Jesus serve to highlight an important point that is sometimes overlooked by anthropologists working on Tanna or amongst traditionalists elsewhere: whatever the original Tannese conceptions of the supernatural realm, they have been so contaminated by external notions that there is little point in trying to disentangle them. The Christian contamination was well under way over a century ago, long before the first baptisms, as Agnes Watt found in relation to beliefs about the afterlife (1896: 110). What is important for our purposes is that by drinking kava on *yimwayim* at the end of the day men are placed in contact with the supernatural world, and that this is said to provide them with their major source of power.

The syncretism of contemporary pagan thought, while denied by the pagans themselves, is patently obvious in a long myth which forcefully expresses kava's role as a power giver. The myth starts with the assertion that once all the world was Tanna, and then recounts how Jesus made Adam and Eve, who broke his Law by eating before they had been told which foods were taboo and which were permitted. When Jesus discovered that Adam and Eve had already begun eating food, he decided that they would not receive the knowledge that he had intended to give them along with the food taboos: the knowledge that would bring them power.

After a series of episodes the myth concludes with an account of Moses, on top of a mountain, finally receiving the knowledge and power from Jesus – who by this stage of the tale had become Wunghin, the Lenakel version of Kumesan – in the form of a stone tablet. Before leaving for the mountain, Moses told his people, who were the Tannese, that they should just think about him and do nothing until he returned. However, one man made an image of a bull which a number of others began to worship. Returning, Moses saw this and in a fury dropped the stone tablet which fractured into ten pieces. At the same time Tanna fractured into all the islands of the world. The Europeans, those who had remained faithful to the instructions of Moses, went off on them, with the power meant for all. The Tannese remained, with no power. However, Wunghin's son felt sorry for the Tannese and gave them the things they have today – foods, magic, and so on. He also gave them kava, which is the source of what power they have, although it is not as much as the Europeans possess.[2]

---

[1] Yet this raises the problem of how women can make their *nelual timavha*, as these are made in the hamlets. I did not think to obtain a clarification of this during my 1986 visit, the first I made since learning about women's *timavha*.

[2] A more complete version, together with the circumstances in which I learnt of the myth, can be found in Brunton 1981b, although this does omit some details. It is also very slightly fictionalized, as I was told the full version not two days after first hearing about it but many months later during my next visit (ibid.: 35). In order to explain the reason for this delay – the

This was presented as a completely traditional story. Although the characters had European names, this was explained by the old, and usually plausible, standby that all the men who knew their Tannese names died before they were able to pass them on – a situation that has regrettably occurred with a lot of traditional knowledge. The importance of this myth to the people who related it was underscored by the circumstances in which it was told to me: the general fuss that was made exceeded that of any other information-gathering session I experienced.

I think that there can be little dispute about the point of this myth. The events it describes were precipitated by the inability of people to keep to the restrictions and taboos that had been laid down for them, and that are necessary for an ordered social life. When the Europeans listened to Moses, they were rewarded. The narrator made it clear, as did others commenting on the myth afterwards, that it was the Tannese lack of self-control, and their general fractiousness, that had been the cause, and its continuance a consequence, of their punishment. Of course, this theme is hardly unique, and is a prominent feature of the myth's biblical source. The twist is that Tannese obtained kava as a compensation for their disadvantaged condition, but that the power it gives them is much less than they could have had. Europeans, who are perceived as being far less troubled by internal divisiveness, do not need kava.

I will be returning to this myth in the chapters that follow, because I think that the attitudes towards kava and Tannese social capacities that it expresses provide a most useful key to understanding not only the role of kava, but its varying fortunes in the post-contact period. In turn, this leads us to more detailed considerations about power, taboo, and the nature of Tannese society, and the question of the pre-contact abandonment of kava in other parts of Melanesia.

combined consequences of the narrator having to visit another part of the island to answer accusations that he had been involved in causing a hurricane, and my departure for Australia – I would have had to introduce too much additional information for a short article directed at a non-anthropological audience.

This is not the only myth that ascribes a supernatural origin to kava. There is another, which describes how the deity Kalpwapen first created the alternation between night and day and gave kava to man, together with the cicada who would announce sunset, and the rooster, who would announce the dawn (see Guiart 1956a: 250–1; Brunton 1979: 97–8).

6

Kava on Tanna: the development of secular patterns of consumption

Perhaps the most far-reaching changes in Tannese kava use relate to the frequency of its consumption. For there has long been a parallel secular form of kava drinking, which was initially adopted as an aggressive response to Christian attacks on the ritual, and which is subject to far fewer constraints. In order to understand this development it is necessary to recount briefly the history of the attitudes of Christians on Tanna towards kava.

Christians and kava

The policies that Christians adopted towards kava in the last century showed some variation, albeit within a framework of overall disapproval. There are no indications that the London Missionary Society (LMS) missionaries, who were the first to work on Tanna, attempted to interfere with kava drinking despite their obvious disgust (Turner 1842–3: 5–11; 1861: 85). Presbyterian teachers from Aneityum, who were first sent to Tanna in 1854, arranged for their relatives at home to send them kava on the mission vessel, the *John Knox*, so that they could maintain satisfactory relations with the Tannese (Adams 1984: 73; Copeland 1861: 171). Initially, this seems to have been tolerated by the mission. However, John Paton, who had arrived at Port Resolution in 1858, saw kava as a great evil and insisted that no more be sent. This caused great resentment among the people of Port Resolution, who then demanded that the *John Knox* take them to Futuna to enable them to obtain kava there (ibid.; Adams 1984: 115; Paton 1965: 180). While this apparent dependence on a European vessel for kava might appear puzzling, it should be understood that certain areas of Tanna, particularly the central eastern coast around the volacano, are regarded as not very suitable for the cultivation of kava, and were probably always dependent on trade with the interior people for an adequate supply (see e.g. Guiart 1956a: 249). Under the military conditions obtaining at the time, Aneityum and Futuna no doubt afforded a more convenient source (ibid.: 98–101; Adams 1984: 36).

114

Some time after the forced departure of Paton from Tanna in 1862, the prohibition on the carriage of kava must have been dropped. In 1873 the synod of the Mission, meeting in Aneityum, agreed that natives could use the mission vessel *Dayspring* for other than mission journeys provided that they paid for their passage. They were expressly forbidden to bring any pigs on board, but the minutes make no reference to kava (New Hebrides Presbyterian Mission 1857–1938, vol. 1: 133). The labour recruiter William Wawn, who visited Port Resolution in 1875, was surprised to see the *Dayspring* landing a number of Tannese who had gone to Futuna and returned with several large roots of kava: 'I should have thought that a missionary vessel would have been forbidden to carry such an article' (1973: 26). A year later, the synod in Nguna decided to end this incongruity, resolving that 'no pigs or kava be carried on the vessel for native passengers' (New Hebrides Presbyterian Mission 1857–1938, vol. 1: 168).

The Presbyterian missionaries who worked on Tanna in the 1870s and 1880s appear to have adopted a slightly more cautious attitude towards kava than Paton had. Writing in 1881, a few months before her husband would baptize the first Tannese into the church, Agnes Watt reflected on the campaign to destroy kava plants on the neighbouring island of Aneityum:[1] 'The kava question will be a grave one on Tanna . . . It will be like plucking out a right eye . . . to give it up' (1896: 203–4). She added, however, that there were 'still graver sins in our midst to war against' (ibid.: 204). Abstinence was made a term of communion, but there are no indications of any concerted campaigns against the custom. In 1885 when Peter Milne, the Nguna missionary, successfully moved a motion in synod that would have led to the dismissal of any teacher who drank kava, it was opposed by William Gray and William Watt, the two missionaries from Tanna. Their arguments, which were also supported by Daniel McDonald of Efate, were based on the belief that the motion was too inflexible (New Hebrides Presbyterian Mission 1857–1938, vol. 1: 272–7).[2] At the 1886 synod they were able to obtain a more flexibly worded resolution, which gave a

---

[1] Although Gregory, Gregory and Peck assert that the kava plant was physically eliminated from Aneityum in the 1890s (1981: 303), some Aneityumese continued to grow it secretly (Anonymous 1916: 19). In any case, the documentary evidence they cite is geographically vague, and there is no justification for thinking that Aneityum is the island referred to (Anonymous 1894: 17). Lawrie, who was the missionary on Aneityum, states only that 'over 1,000 kava plants were destroyed' (1895: 10) in the campaign, and gives no indication that the destruction was total.

[2] For further details see Gregory, Gregory and Peck (1981: 302–3). However, their statement that the matter was a side issue to a territorial dispute between Milne and MacDonald is questionable. While this territorial dispute was a serious matter which dragged on for many years, it is more likely that the differences over kava were related to genuine differences in perceptions of the strategic implications of the motion. The three missionaries who opposed Milne also appear to have had a slightly more detached attitude towards traditional culture, and unlike him, all published serious articles on aspects of the ethnography of the islands on which they worked (Gray 1892, 1899; MacDonald 1892, 1898; Watt 1895a).

missionary the possibility of discretion, and the opportunity of first exerting strong moral pressure on an offending teacher (ibid.; vol. 2: 17). The opposition to Milne's motion was led by Gray, who was later to provide a detailed and very useful description of kava drinking, distinguished by the absence of any moral condemnation (1892: 661–3).

Despite these modulations in missionary opinion, in practical terms a man's conversion to Christianity generally put an end to his kava drinking (Watt 1896: 258; Nicholson 1916b: 11). The great increase in the number of Christians that occurred in the first decade of this century brought about a situation in which kava became a prime focus of contention (New Hebrides Presbyterian Mission 1908; Nicholson 1907b: 42–3; 1909d; 1910b: 7). Frank Paton – John Paton's son – who was based in Lenakel on the west coast for six years from 1896, saw it as a major evil, a 'horrible concoction' which made men 'dull and stupid' (1897: 12; 1903: 13). Lomai, a stalwart of the Lenakel mission until his death in 1917, and the subject of much inspirational writing, gave up kava about eighteen months before being baptized in 1898 as a consequence of two dreams in which Mrs Paton and Mr Hume, a lay mission helper, warned him that he would become very sick if he continued to drink. When he became ill after drinking on the night following the second dream, he realized that abstinence was the only course of action open to him (Paton 1897: 12; 1903: 142–3).

The notion that Christianity and kava were incompatible did not go entirely unchallenged by Tannese converts, however. Frank Paton wrote of his dispute with a man who had been baptized in Queensland, yet who continued to drink kava on his return to Tanna. When admonished, the man produced the New Testament in English and asked to be shown the precise passage where it was stated that kava was prohibited. Until this could be done he could only assume that there was nothing wrong with the drink, and he refused to yield to Paton's attempts to explain the situation away. Paton recognized the danger of these arguments, and was relieved when others suggested that kava may have unhinged the troublemaker's mind, thus providing an additional ground for abstinence (ibid.: 165–6). But the reassurance Paton thereby gained was not fully justified. The man's argument appears to have gained an underground currency, and to have been extended to some other elements of traditional culture opposed by the mission. Informants have told me that it was one of the justifications used by some Christians in their attempts to participate, usually secretly, in certain aspects of traditional life (see Brunton 1981a: 370–1). Ironically, it is possible that Paton contributed to this himself by writing about the incident, as my informants recounted the man's arguments in words identical to those set down in Paton's book.

Nevertheless, all the indications are that such a position was always very much a minority one among Tannese Christians. Converts, using the vehicle of native courts, generally displayed an even greater zeal for attacking kava than did their missionaries. These courts had been set up after the Mixed Naval Commission visited Tanna in 1906 in an attempt to put an end to warfare (Nicholson 1907b: 40–1). Guiart suggests that the impetus for their establishment came from the warship commanders' response to Tannese requests for guidance on how they could resolve their disputes peacefully (1956a: 139). But the status of the native courts was initially clouded. They operated under mission auspices, although at first the pagans appear to have believed that they had a wider authority (ibid.: 138–9; see also Watt 1908; Brunton 1981a: 368–9). The courts were usually manned by, and under the control of, prominent Christians. Occasionally, however, pagans would also participate in cases such as adultery, which were equally condemned by both camps (Guiart 1956a: 134, 139). But the Tannese converts used the courts to extend Christian restrictions into new domains, seeking to prevent even non-Christians from, amongst other things, drinking kava and carrying the plant along the roads (ibid.: 132–5; Guiart 1956b: 108; Gregory, Gregory and Peck 1981: 303–4). This was the period that the pagans refer to as 'Tanna Law', in recognition of their belated realization that the authority for the Christians' actions did not derive from the metropolitan powers. (For further details see Brunton 1981a: 369.)

The restriction on the carrying of kava expressed a cunning iconoclasm that could have come only from ex-pagans. This is because every traditional ceremonial event is always preceded by sending kava root along the roads (*suatu*) connecting the *yimwayim* of all those who are being invited to participate. Kava actuates the *suatu,* and enables circumcision, marriage, the first fruits ceremonies, dances, and every other activity of any significance to proceed. In effect, had it been possible to enforce this restriction completely, the whole structure of pagan society would have come tumbling down. (Keesing and Corris describe a similar strategic attack on the fundamental basis of a pagan culture by ex-pagans in Malaita, 1980: 166. See also Strathern 1984: 35; Tippett 1967: 102–6.)

The pagan response

The pagans responded to these attacks on their customs in two quite separate ways. The first, which commenced in 1908, was to get the traders R. Humes and J. Truss to write to the British Residency on their behalf complaining about Christian abuses, and requesting information about their legal rights under the Condominium Convention. Complaints about attacks on kava were prominent in these letters. One of Humes' letters noted that the pagans were demanding the right to transport kava along the roads, and asked under what authority were the roots confiscated and burnt, and Truss protested against threats by Christians to destroy kava gardens (Guiart 1956a: 132, 135; Gregory, Gregory and Peck 1981: 304). Humes' letters, and the counter-claims they occasioned from the Presbyterian missionaries on Tanna, led to a visit from the British Resident Commissioner, Mr King. While King upheld the jurisdiction of the native courts in general, thus giving great comfort to Dr Nicholson, the missionary at Lenakel, there is no evidence that he supported their interference with kava (Nicholson 1908: 10). Certainly, later visits from British officials brought criticisms of this interference, as there were no regulations against kava. At least one missionary, William Watt, was defensive about such actions of the courts, and claimed that they took place without his knowledge (Guiart 1956a: 133).

Finally, the appointment in 1912 of a British District Agent, W. Wilkes, put an end to the 'Tanna Law' period.[1] The native courts were re-organized, and both Wilkes and the two Resident Commissioners made it clear that pagans could not be prevented from using kava (Guiart 1956a: 141–4; Gregory, Gregory and Peck 1981: 304). When I first started to work on Tanna, a number of men who were youths and young men during Wilkes' three-year stay on the island were still alive, and without exception he was remembered as someone who 'helped kastom', a claim given additional support by the vehemence of the attacks on him by the mission (ibid.; Nicholson 1913c: 8–12; Guiart 1956a: 144–5). These old men were convinced that Wilkes' appointment had been brought about by the traders' letters and the subsequent meetings between important pagans and Condominium officials. The details were chronicled in a song about Tanna Law that was still sung occasionally by my older informants, although it refers only to Truss,[2] and not Humes.

Even though the pagans' recourse to the Condominium authorities ultimately ensured their right to continue those of their customs which were not specifically prohibited by law, in many ways it was their other response to the Christian attacks on kava drinking which had the greatest long-term

[1] Gregory, Gregory and Peck state that the term 'Tanna Law' is applied to the 1920s and 1930s (1981: 305). As will also be clear from Guiart's work this is simply wrong and, among other things, indicates a lack of awareness of the etymology of the term (1956b: 108–9).
[2] Truss has also acquired a supernatural persona. Rice presents a text dictated to him by John Kalate, in which 'Jake Kratis' is said to be the son of God (1974: 223). My pagan informants pronounced Truss' name as 'Kratis', and this has caused some confusion, as a similar pronunciation is used for Carruthers, a lay trader/evangelist who worked in Lenakel in the early years of the century (Guiart 1956a: 129), whereas Truss lived on the other side of the island in the White Sands area. A possible explanation of my informants' unlikely pronunciation of Truss' name is the fact that in many Lenakel words 'r' occurs where the White Sands language has 't' and vice versa: e.g. Lenakel *kuvir*, White Sands *kuvit* ('four'); Lenakel *katilum*, White Sands *karilim* ('five'). While it is by no means invariable, Lenakel speakers, if asked about the differences between their language and that of White Sands, nearly always refer to this alternation of the two sounds. (For an account of the rules governing sound changes in these languages see Lynch 1978a: 734–49.)

consequences for the practice. At some time during the Tanna Law period two restrictions on the use of kava were relaxed. The first innovation, which was of lesser importance, allowed a wider use of kava *topunga* and kava *nousumiriang*. Previously these types of kava could be drunk only by the occupants of a particular title – the *yeremira*, a title contemporary Tannese translate as 'chief'. These kavas also became incorporated into the final stage of the circumcision ceremony, the *naupwinaan*, in which the boys who have been in seclusion for a number of weeks are led onto the *yimwayim*, and returned to everyday life. The boys walk out as part of a long line of men, the first few of whom now began to carry kava *topunga* or *nousum-iriang*, specially decorated with leaves and flowers. The point of this innovation, informants claim, was to win back the allegiance of those who had converted, or were thinking of converting, by making two of the more esteemed items of the traditional culture available to more men. (As well, this overall strategy contained other measures which did not directly involve kava. Thus some pagan centres markedly increased the frequency of *nikoviaar*, the most prestigious and spectacular Tannese ceremony.)[1]

The other, and major, innovation was to break the nexus between sunset and kava drinking, allowing kava to be consumed at any time of the day or night. My informants state that the initiative for both these innovations was taken by Manga, a very influential *yeremira* from Lamwinaura, in the centre of the island. Manga plays a significant part in a number of songs and stories recounting the pagan resistance to Christianity, and was one of the pagan leaders who is said to have met with the British Resident Commissioner. Nevertheless, as he came from a *yimwayim* with close links to those of a number of my informants, it is always possible that they have exaggerated his pivotal role, which may have been confined only to introducing or winning acceptance for the innovations within his own region. Whatever the exact details, the process of making the change would have been similar to what occurred in another significant change that was introduced during the Tanna Law period, the expansion of the range of permissible marriage partners (see Brunton 1981a: 368–9). Invitations to attend meetings to discuss the issue would have been sent along the *suatu* network to important pagans, and the end of warfare would have made it feasible for the attendance to be drawn from a reasonably wide geographical area. Once agreement had been reached, the men involved would have organized meetings in their own area, bringing in those who had not attended the original meetings. In this way the innovation would have spread to encompass the whole pagan population of Tanna. By 1913, an increase in

[1] As these ceremonies involve a massive distribution of pigs, kava and food, their increased frequency would obviously have been facilitated by the ending of warfare. For descriptions of *nikoviaar* see Guiart 1956a: 17–36; Lindstrom 1981a: 119–22. I have included two photos of a major element of the *nikoviaar*, the entry of the *yeremira* wearing the symbols of their title, in Chapter 7 (Plates 1 and 2).

kava drinking had come to the attention of Dr Nicholson, who attributed it to the coming of peace and the decline in pagan numbers which left more kava for those remaining. During a visit to the inland villages in the extreme north of the island in 1915, he noted a similar upsurge (1913c: 13; 1916b: 12). Certainly, an end to the ever-present threat of surprise attack meant that men who were drunk on kava would no longer be in any danger of their lives, but I think that the real cause of the upsurge lies in the events I have outlined. By 1921 the old rule had been completely set aside; Humphreys found that 'all agree that [kava drinking] may be done at any time as it is in Tonga . . . there is no rule about the matter' (1926: 83).

If there was any major opposition to the change among pagans, my informants do not know of it. The main reason my informants give for the breaking of the nexus was to spite and challenge the Christians. An additional reason was the hope that, by allowing kava to be drunk at any time rather than during a brief period at the end of the day, many erstwhile pagans would be faced with a continual temptation too great to resist.

There are two points that need to be made about the decision to change the rule about the time of drinking kava. The first is that as a tactic to reverse – or even halt – the defections to the church it cannot be said to have been very successful. Thus, despite an occasional hiatus such as occurred in 1912–13, the percentage of pagans continued to decrease until it dropped to just over a quarter of the population around 1920 (Nicholson 1913b: 9; 1913c: 12; Guiart 1956b: 110; see also Rae 1920b: 12). In 1939 the ratio of pagans to Christians was similar, though perhaps marginally higher (Armstrong 1939: 7–8). So it was only during the twenties that the pagan decline appears to have halted, and as this was a decade or so after the change to the kava-drinking rule the causal links are likely to have been tenuous.

The arrival of Catholic and Seventh-day Adventist missions in the early thirties changed the composition of the Christian side. The Adventists, who had even more restrictions, concentrated their efforts on the Presbyterians, and were quite successful, gaining over 10 per cent of the population in seven years (Armstrong 1939: 7; Guiart 1956a: 148–51). The Catholics, whose attitude towards kava and other elements of traditional culture was considerably more tolerant than that of their rival denominations, made little headway and had gained only 72 adherents by 1939 (Anonymous 1947: 10; Wilkinson 1979: 258; Armstrong 1939: 7). It should also be noted that the similarity between the 1920 and 1939 figures for the pagan proportion of the population disguises the considerable extent to which individuals and communities changed their affiliation backwards and forwards (see e.g. Guiart 1956a: 150; Nicholson 1914: 11; Macmillan 1923a: 13; 1929: 6–7; Bell 1938: 8). I will return to this matter in the next chapter.

The second, and most important, point about ending the restriction on the time of drinking is that it created a secular practice of kava, one that has had repercussions for the stability of the ritual practice. As will be obvious from my comments in the last chapter, women are still forbidden to participate or watch. The age restrictions also apply, but the other restrictions are lifted. (The restriction on any man who has had sexual experience kneading the kava remains as well but, as I explained earlier, this is an expression of a more generalized rule about pollution.) There are no taboos on handling fire or mentioning women's names while the kava is being prepared, no one bothers to touch the bowl to the ground before handing it to another, and there is no need to eat after drinking. There is no point in making *timavha*, as the spirits are not thought to be around. As one man stated, 'it is just like drinking beer, men only drink in the day because they like getting drunk'. But if they do get drunk, it is in a setting quite different to that in the evening: social interaction continues, and no attempt is made to maintain silence. If anything, some drinkers become quite loquacious.

Abstinence and excess

It is difficult to assess the effect that the absence of restrictions during secular kava-drinking sessions has had on the evening kava ritual, because some effects are likely to have been gradual and thus not necessarily perceptible to the Tannese. Some men do not appear to worry about particular restrictions, but it is not possible to know the extent to which such an indifference was always present, as the early missionary descriptions of kava drinking do not provide sufficient detail. Thus, although the importance of the taboo on touching fire is verbally stated, and assistants usually shout a warning as soon as preparations start, on a number of occasions I noticed that the taboo had been broken without any fuss being made. As I stated in a footnote to the previous chapter, on occasions I have seen the prohibition against the return of *nahunu* to the hamlets broken; again this did not seem to cause any bother. Also, quite a few men ignore the rule on touching the bowl to the ground after drinking, although it does need to be remembered that this rule is an innovation adopted to deal with the replacement of the extemporaneous banana-leaf cups by durable bowls.

What has definitely occurred, however, is a tendency for kava use to get out of hand, with some men spending much of their time drinking or drunk. There also appears to be a cyclical pattern to this, with periods of heavy use followed by periods of more orderly use, or even complete abstinence on the part of individuals and communities.

I cannot claim that my evidence for this proposition for the time between the Tanna Law period and the coming of John Frum is particularly strong, but I can point to some very suggestive data. There are the reports of increased kava drinking soon after the end of Tanna Law, and Humphreys' statements that kava could be drunk at any time, both of which I referred to previously. Nevertheless, although it was they who told me about Manga's innovation allowing kava to be drunk at any time, nearly all of my oldest pagan informants in the early 1970s – men who were then in their sixties and seventies and who had come to maturity between 1920 and 1940 – were sparing in their consumption of kava. Unlike most, though not all, of the younger men, they generally drank only at sunset, and then only once.[1] The only times I ever saw them break this practice were when dances were held, when they might drink two or three bowls beforehand, and another immediately after the final dance at sunrise. The explanation they gave me for their restraint was that when they first started drinking kava their elders had told them that they should not drink it *olbaot*,[2] but should adhere to the ways of the past. These men often spoke to me of their annoyance at what they saw as the abuse of kava by the younger men.

The evidence for the post-John Frum period is stronger. The appearance of John Frum at Green Point, and the subsequent spread of his message throughout the island, was accompanied by an upsurge in kava drinking, as Presbyterians and Seventh-day Adventists abandoned their churches. Guiart says that all the evidence shows that in the first years of the John Frum movement the kava-drinking bouts were anarchic ('les beuveries de kava étaient anarchiques', 1956a: 249). Rice's summary of Government files notes that District Agents reported excessive kava drinking in April 1941 (but a report in December 1941 stated that it had diminished), and again in August 1943 and September 1946 (1974: 251–6).

For most of the erstwhile Christian men it was the acceptance of the roots of kava that had been transmitted along the *suatu* from Green Point, and the drinking of kava, that symbolized their break with Christianity. Guiart, while providing strong evidence to support this interpretation, evidence which is confirmed by my own informants, has nevertheless questioned the extent to which the John Frum movement was responsible for the return to kava (1956a: 166–7, 171–2). His point seems to be that a number of villages had left the Presbyterian church and returned to paganism before the appearance of John Frum, a consideration which also appears to be behind the Gregorys' raising of the same question (ibid.: 181; Gregory, Gregory and Peck 1981: 307; Gregory and Gregory 1984: 84.) But this is something of a *non sequitur* which ignores the fact, referred to earlier, that there was a continual backwards and forwards movement between paganism and the Christian denominations. Thus while Guiart could point, with justification,

---

[1] Now, the heaps of chewed kava are invariably set aside after the first squeezing, and used to prepare additional bowls as required. After two or three squeezings the resulting kava is usually too weak, and if men still wish to drink – not an unusual occurrence – further kava will be chewed.

[2] A Bislama word meaning 'haphazardly, not in the appropriate manner' (see Camden 1977: 77).

to the disaffections with Presbyterianism beginning well before John Frum (1956a: 226–7), in 1939 when John Frum had already made his presence known to at least a few Tannese, Dr Armstrong was still able to report on the great success of an evangelical campaign in the Lenakel area which had brought in eighty new members (1940: 6; Bell 1941: 9).

At this point, I think it is appropriate to note as an aside that the John Frum movement may well have been triggered by the success of a Presbyterian move to undermine traditional practices to an even greater extent than before. As I have argued in a previous paper, there are strong grounds for seeing the movement as an attempt by pagans to reverse the social disintegration brought about by Christian interference with traditional marriage exchanges (Brunton 1981a). When I prepared that paper, I had not yet examined the mission reports published in *Quarterly Jottings from the New Hebrides*. In 1937 Dr D. Macleod, who was stationed at Lenakel, wrote that a committee of four influential men had been appointed by the Church to determine the best way of abolishing 'a blot on the life of the community, viz. the system of exchange of children' (1937: 11). This exchange of children was essential for both the operation of the marriage system, and the continuity of traditional social groups and their corporeal and incorporeal property. Although sister exchange is the Tannese ideal, with two men marrying each other's sisters, demographic and other circumstances make this impossible, even using classificatory sisters, and many men marry on the promise of returning a future daughter for their wife. In cases where men have no sons of their own to take their place, boys also may be exchanged, either as the return for a woman in a previous exchange, or with the promise that eventually a son of the adopted boy will be sent back to the original family. (For further details see Brunton 1981a: 358–66; Lindstrom 1981a: 126–50.) I think the fact that the Presbyterians had embarked on this course of action serves to strengthen my original argument. It also provides some justification for pagan comments – which I dismissed as exaggerations – that had John Frum's appearance been delayed by even one year it would have been too late to save *kastom* (Brunton 1981a: 374).

By the time of Guiart's fieldwork in 1952–3 the excessive kava use of the 1940s had passed, and he reported that there appeared to have been a return to the traditional form which was as complete as possible (1956a: 249). This settling down must have occurred not long before his arrival, as an interview that the British District Agent had with a Tannese assessor[1] in 1950 seems to indicate that kava was still being drunk at any time of day or

[1] Gregory, Gregory and Peck state that this man, James Iehnaiu, was a 'staunch Presbyterian' (1981: 310). But he is almost certainly the man Guiart refers to as James Yehnayeu, an assessor who maintained a good relationship with the British District Agent, but who left the Presbyterian Church for the Seventh-day Adventists, and who played a major role in the post-war attempts to rebuild support for the latter (1956a: 196, 202).

night (Gregory, Gregory and Peck 1981: 310). Guiart says that in early 1952 a man from Imay on the west side of the island claimed to have received instructions from the spirits that kava should be drunk only at sunset (1956a: 212–13).

Although the Presbyterian church unsuccessfully attempted to persuade the Condominium authorities to ban kava in 1949, in practice its attitude towards the custom moderated somewhat from its pre-John Frum position, if only because it had no real alternative (Gregory, Gregory and Peck 1981: 308–10). Guiart states that by the time of his visit, the missionary at White Sands was inviting kava drinkers to attend Sunday services, but they were not allowed to take Communion (1956a: 195, 254). By the early 1970s this policy had been liberalized further and, with only two exceptions, all the Presbyterians I met during my early visits, including a number of elders, drank kava. To the best of my knowledge the Seventh-day Adventists have made no attempts to relax their ban on kava drinking, although a number of their members grow the plant to enable them to participate in exchanges.

From the time of my first visit to Tanna in 1972 I noticed that there was a fair amount of kava drinking during the day. Given Guiart's comments about the return to the traditional pattern, I was surprised by this. From what I was able to gather from my informants, daytime kava drinking never completely disappeared, although its incidence was considerably reduced for a time. But it steadily increased again, with many of the younger men, once they were permitted to drink, refusing to confine it to the evening. Traditionalists complained, but the young men were *stronghed*, and would not listen.

Over the eight-year period during which I made regular visits to Tanna – from 1972 until 1980 – there was no decline in the extent to which kava was consumed at non-traditional times. If anything, the opposite seemed to be occurring. During my brief visit to the island in 1986, after some years of Government promotion of kava as an alternative to alcohol, I was struck by the almost continual kava drinking at the *yimwayim* I visited, starting from quite early in the morning. Nor were my impressions idiosyncratic. When I remarked that I could not remember such enthusiastic kava drinking from my earlier trips, men agreed.

Yet at the same time a counteracting process had started, which would reduce the proportion of kava drinkers in the Tannese population. In 1974 pagans were expressing their concern to me about the interest many of their neighbours were taking in the new Christian sects and movements – fundamentalist and charismatic – that were being brought to the island. The specific catalyst for their anxiety was the recent conversion of Lounapektuan, a *yimwayim* not far from the airfield and about 4 km from Irakik, to the Assembly of God church. The people of Lounapektuan had previously comprised pagans and rather indifferent Presbyterians, who had drunk kava and fully participated in the usual round of traditional rituals, dances and exchanges. But after their conversion everything was abandoned; a situation graphically expressed by one man's comment that the grass on their *yimwayim* was now knee-high. An additional edge to the pagans' concern was the fact that one of the leading Tannese evangelists for the Assembly of God was a man from Ikasuk, which had direct *suatu* links to some of Irakik's immediate neighbours, and which was much closer than Lounapektuan. This man had been sent to Fiji for training, and on his return began an active campaign to convert the people in the Lenakel district. I suggested that the pagans' fears were groundless, that whatever the specific motives for Lounapektuan's apostasy, a religion which prohibited so many of the worthwhile aspects of Tannese culture would surely have limited appeal for the remainder of the island. The response from all of the half-dozen men with whom I was discussing the matter was immediate. And, given the frequent complaints I had heard about Presbyterian interference in traditional culture, it was totally unexpected. They said that it was just these prohibitions which made the Assembly of God so attractive; their purpose was to pull people into the church.[1]

The Assembly of God has become one of the major churches on Tanna. Concern about the burgeoning number of religious groups active on Tanna – one count put the number at twenty-three by the mid-eighties[2] – has led to the Local Government Council passing regular resolutions, which are nevertheless ineffectual, that all but four of these groups should be thrown out. The Assembly of God is one of these four, along with the Presbyterians, the Adventists and the Catholics (Monty Lindstrom, personal communication).

As it turned out, the Assembly of God did not have very much success with the people of Irakik and their neighbours, and obtained only a handful of converts there. Nevertheless, after the death of a number of influential and knowledgeable pagans in the mid-1970s, especially David Nasu from Irakik and his brother Yasgapel from Inapukil, a growing interest developed in other Christian movements. By 1986, the area had been transformed, with a large number of pagans joining, or planning to join, one of the churches. The people of Lopnumwin, 1 km from Irakik, had joined the Holiness Fellowship. The people of Irakik, along with many from nearby

[1] Cf. for instance Wetherell's account of Revd J. Fisher, an Anglican missionary in Wanigela, 'who had few illusions about Papuan culture . . . [and who effected] a general reforming of manners and morals, so that by 1916 he could say that the people had definitely forgone "their hideous native customs"' (1977: 146). While he was strongly criticized by his fellow missionaries, 'the Wanigela people did not criticize Fisher, and paradoxically, some of them liked the man best who turned against their fathers' customs' (ibid.: 147).
[2] This was the number given by Shirley Fenton Huie, who has been carrying out research in Vanuatu for a book on women in isolation, during an interview on the radio programme 'Profile' broadcast on the Australian Broadcasting Commission station 3AR on 11 March 1986. This would also include non-Christian groups such as the Bahai.

yimwayim, were involved in the New Life movement, a charismatic movement within Presbyterianism, and were planning to build a church. The few remaining staunch pagans that I was able to speak to during my brief visit said that they felt completely beleaguered, and that while the majority of the new Christians were still participating in *kastom*, they could not be sure that this would continue.

At Lopnumwin kava had been abandoned completely. Most of the men at other *yimwayim* in the area were still drinking and, as I have already noted, a considerable number were drinking to excess. But specific individuals had given it up, although they continued to grow kava (for sale as well as for use in exchanges: kava has become an important cash crop, Ellis 1984; Lebot and Brunton, n.d.). The reasons given were nearly always religious. However a couple of men said that kava drinking interfered with their gardening and business ventures and, while they did not express it in quite these terms, the implication was that, just as most cigarette smokers in the West find, complete abstinence was easier to achieve than controlled consumption. One of these men, who had been a particularly heavy drinker in the 1970s, told me that he had chosen the day Vanuatu gained its Independence in 1980 as the appropriate commencement date for his abstinence. Nevertheless, as I discovered later, he had become involved with the Seventh-day Adventists, an affiliation he may have wished to hide from me, both because I was presumed to be a 'man of *kastom*', and because he probably remembered making a number of disparaging comments about Christianity to me in earlier days.

Another source of pressure on men's kava drinking comes from their wives. Over the years, a number of men have told me that their wives often nagged them to give up kava. Women resent the idleness that it induces in their husbands, and the extra burden that falls on themselves. While men strongly deny that they respond to this pressure, some of the men who had become Christian abstainers in 1986 were those who had told me about their wives' complaints in the past.

Discussion

As I noted earlier, my informants state that the major reason that the pagans of the Tanna Law period permitted kava to be drunk at any time was to challenge the Christians. While it is not possible to recover the precise motivations and arguments involved, it is important to consider this matter further, even though it requires some conjecture.

Irrespective of whether the syncretic myth of the origin of kava was known in Tanna Law times, its themes of the connections between prohibitions and power, and the imbalance between the European sources of power and the Tannese source, kava, are central to our understanding.

Insofar as the European sources were perceived to be accessible through obeying the prohibitions the Christians had laid down, the attractiveness of Presbyterianism over paganism would have increased considerably. To anticipate some of the discussion of the next chapter, the arrival of a medical missionary, Dr Nicholson, at Lenakel in 1903, the subsequent construction of a hospital and the great improvements in health care that resulted, together with the abolition of warfare in 1907, must have made it look as though that power was within reach (Nicholson 1909a: 9, 12; 1909b: 11; 1909c: 6; Wilson 1948: 10). Growing numbers of Tannese were only too willing to abandon paganism, telling their former co-religionists that they were now being helped by God. By 1909 the missionaries, reminding themselves that this island was once 'dark Tanna', were writing that it was 'not merely the dawning of a new era, but we might also say the birth of a new Tanna' (New Hebrides Presbyterian Mission 1909; Nicholson 1909d). A conversation that Nicholson had with a Tannese 'chief' on the east coast shows that these were not just their own sentiments: 'Since you missionaries who obey the word of Jesus brought us the light and healed the sick, *we are living in a new country*' (1910a: 11; emphasis in original).

Those Tannese who, for whatever reason, wished to remain pagan had been presented with a major challenge. It can legitimately be seen as the culmination of a long series, in which missionaries challenged pagans to a ritual contest, with the pagans responding with challenges of their own. My pagan informants gave me accounts of a number of these contests, and others have been recorded in the missionary literature (F. Paton 1903: 282; J. Paton 1965: 140–3; Watt 1896: 214–15; see also Tippett 1967: 107). This method of handling questions of relative power also had a traditional basis. Men attempt to send downpours to wash out major feasts – or volcanic ash to spoil the gardens – of their rivals or enemies, who in turn attempt to thwart these acts. The outcome is interpreted as a kind of meteorological tug-of-war, with the 'winners' being those whose power prevails over their 'victims' (cf. Nachman 1981).

I would suggest that, whatever their understandings and expectations of the connection between prohibition and power, the pagans had no alternative other than to relax the restrictions on kava along the lines I have described. The terms of the contest had been determined for them. Had the pagans *increased* the restrictions – either by limiting kava to particular categories of men or limiting its consumption to specific occasions – they would have played into their adversaries' hands by making the Presbyterian requirement of abstinence from kava correspondingly easier to achieve. By showing that the consumption of kava could be increased without any ill-effects, the pagans were trying to make the point that the taboos that the Christians were imposing had no substance behind them. I saw a similar principle operating in the mid-1970s when a number of men from Laruanu,

Loutahiko, and Lowun, angered by the evangelism and sabbatarianism of the New Life movement, formed 'companies' whose sole purpose was to work in each other's gardens on a Sunday.

Although no one has phrased it in quite such terms, the easing of the restrictions on kava also created problems for the Christians themselves. It made it easier for Christians to drink kava without their co-religionists being aware of it, and at least a few took advantage of this possibility.[1] Given this, it would have become more difficult for Christians to be sure that converts were actually abstaining from kava, thus introducing elements of suspicion that would help to undermine the Christian desire for a society based on love and trust, a re-creation of the mythical time of *niproou*.[2]

Nevertheless, I think it is fair to argue that, viewed from a long-term perspective, the development of a secular pattern of kava consumption and the consequent abuse of kava has diminished its effectiveness as a source of power, and thus increased the appeal of restrictive Christian sects. There is an indication of this in the syncretic myth of origin, with the statement that kava was a lesser substitute for the power that was given to Europeans. Philibert has made a comparable point in a slightly different context, arguing that the promotion of kava by the Vanuatu Government is undermining its symbolic potential, to the extent that for most Vanuatuans it is becoming simply a means of getting drunk without having to suffer the harmful effects of alcohol (1986: 5–7, 10). The cycles of intemperance that were triggered by the pagans' decision in Tanna Law days have become more and more difficult to contain. At first they were at least partly reversed by mechanisms within paganism itself – admonitions from older men or messages from spirits stating that kava should be drunk only at sunset. But these mechanisms seem to have lost their force, and the only means of control available at present appears to be a religiously underpinned abstinence.

---

[1] Gregory, Gregory and Peck's statement that 'there are references to men drinking kava during the day to keep their use of kava secret' (1981: 305) might appear to provide additional confirmation of my informants' statements. However, these unspecified references may well be to an early, unpublished paper of mine, in which I noted that some Christians secretly drank kava (1974: 7). They have listed this paper in their bibliography.

[2] It is true that some Christians would voluntarily abstain from Communion after committing some delict usually known only to themselves, either out of guilt, or more probably accepting that God, like a number of traditional spirits, would know about and punish transgressions (Rae 1920a: 9). But as I have already mentioned, the known absence of any biblical injunctions against the custom permitted the existence of a minority counter-tradition which denied the incompatibility beween kava and Christianity.

7

The problems of Tannese society

In this chapter I intend to bring together and develop issues relating to social order, power and taboo that have been raised in the previous two chapters, in an attempt to explain the religious volatility that has characterized Tanna over the past one and a half centuries. Although, of necessity, I will be discussing institutions that are specific to Tanna, my overall intention is to point to social processes which were shared with other Melanesian societies, in preparation for dealing with the central topic of this book: the pre-contact disappearance of kava from a number of places in Melanesia.

Traditional social organization

Several writers have discussed Tannese social organization (Guiart 1956a; Brunton 1979, 1981a; Lindstrom 1981a, 1985; Bonnemaison 1985a, 1985b; Wilkinson 1979; Adams 1977, 1984, 1987; Bastin 1981). The most comprehensive treatment to date is the one given by Lindstrom. He describes a segmentary system with six levels of social grouping. At the lowest level of inclusiveness is the household and then, in ascending order, the name set, the *yimwayim* side, the *yimwayim*/village, the place,[1] and the moiety. While I would not dispute his statements about the household, which typically consists of a married couple and their natural and adopted children, there are important shortcomings in his discussion of the other levels and these need to be considered.

It is misleading to present the relationship between the different groups as different levels of a segmentary structure. From the way Lindstrom has treated the *yimwayim*/village group, he must be aware of at least some of the difficulties, although he does not make these clear. Thus, in a diagram, this is treated as a single level although, in the text, *yimwayim* is separated from village[2] without any attempt to locate the latter within the segmentary system (1981a: 34, 59–60, 65–6).

[1] This is referred to as 'tribe' by Guiart 1956a: 11–12.
[2] His description makes it clear that what he calls 'village' (*rokwanu*; Lenakel: *lauanu*), I have called hamlet.

Although Tannese use kinship idioms to refer to most of their groups, their social organization is more accurately understood as being locality based. On this point at least, Lindstrom and I agree, although he does not carry through the full implications of this understanding (see Lindstrom 1985: 28–31). Such a perspective is justified on three main grounds. Firstly, it accords with the way in which the Tannese themselves describe, and appear to conceptualize, their society. Secondly, it is only in these terms that one can adequately incorporate the central role of the *suatu*, which are both enduring relations of alliance between *yimwayim*, hamlets (*lauanu*), and their members, and physically existing roads connecting these places. Finally, it is through this local group affiliation that a man acquires the rights and obligations which enable him to participate as a full member of society. Under certain circumstances, which despite being unusual are nonetheless significant, this affiliation will be incongruent with his kinship status. Demographic considerations may result in a boy being adopted into a *lauanu* which should not contain anyone in his kinship category. In such a case, he becomes a full jural member of the *lauanu*, with just one proviso: were he to be involved in serious and continuing conflict with the other men of his *lauanu*, they might try to strip him of his membership, and force him to return to his natal hamlet.[1] But his kinship status is not affected; and he is subject to the same marriage restrictions and requirements that he would have been had he remained in his original *lauanu*.

While the possibility of an adoptee losing his *lauanu* membership indicates the relevance of at least a qualified principle of descent, such attempts are nevertheless rare, at least in the area in which I worked.[2] My informants simply told me that they were a possibility, without being able to give me a concrete instance. And although Lindstrom does describe some attempts, none of these appear to have been successful (1981a: 52–4; 1981b: 387–8; 1985: 36–7).

Kava grounds and hamlets

The most satisfactory way of commencing the analysis of Tannese society is to examine the *yimwayim*, the *lauanu* which are scattered in their vicinity and whose members make up the membership of the *yimwayim*, and the network of major and minor *suatu* which intersects the island, linking *lauanu* to *lauanu*, and *yimwayim* to *yimwayim* in perpetual relationship. These are the essential elements in what the Tannese represent as a

---

[1] I should point out that such an attempt could also occur in the case of a man who stood in a 'brother' relationship to the other men, but who had also been adopted from another hamlet.
[2] In the Waesisi area, pressure of land, the extermination of most of the original inhabitants in warfare, and loss of traditional knowledge has brought about a situation where descent has become the paramount principle of group formation (Lindstrom 1985: 39; Wilkinson 1979: 56–62; Bastin 1981: 338–41).

perpetually enduring structure laid down, as they say, 'by God' in the distant past. While it is recognized that certain *yimwayim* and *lauanu* have actually been created by men, or that new *suatu* may be cleared, strictly speaking these innovations cannot enter into the cycle of marital and ceremonial relations that constitutes the essence of Tannese sociability.

Following my arguments about the fundamental importance of locality, I think that it is more appropriate to use the term 'hamlet' (*lauanu*)[1] for the group that Lindstrom calls 'name set' (which he also says is referred to by the phrase *nimwipwi* X, 'grandchildren of X', 1981a: 39; Lenakel: *namwipwi*). 'Name set' does not convey the fact that names are inextricably tied to hamlets. Furthermore, Tannese personal names also function as titles, and this is the term I prefer to use, as it is by virtue of having a particular title, allocated from the stock possessed by a hamlet, that a man owns specific plots of land, occupies political and ritual office, possesses magical paraphernalia and knowledge, and has the right to activate particular *suatu*. It is also important to note that, as will have been apparent from my earlier comments, while members of the one *lauanu* are usually agnates, this is not invariably the case. Young boys, and sometimes older men, may be adopted into *lauanu* which were previously empty or diminished in numbers (see ibid.: 50–1). Occasionally, although men try to avoid it if at all possible, boys who stand in a cross-cousin relation to the other men of the *lauanu* may be adopted. More commonly, while the adoptee may be in a brother or son relation to the others, the precise agnatic links may be quite distant.

The application of the term *namwipwi* to the 'name set' or hamlet is not as clear cut as Lindstrom claims, at least not in the Irakik area. Firstly, the phrase '*namwipwi* X' is not applied to all hamlets. It is said to be a classification 'put by men' rather than 'by God', and indicates that at some time in the past all the men of the hamlet were the grandchildren or descendants of X.[2] Secondly, the phrase may be applied to more than a single hamlet or 'name set'. Thus, at Irakik, *namwipwi* Plaha refers to Louyerabou hamlet and Yimetang hamlet, both of which are divided into two sides, each with its separate stock of titles, which give their holders rights to, *inter alia*, quite different *yimwayim* sides and *suatu*. Thirdly, although the same title appellations may recur in hamlet after hamlet, but with different sets of rights,[3] this is not so true of *namwipwi* names. In the

[1] In fact, many hamlets are divided into two 'sides'. For purposes of exposition, however, these can be regarded as two separate hamlets, even though they share the same name.
[2] Yet this still leaves a puzzle which no one was ever able to explain. In some cases the title 'X' may be one of the titles owned by the hamlet concerned, yet in other cases it does not form part of the stock. The most plausible explanation is that once it did, but that knowledge of the associated rights has been lost. Without this knowledge there is no point in allocating the title.
[3] Men with the same title appellation call each other 'my namesake' (*yanhinok*). Lindstrom states that this constitutes a significant social link, which ideally makes for easy relations

occasional cases where they do recur, men assume that there is some connection, although they may be at a loss to describe it. For instance, the appellation *namwipwi* Plaha also applies to some hamlets at Lounepuk yimwayim, a couple of kilometres away, and the men of Irakik think that this is because the members of those hamlets must originally have derived from Irakik (cf. Guiart 1956a: 314). However there are no particular social links between the two places.

While every *yimwayim* has its affiliated *lauanu*, the relationship between the two admits of some complexity. The status of *yimwayim* varies. The most important are those which can be used for the major rituals and exchanges such as the *nikoviaar* or the *niel*, as well as for kava drinking and minor rituals (see also Guiart 1956a: 15–16).[1] These will usually have a number of secondary *yimwayim* associated with them in a single cluster as 'witnesses' or supporters (*rol il nasis*), who are supposed to assist them in these exchanges, although theory and reality do not always coincide. Men from the hamlets of these secondary *yimwayim* may speak of themselves as belonging to the major *yimwayim* in their area as well. But the converse does not apply to the hamlet members of the major *yimwayim*. In addition, there are some very minor *yimwayim* which are not used as a focus of affiliation, but which belong to the men of one or two *lauanu*. These may be used only rarely: as a place where boys are circumcised and then secluded until their wounds heal,[2] or as a temporary kava ground for men who may be angry with others at their *yimwayim* and wish to withdraw from them.

An illustrative example of the complexities involved can be taken from the area in which I worked. Lomtihekel is the major *yimwayim*, and it has a number of secondary ones associated with it: Irakik, Inapukil, Yuneras, Lopnumwin, and Lounepuk. As well, the men from two Irakik *lauanu* have a minor *yimwayim* called Lenuknim. Furthermore, the secondary *yimwayim* do not all have the same status. Thus, while Irakik men readily admitted to the pre-eminent position of Lomtihekel in matters of ritual and exchange, they also asserted that, unlike the other secondary *yimwayim*, they had the right to hold *nikoviaar* themselves. Yet this was contested – in private – by men from other *yimwayim*. They said that while there had been a *nikoviaar* at Irakik in the distant past, it had been held in the 'name

between the men involved (1985: 32, 43). In my own experience, however, this is something of an overstatement.

[1] There are also important differences in the ritual status of these major *yimwayim*, which are explained by reference to specific myths (see Bonnemaison 1985b: 32–7). For instance, there appears to be general agreement that there are twelve *yimwayim* of paramount importance, because of their association with the initial appearance and subsequent dispersion of the political moieties. However, Bonnemaison's map indicates that there is not the same agreement on the actual *yimwayim* which should be included (ibid.: 35). My informants always included Lomtihekel, his informants obviously did not.

[2] For an account of circumcision on Tanna see Mills 1961.

of Lomtihekel', the people of whom had been unable to use their own *yimwayim* for some unspecified reason.

While the members of most – though certainly not all – *lauanu* are agnates, this is not the case with the majority of *yimwayim*. The Tannese use a Dravidian kinship terminology in which all male kin of the same generation are either brothers (*pwian* – older; *norhin* – younger) or cross-cousins (*taniel*). This, in conjunction with the system of prescribed cross-cousin marriage, creates implicit moieties which cut across the *niko*, the explicit political moieties (which will be discussed below). With the exception of Irakik, all of the *yimwayim* for which I possess information contain members of both implicit moieties. The Irakik situation was perceived as anomalous, the possible result of a loss of knowledge about the correct composition of some *lauanu* brought about by the extensive depopulation of the last century.

The roads of alliance and exchange

Roads and paths are an obvious and commonly used metaphor for alliance in Melanesia (see e.g. Campbell 1983: 202–5; Deacon 1934: xl, 62–4; Feil 1984: 58–65; Harding 1970: 97; Layard 1942: 132–3). But what is so distinctive about Tanna is the theoretical unalterability of the *suatu*, and the manner in which they constrain all social relations of any significance. I think it is fair to say that they comprise the central element in the Tannese model of their own society. All communication – messages, resources, actions – relating to marriages, exchanges, rituals, meetings and warfare had to be transmitted along given *suatu* by men whose titles gave them the right to actuate the particular road being used. As an informant once put it, 'Laef blong mifela i go i kam long suatu.'[1]

There are a number of different types of roads, each serving to channel a certain range of interaction. *Suatu* is used both as a generic word, and to refer specifically to the major roads. In the latter usage the word *asuul* (big, important) is added should the context require it. The *suatu asuul* are the named roads which link the *yimwayim* (as opposed to the individual *lauanu*), for the major exchanges and dances, especially the *nikoviaar*. Most of the *yimwayim* for which I have information are on more than one *suatu*, and are thus linked to other *yimwayim* in a number of possible ways. Map 16 shows the major *suatu* passing through Irakik.

I should note that this map does not completely correspond with the maps of the major *suatu* on Tanna presented by Guiart (1956a) and Bonnemaison (1985a: Map 3), just as there are differences in detail between these two researchers themselves. I suspect that the responsibility for these differences lies more with the Tannese than with our carelessness. On quite a few

[1] 'Our lives come and go along the roads.'

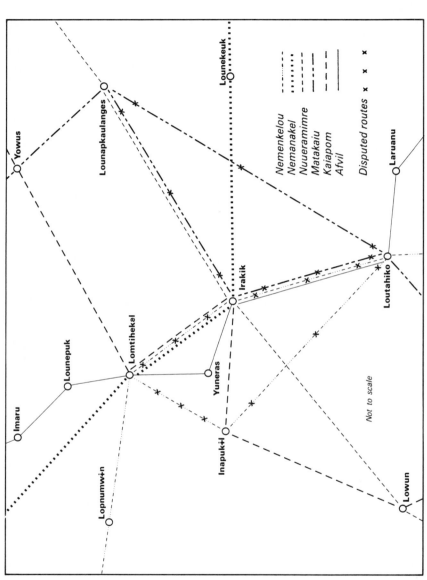

Map 16 Suatu passing through Irakik

occasions men would come to tell me that I should ignore what they had said to me earlier; they had discussed the matter with others and realized they had been wrong. But my data still contain discrepancies, and while I have no doubt that there were some who were not concerned about correcting any errors, there is more to it than this. There are major disagreements as to whether a particular *suatu* joins two *yimwayim* directly, thus allowing the appropriate titleholders to transmit messages and gifts to each other without the involvement of any other *yimwayim*, or whether it passes through intervening *yimwayim*, whose agreement and participation must first be sought. For example, some of the men from Inapukil claim that Nemenkelou goes direct to Loutahiko, but this is denied by men from Irakik who assert that it first passes through their *yimwayim*. Such disagreements are a common cause of serious quarrels, and in the past often led to warfare.

Contemporary Tannese tend to explain these disputes in terms of the loss of knowledge caused by the major population decline of the latter part of last century. This is certainly a factor, but common sense, various accounts about the origins of particular wars, and the fact that some *suatu* are said to be split into two or even more branches along part of their route, all suggest that similar disputes played a major role in the past as well.

The second type of *suatu*, known as *nukulu*, underpins the marriage system: it is along these that women are transmitted, physically as well as metaphorically. These roads link two hamlets whose inhabitants are in a *taniel* relationship to each other. The hamlets may be from a single *yimwayim*, from ones that are part of a cluster, such as Irakik and Lomtihekel, or from distinct *yimwayim* which are relatively close geographically. Normally, the men of a single hamlet (or hamlet 'side') will have only one *nukulu* to a *yimwayim* outside of its own cluster, and the men who are thus linked are called *nipwagniel* (literally 'hole'-*taniel*) or *nipwagnoukausik* (which informants translate as 'dry hole'). The *nipwagnoukausik* is spoken of as the 'true' *taniel*.[1]

One way in which Tannese explain the difference between the two kinds of roads is by saying that when a man goes to another *yimwayim* he is using a *suatu* (*asuul*), but if he has a *taniel* there, and he visits this man's hamlet, he is using a *nukulu*. Another way of expressing the difference is to see the *suatu* as a rope connecting a series of *yimwayim*, but which is made up of individual strands – the *nukulu* – which stick out to connect pairs of hamlets (see Diagram 1), although this is my own rather than my informants' metaphor. Nevertheless, this way of thinking about *nukulu* is given some justification by a point communicated to me by Monty Lindstrom. In the Kwamera language of south-east Tanna, *nukuru*, which is the cognate term, means 'knee' or 'elbow' (in Lenakel it means 'gate').

---

[1] Some men make a terminological distinction between the *nukulu* and the road linking *nipwagniel* or *nipwagnoukausik*, although this does not affect my overall presentation.

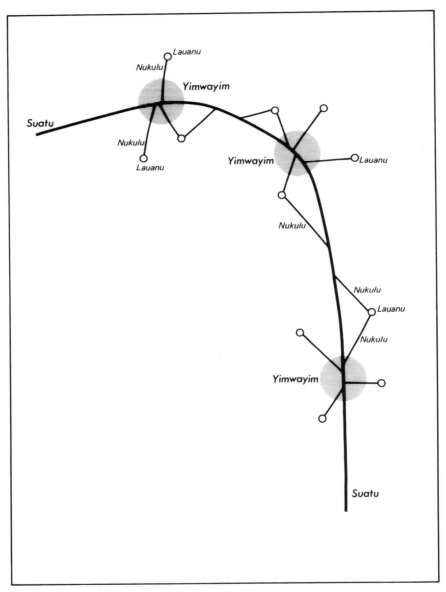

Diagram 1   *Relationship between* suatu *and* nukulu

Traditionally, with only one exception which will be explained later, *nukulu* set the limits of marriage. A man could take a wife from a hamlet only if either he, or someone else from his *yimwayim*, had a *nukulu* link with that hamlet, or another one at the same *yimwayim*. The main reason for this lay in the nexus between marriage and other exchanges, and the interdictions on establishing links outside of the existing network. Marriage is the starting point for a long series of important life-cycle-based exchanges between the men of the two hamlets – and the other members of their *yimwayim* – linked by the *nukulu* along which the woman was transmitted. These continue until the death of the children of the marriage. If the woman were to be passed on to a hamlet at another *yimwayim*, the original givers would not be able to act as the principals in these exchanges, which would then take place along the *nukulu* linking the original and the new wife-receivers. The original givers would be able to play only a minor role as helpers. As well, a man has the right to obtain food, kava and other services from the hamlet to which he has sent a woman. But in the days before pacification, while a man might well be in some danger when visiting other *yimwayim*, the danger was even greater if there were no direct *nukulu* links, even if his daughter or sister was married to a man there. Consequently, in the past, attempts to send a woman on usually led to serious disputes. Although, as I mentioned in the previous chapter, the exigencies arising from the Tanna Law period and conversions to Christianity forced the Tannese to expand the range of marriage links, the transmission of women along more than one *nukulu* still has the potential for creating difficulties.

The *nukulu* create the pivotal relationships in Tannese society. An English-speaking informant once said to me 'A man's *taniel* are his banks. From your banks you get money, from ours we get women.' Tannese say that a man is entitled to a high degree of access to the hamlet and resources of his *taniel*, particularly those of his 'true' *taniel*. *Nipwagnoukausik* could not refuse each other's requests, and they have the right, denied even to a brother owning a different side of the same *yimwayim*, to make fires at the sides of each other's *yimwayim*. Some men included their *nipwagnoukausik* as an owner of their side, and themselves as an owner of his side. But on the other hand, the mutual dependence and the load that the relationship must carry creates a great potential for conflict. Tannese claim that in the past men would not kill close *taniel* themselves (see also Humphreys 1926: 49). But when disputes broke out they would send requests along the network of *suatu* for others to do the job, for which the killers would later be recompensed. Such disputes were not infrequent, for even if men intended to keep promises made to those with whom they were linked by *nukulu*, the vicissitudes of climate and disease frequently prevented them from doing so.

The *kualinapwir*, which is the third type of *suatu*, is of much lesser significance than the *nukulu*. It is the road between a man and any of his cognates, and cannot be used to transmit women, but only goods and requests to perform services. Furthermore, the flow of goods between men linked by *kualinapwir* cannot be too great, lest it provoke the jealousy of their *nukulu* partners.

The final type of *suatu* are called *niko*, because of their connection with the political moieties. These were links between relatively distant *yim-wayim* of the same moiety which could be used as places of refuge after defeat in warfare, and they afforded the one exception to the rule that women could be exchanged only when there was a direct *nukulu* link between giver and receiver. When the defeated group finally returned to their own place they would exchange women with their hosts. But because of the distances and the different conditions that were sometimes involved, these exchanges were not always successful. About a century ago, the people of Irakik took refuge at Ipïkïl, a *yimwayim* about 16 km away on the east coast near the volcano. After residing there for a few years, they returned to Irakik with an Ipïkïl woman, having left one of their own women in return. But the woman, unused to life in the interior, far from the sea, and lonely for her kin, ran away and returned to Ipïkïl. The Irakik men then demanded that the woman that they had left in exchange be returned to them. A heated – though supposedly non-violent – argument broke out, and the road was 'blocked'. It was only many years later, after the complete pacification of the island in the early years of this century, that the road was 'cleared', at the instigation of the men from Ipïkïl – or so I was told – by a reciprocal exchange of pigs, kava and *nelual*.

Moieties and districts

The names of the moieties (*niko*: canoe) are Numrukuen and Koiameta. Their main traditional significance was military, and although their role in terms of present-day social action is limited, they provide a potent model of dualism which pervades Tannese thinking about their own – and other people's – disputes, a point noted by most recent researchers on the island (Lindstrom 1981a: 74; Bonnemaison 1985a; Wilkinson 1979). They are given some minor contemporary expression in ritual: when the men come to lead the circumcised boys on to the *yimwayim* at the end of their period of seclusion, they carry kava decorated with leaves that show their moiety affiliation. There are also said to be various differences in custom and ability, although there is little consistency between informants in this regard (see also Lindstrom 1981a: 72–3; Guiart 1956a: 91–2; Gray 1892: 648–9).

Before pacification, however, the situation was very different. As I indicated in a previous chapter, it was the arrival of Numrukuen and Koiameta that ended *niproou*, the original pre-social state of peace. The early writers on Tanna thought that the moieties were largely based on territory (ibid.; Humphreys 1926: 13–14, 59). However, Guiart realized that they were not territorial units, and in those areas where one or the other were either predominant or the sole occupants it was as a result of the fortunes of war. While the intensification of fighting following the introduction of European diseases and firearms almost certainly accelerated the process whereby one moiety was exterminated or driven out of a given area, the process itself probably commenced earlier (1956a: 90–104).

Lindstrom writes that he was told that the hostility between moieties caused them to be endogamous traditionally (1981a: 73). My own data, however, indicate that this was not the case, and that the *niko* did not have a specific rule of marriage (a point also confirmed by Guiart 1956a: 113–15). Indeed, some *nukulu* connected men from opposite *niko*. Even so, marriages between moieties carried their dangers. A woman might be given by, say, a Numrukuen group to a Koiameta group as compensation for a previous killing, but solely for treacherous reasons, with the intention that the woman would eventually betray her husband to her brothers.

All the information that I have obtained indicates that most *yimwayim*, especially the larger and more important ones, were divided between Numrukuen and Koiameta. This joint occupancy meant that even on the level of a basic local group there was a persistent threat of strife and violence. While men assert that members of opposing *niko* residing at the same *yimwayim* would not attack each other directly, what did occur – and by all accounts, occurred quite frequently – was that *niko* members from other *yimwayim* would be asked to do the fighting instead.

The early European observers on Tanna often spoke of fighting as taking place between 'tribes' or districts (*yimwa*), consisting of a group of up to eight or so *yimwayim* (e.g. Nicholson 1907b: 39; Paton 1903: 94–5; Turner 1861: 39, 85).[1] Yet, as far as I have been able to determine, while all those in a district might join together to fight another district (or a more haphazard assortment of men), they were just as frequently divided in battle (see also e.g. Gray 1892: 649; Nicholson 1907a: 9). My informants play down the significance of the districts, both in the present and during the past. In the words of one, 'men didn't think much about them'. The only occasions in which they seemed to play any role were during dances and the *nikoviaar*. Thus, different groups of dancers might be spoken of by a district name, for example Rakavilne or Numatane. But this is simply as a point of reference, and does not reflect a rule of composition (see also Guiart 1956a: 29). Or people might speak of a *nikoviaar* as being held in the name of a district,

---

[1] The names of these districts usually consist of a name of a person or thing to which the suffix *mine* ('and') or its shortened form *ne* has been added. Thus the district in which Irakik is located is called Nauiliangmine. *Nauiliang* is the word for a vine that grows around coconut palms.

without this meaning much in practical terms. In 1974 a *nikoviaar* was held at Imaru which, like Irakik, is a Nauiliangmine *yimwayim*. The people of Irakik spoke of it as 'their *nikoviaar*', but I was never able to detect any difference between their involvement and the involvement of their Rakavilne neighbours from Loutahiko and Laruanu.

Nevertheless, district boundaries are precisely delineated, apparently without involving substantial disagreements between informants. Both Guiart (ibid.: 11–12) and Bonnemaison (1985a: Map II), working almost thirty years apart, enumerated the same number of districts: one hundred and fifteen. Part of the explanation for this uncharacteristic certainty must lie in the relative insignificance of the districts as a means of organizing social action; consequently there are fewer incentives for manipulation. Yet at the same time there is an important myth detailing their origin. This myth tells of Semsem, an ogre from Aneityum, who ate all the Tannese, with the exception of one woman who later gave birth to twin boys. When the boys matured, the three lured Semsem back to Tanna where they killed him and carved up his body, freeing all the people he had eaten. The twins then defined and named all the districts of Tanna, and assigned every one of the freed people to a specific district.[1]

Bonnemaison states that the Semsem myth expresses the idea of a divided society 'held together by the death of an initial victim and the dispersion of the body. Tannese cultural unity is a direct consequence' (1985b: 36). Although the actual phrasing of this comment is perhaps misleading, because no matter what the level of Tannese society, unity is only an ideal, I think it is based on a sound insight. One way of explaining the existence of an apparently otiose level of grouping which is nevertheless legitimized by a major myth is that it was an attempt – albeit one which was not successful – to provide a stronger basis for unity.

The principles of organization that I have examined so far do not exhaust the list. Gray refers to the division between coastal and inland people, and the disdain in which the latter were held by the former (1892: 649; see also Humphreys 1926: 14; Guiart 1956a: 92; Lindstrom 1981a: 79). This division was also mentioned by my own informants, but although it appears to have been emotionally charged in the past, it was no longer of relevance.

Furthermore, some time during the last century a new moiety division was created between Manuwar (man-of-war) and Sipi (ship). There are many confusing aspects about this new system, which appears to have been strongest in the eastern side of the island around White Sands. Lindstrom was told that these moieties were invented by four men (1981a: 74). But it is

[1] Identifiable versions of this myth have been recorded and published by Gray (1892: 657–9), Humphreys (1926: 95–7), Guiart (1956a: 12–13), Lynch (1978b: 123–30), and Bonnemaison (1985b: 36), although they do not all go into the details of the creation of the districts. I have summarized a version told to me by David Nasu, which is very similar to the one Guiart presents.

140

not clear whether Manuwar and Sipi were simply new names for Numru-kuen and Koiameta, whether they completely cut across the old moiety divisions, or whether the bulk of their respective membership came from a single moiety with the remainder coming from the other. Guiart states that in the east the new names were superimposed upon the old, with Numru-kuen becoming Sipi and Koiameta becoming Manuwar. In the south, where the Koiameta had been driven out earlier, they were imposed upon the coastal–inland division (Guiart 1956a: 92). Yet Lindstrom writes that in the south-east it was Manuwar that emerged from Numrukuen and Sipi from Koiameta (1981a: 78). Wilkinson offers yet another interpretation, in which the Manuwar were the coastal supporters of the missionaries and the Sipi the inland pagans (but cf. Macmillan's comments that church membership was freely distributed amongst both moieties, although it was only in 1926 that Sipi office-bearers were appointed, 1927a: 7). Wilkinson specifically states that the new moieties did not coincide with the old (1979: 18–19, 26–7). It is hardly surprising therefore that I received contradictory state-ments from my own informants. Some gave information that corresponded with Guiart, others said that each of the new moieties contained members from both Numrukuen and Koiameta. However, there was one point on which there was general agreement: that the basis of the contention between Manuwar and Sipi were claims about which had been the first to see European ships coming to White Sands, with Manuwar maintaining that they had seen the first vessel, which had been a warship, and Sipi claiming that it had been a merchant ship, seen by them.[1]

I would suggest the most appropriate perspective from which to view Tannese society is one that recognizes that, far from it being a segmentary system, it was one which incorporated a series of cross-cutting principles of organization, in which those divided at one level were united at another. Thus, members of the one *lauanu*, even if they were all agnates, were divided by their close relations with different *nipwagnoukausik* who came from separate *yimwayim*. The *niko* united men from different *yimwayim* and different districts, as well as dividing members of the one *yimwayim*, and sometimes men in a *nipwagnoukausik* relationship. Most districts, with the exception of the very small ones just north of Lenakel, were divided by the coastal–inland distinction, which united men of different *niko*.

Furthermore, these principles of organization almost certainly varied in their extension and significance, in the extent to which allegiance to one overcame allegiance to the others, at different times, and in different parts of the island. This has made the task of presenting a social morphology of Tanna such a difficult one (Guiart 1956a: 115; Adams 1987: 8–10). Although we may never discover the way in which the various groupings

[1] For an example of the continued relevance of the Manuwar–Sipi division in the 1920s, see Macmillan 1927a: 7–8.

were established, or their chronology, I think that it is possible to see them, at least in part, as attempts to create a workable degree of social harmony. It should not be necessary to argue that people in traditional societies attempted to modify their institutions in order to achieve certain goals,[1] although the successful legitimation of major innovations might require that individual agency be disguised. Yet Facey notes that in Nguna, in central Vanuatu, 'certain chiefs are said to have instituted [totemic matriclans] in order to reduce a disastrous level of warfare and intergroup enmity' (1981: 298).[2] While I have not come across anything quite so conclusive on Tanna, historical material, as well as statements from contemporary informants, suggest that the maintenance of an acceptable degree of social harmony and order has long presented the Tannese with an intractable problem.

Traditional political hierarchy

When making general statements about the pre-contact political structure, my informants usually drew a number of contrasts with the contemporary situation. While people now did what they pleased and did not listen to their chiefs, in the past, they claimed, the *yeremira* were very powerful. Their views, which were conveyed at public meetings by their subordinates, the *yeniniko* ('spokesman of the canoe'), had to be reckoned with, and their orders obeyed. If they were not, the *yeremira* would command another of their subordinates, the *yolatkokunar*, to perform sorcery (*netik*) against the offender. Initially, the intention would not necessarily be to kill, but to warn by inflicting pain and suffering. If the person who had angered a *yeremira* desisted from his or her course of action, the sorcery, which involved the slow burning of something which had been in contact with the victim, would cease. Otherwise, the burning would continue until the offender's death. *Netik* was said to have been the punishment for 'breaking the law' or, more graphically, 'kalabus blong mifala'.[3]

Because of the central role that marriage played in the exchange system, and the potential of any disputes to disrupt all other relations along the *suatu* involved, a *yeremira* was concerned to ensure that the marriage

[1] See Rodman (1985) for a very useful discussion of anthropologists' neglect of legal innovation in small-scale societies. Yet Rodman's case study and subsequent argument relates to the post-contact period. A more appropriate case is Pospisil's account of a change in rules of exogamy among the Kapauku, in particular his suggestion that this change was accepted because of its positive consequences for the maintenance of social order (1969: esp. 223–5; see also Errington 1977: 36). Tuzin, referring to the 'uncommonly acute awareness of generations of leaders that security lay in numbers' (1980: 287), suggests a much broader process of innovation and development aimed at maintaining social cohesion that may have been at least partly deliberate (1976: 82, 148, 319–21; 1980: 254–7).
[2] The examples of the changes in marriage practices, the ritual innovations in which Manga of Lamwinaura was involved, and the creation of the new moieties, show that successful innovation and individual agency were not incompatible on Tanna either.
[3] 'Our (traditional) prison'.

142

exchanges that his people were involved with proceeded smoothly. The wishes of the young people concerned were said to have been irrelevant, and if they protested, they would be threatened with *netik*. As informants explained it, 'Once the men responsible for the road had come to an agreement it didn't matter how ugly the boy or girl was, or how much they smelt. If they refused the *netik* would start. Once the pain started they would usually agree, otherwise the *netik* would continue until they either changed their minds or they died.'[1]

A *yeremira* was not expected to work in the gardens, as his people would feed him. In times of war he would not fight, but would remain in his *lauanu* where he could be better protected from being killed. Only a *yeremira* could wear the *kueria*, a very tall cylindrical feather head-dress built on an armature of coconut palm ribs, at *nikoviaar* (see Plates 1 and 2). This was made for him by his *yolatkokunar*. Polygyny was restricted to *yeremira* and *yeniniko*, with the *yeremira* allowed five or six wives and the *yeniniko* two or three.[2]

All the political offices were held as a consequence of possessing a particular title. There were various other ritual privileges that were restricted to individual *yeremira* or the occupants of other titles, such as eating the head of the turtle, or the flesh of the *kipwia*, the hairless pig, which is particularly valued on Tanna. Using language drawn from the colonial political structure, men said that the *yeremira* was a 'high commissioner', the *yeniniko* a 'district agent', and the *yolatkokunar* an 'inspector'. One man put it even more dramatically. 'If you could see our chiefs from the past', he said, 'you would cry. You would be too frightened to look into their eyes.'

But this general picture does not accord with other evidence, both historical and ethnographic. It is also at variance with comments the same informants would make at other occasions about particular incidents and conflicts in the distant past.

The most important point to note is that titles to political office were extremely numerous, and this alone suggests that the power associated with them was diffuse and insubstantial. Guiart counted 472 *yeremira* in his island-wide survey, and 129 *yeniniko*. There were many *yimwayim* which had more than one of these titles, particularly *yeremira* (1956a: 9, 262–402). These figures almost certainly understate the traditional situation: after it became known that I possessed a copy of Guiart's work, I was visited by a number of delegations of men from various *yimwayim*, wanting to know

---

[1] *Netik* was not the only punishment used in such cases. Thus a woman who refused to marry a particular man might have the needles from the black palm jabbed into her legs.
[2] Contrary to contemporary claims about *yeremira* having up to six wives, Turner stated that 'he does not know of any chief with more than three wives' (1842–3: 8). The maximum number of wives I recorded in genealogies was five, but my informant was not able to tell me whether the *yeremira* had actually been married to all of these women at the one time, or whether the figure represented the total wives during his life.

whether he had recorded particular titles, the names of which they had lost. There was not a single occasion on which I could help them with this, so the knowledge had obviously disappeared well before the time of Guiart's research. I was never able to obtain a satisfactory explanation of the fact that there were fewer *yeniniko* than *yeremira*, and the effect that this had on the relations between the two titles, particularly when there were disagreements among a number of *yeremira* who had the one *yeniniko*. Some men thought that the reason might lie in a much higher mortality rate amongst *yeniniko* during the vicious fighting of the last century. But this does not explain why knowledge of the title itself was lost, although it is true that the men seeking information from Guiart's work always inquired about *yeniniko* titles (or titles relating to the performance of particular kinds of magic), never *yeremira*. Guiart obviously had similar difficulties, and he suggested that the *yeniniko* had more secular power, at least in the southern part of the island, and the *yolatkokunar* carried out his instructions, not those of the *yeremira* (1956a: 86–90, see also e.g. 311–28). But my informants were adamant that the *yeniniko* had a subordinate position, and said that, even in warfare, it was the *yeremira* who made the important decisions and the *yeniniko* who carried them out. Lindstrom received similar information to mine about the relative position of the two titles (1981a: 69).

Nearly all the early European observers were struck by the rudimentary nature of political authority on Tanna (Forster 1968: 528, 540; Cook 1961: 507–8; Turner 1861: 84–5). Cook noted that 'one of these Kings had not authority enough to order one of his people up into [a] cocoa nutt [sic] tree to bring him down some nutts, altho he spoke to several, and was at last obliged to go himself' (1961: 497). In 1870 Agnes Watt commented: 'Chieftainship may be said to exist only in name. In a village of eight or nine men, six will claim to be chiefs' (1896: 110). This ratio is not so different from the one Guiart obtained from his 1952 survey: out of an adult male population of 1,790, eleven hundred claimed to hold titles which gave them some kind of authority (1956a: 107).

Nineteenth-century accounts of *netik* portray a far more capricious use than contemporary Tannese admit, and suggest that if punishment for disobeying the commands of a *yeremira* was a factor, it was no more frequent than attempts by *netik* performers to obtain personal advantage (Watt 1896: 109; Nisbet 1840–51: 77–8; Turner 1861: 89–91; Gray 1892: 653–6). While the fact that all these early descriptions come from missionaries might seem to compromise their veracity, one of the details in Gray's account is particularly revealing. After pointing out that *netik* required obtaining something which had been in contact with the victim, he states that great care is taken to ensure 'that the original taker may not be known' (ibid.: 654). These efforts at concealment are very difficult to reconcile with my informants' claims that *netik* was used only as a legitimate form of punishment on the instructions of a *yeremira*. This is not a detail that Gray, who in any case was a careful and quite objective reporter,[1] would have seen any point in distorting. Gray offered a number of motivations for carrying out *netik*, but none related to the exercise of any legitimate authority, although he does refer to other magical techniques used to prevent crops from being stolen or harvested before the first-fruits ceremonies had been performed.

Specific events that informants recalled from the past also indicated that the system did not work as their general picture would have it. There were accounts of *suatu* being 'blocked' because, despite the threat of *netik*, women ran away rather than marry particular men. Even *suatu* Afvil ('wide road'), the road linking Irakik and Loutahiko, whose name was always cited as an expression of the close ties between the respective *taniel*,[2] was blocked for a considerable time in the last century because of such an incident. There were references to *yeniniko* who, far from carrying out the instructions of their *yeremira*, acted independently and treacherously. And explanations of the causes of past conflicts showed that the relation between individual *yeremira* was very fluid. Some titles gave their holders the right to wear taller *kueria* than others. However, these relative differences in status often appear to have been ignored, either accidentally or intentionally, and fighting almost invariably followed. Although the details of such fights are usually sketchy, they suggest that for many *yeremira* the number of men who could be relied on to provide automatic support was very few.[3]

It is hardly surprising to find such a discrepancy between a generalized model of a traditional polity and what appears to have been the actual situation, especially as the amount of authority available to traditional leaders has a bearing on both contemporary political issues and Tannese evaluations of their own culture in relation to their perceptions of the colonial hierarchy. (Although I heard many criticisms of the actions of particular colonial officials, the people in my area always seemed very impressed by the pomp and hierarchy of the colonial governments.) Yet at the same time, I do not think that this model can simply be dismissed as a contemporary exaggeration of a very rudimentary traditional hierarchy. Something rather similar may have inspired social goals in the pre-contact period.

---

[1] Adams, whose attitude towards the nineteenth-century missionaries is not particularly charitable, approvingly calls Gray 'a cultural relativist' (1984: 14).
[2] Although their explanation of the etymology is probably false, as this road links many more *yimwayim* than just these two.
[3] Referring to two incidents in 1861 when *yeniniko* were unable to persuade their people to join them in fighting, Adams states that 'traditional authority relations had been upset by European intervention' (1984: 17). But then, as examples of the supposed traditional authority of the *yeniniko* in matters of war, he cites incidents which occurred *thirty-six years later* (ibid.).

I make this suggestion on two separate grounds. Firstly, the way that the titles are interconnected seems to point at attempts to buttress the authority of the existing holders. *Yeremira* were linked to their *yeniniko* and *yolatkokunar* through the theoretically unchangeable network of *suatu*, and these latter titles were allocated by the men of *lauanu*, and often *yimwayim*, other than their own. In other words, an ambitious and able man who had collected a following could not readily claim to be a *yeremira* or *yeniniko*. He would have had to plug into an established system in which the complementary titles to the one he was claiming would normally be residentially dispersed. Spurious claims were further hindered by the mechanism of 'witnessing'. Although specific details of magical techniques, etc. were given to the heir in secret, the public aspects of the rights associated with a title – the land, the *suatu*, the privilege of performing certain actions – were not privately transmitted. There had to be at least one witness from an allied *yimwayim* who was familiar with these rights, and who could vouch that they had not been embellished either during the process of transmission or subsequent to the death of the original holder.[1] These mechanisms almost certainly predate European contact. While there can be no doubt that they were not very successful, given that the hierarchy did not depend on the monopolization of more tangible resources, they at least would have made the creation of new titles and the fragmentation of the old ones rather more difficult (cf. Brunton 1975).

The second reason is based on one of the central events of the *nikoviaar*, which is the most important of the Tannese ritual exchanges. In the early morning, at the beginning of the *toka* dance, a number of the *yeremira* from the performing groups enter the *yimwayim*. The *kueria* is on their shoulders, and they are surrounded by men and youths from their own associated *yimwayim* who carry vines and hooked poles to support it (see Plates 1 and 2). Without these supports the structure, which can be up to six metres high, would topple over. It is a striking image of the hierarchical ideal. Wearing the *kueria* as the symbol of his title, the *yeremira* is at the centre of his people, integrating and towering over them, while they are bound to him, and protect him. In making this statement, I am simply communicating the tenor of various comments Tannese offered about the ritual. Yet a discordant undercurrent appears to be present as well, although it was not one that my informants ever accepted. The almost comically exaggerated height of the *kueria* and its consequent instability can also be read as an expression of the frailty of the *yeremira*'s powers, and his vulnerability should his people decide to abandon him.

---

[1] It is rather surprising that Lindstrom makes no mention of this mechanism in his article dealing with knowledge transmission and control (1984).

Plates 1 and 2   *Entry of the* kueria *during the* nikoviaar

Fighting and social order

The interpretation that I am developing of the tenuousness of social order and authority on Tanna, an interpretation which is central to the argument of this book, is not easily reconciled with the view of Tannese culture which informs Adams' history of the island. He sees the Tannese as living under a sacred order of reality, 'an intricate and seamless spiritual web which invested every object and every event with a transcendent, other-worldly significance' (1984: 14). Sacred stones 'manifested a transcendent reality which encompassed both the material and spiritual realms, revealing the true essence of life' (ibid.: 21), and social harmony and balance were maintained through the 'ritual exchange of gifts . . . transforming apparent chaos into cosmos' (ibid.: 8).

Underlying this lofty prose is an untenable view of an essentially homogeneous and closed culture (see e.g. Keesing 1987). Certainly, there are good grounds for presuming the general stability of Tannese epistemological and ontological assumptions, the kind of evidence necessary for something to be accepted as believable or real (Ernst 1987). But Adams is not dealing with anything as fundamental as this. For him, Tannese culture appears to offer no room for individual doubt or reflection, no possibility of new situations and ideas evoking creative responses which go beyond pre-existing categories. The *culture* is presented as paralleling, in its rigidity, the *individual* conceptions of the most obdurate missionary (e.g. 1984: 59, 66, 110). Quite apart from the theoretical difficulties of maintaining such a position, it is also one that is hard to reconcile with the texts that Adams has used to construct his account.

For instance, Adams argues that the Tannese saw Cook and his party as returned ancestors or gods (1984: 25–9). While it is impossible to recover the Tannese interpretations with certainty, what the contemporary texts indicate is the *diversity* of Tannese reactions, which strongly suggests that a number of interpretations were current, none of which were final. This is apparent in incidents such as the attempts by some to cheat in exchanges and make off with equipment from the ship, the attempted seduction of sailors and the sheepishness of the Tannese on discovering that the sailors were men, not women, and in the varied and changing responses of defiance and friendliness, cowardice and hostility (Cook 1961: 482–500; G. Forster 1968: 486–536; J. R. Forster 1982: 584–613; Sparrman 1944: 151–9; Wales 1961: 852–62).

Adams portrays traditional Tannese society as characterized by balance and order. He asserts that 'fighting was not the denial of a social order, but its very affirmation' (1977: 78) and suggests that warfare was 'essentially an exchange ritual' (1984: 12). He claims that if they are 'carefully read' (1977: 79), the contemporary reports justify such an interpretation.

148

But the issue is not so easily settled. The reports Adams uses contain accounts of individual battles as well as general statements about the characteristics of warfare on Tanna. While there is no need to question examples such as Captain Erskine's 1849 observations of fighting at Port Resolution as 'a war party marching out daily to the boundary-line to exchange a few spears or stones, without any very serious result' (1853: 304; cited in Adams 1984: 12), it needs to be shown that this was true of *all* military engagements. It is necessary to consider the general accounts, particularly those relating to the period up until the mid-1850s before traditional fighting was transformed by the increasing use of European weapons (ibid.: 35–6; Gray 1892: 649–50).[1]

Certainly, there are general statements that appear to lend support to Adams' view. Charles Hardie, an LMS missionary who made a brief visit to Port Resolution in 1849, wrote: 'Not a month passes without war between some of the tribes on the island; but their wars are comparatively harmless, for it seldom happens that any are killed' (1981: 5). And after touring the New Hebrides on board the *Havannah* in 1850, John Inglis, the Presbyterian missionary who was later to work on Aneityum, claimed that 'there did not appear to be much loss of life' in warfare (cited in Adams 1977: 79).

Against these, however, there is other evidence. In his thesis, Adams uses a statement from George Turner, who learnt the Port Resolution language after spending seven months on Tanna in 1842–3 (and who made a number of brief return visits in the 1840s and 1850s), as a starting point for his assertion that fighting was the very affirmation of social order (1977: 78). But Adams has taken this quotation out of the context in which it was made: a comparison with Polynesia (Turner 1842–3: 6). Turner's position is more accurately conveyed by the following:

The men are constantly taken up with war. A state of peace is evidently an exception. During the last [four months] the people have been at war, and now the matter is as unsettled as ever. This war is between the people on this side of the bay and some tribes about 3 miles inland from us. About 4 miles to the eastward of us on the sea coast there is another war going on which is much more deadly than this one, and which has been going on from time immemorial. No-one knows . . . when or how it commenced . . . There are no doubt many more going on at other parts of the island.
(ibid.: 5)

Few fall in their daily skirmishes. Many, however, are cut off after lingering for weeks under fatal wounds.   (1861: 82; see also Nisbet 1840–51: 60–1)

In any case, the actual destruction and mortality from war is not the only point that needs to be considered. Although Adams belittles Paton's

---

[1] Adams suggests that 'even if there were an influx of weapons at the end of the 1850's, it is by no means clear that there was a corresponding rise in mortality. After all, the firearms available were notoriously unreliable and inaccurate' (1984: 36; see also Shineberg 1971). If this is true, it strengthens my case, not his, as it means that the accounts of widespread death and

remarks about 'heathen treachery', saying that Paton did not understand the 'complex interplay of political factors . . . [and the] different webs of alliances' (1984: 140–1), this is simply obfuscation. When former military allies go over to the other side, events which Adams does not dispute, this is treachery, and it is invariably the outcome of a 'complex interplay of political factors'. Turner wrote:

> If a chief sees that his is the weaker party, he will very likely turn around upon his own people, kill one or two of them, and then run to the other side. In such circumstances the enemy will receive him and protect him. This treacherous spirit makes all jealous of the movements of their dearest friend.
> (1842–3: 6; see also e.g. Gray 1892: 663; F. Paton 1903: 176; J. Paton 1965: 109)

Although the prose may be exaggerated, the overall assessment accords with the references that informants made to specific conflicts and murders. Furthermore, while battles may have been pre-arranged, and sometimes averted through gift exchange, they were not the only form of military encounter. There was a constant danger of kidnap and ambush (Nisbet 1840–51: 59; Paton 1965: 199; Turner 1861: 82; Watt 1896: 110). As the earliest European observers concluded, Tannese social relations were characterized by a high degree of distrust, a distrust exacerbated by the fears of sorcery (see e.g. Cook 1961: 501; G. Forster 1968: 539, 542; J. R. Forster 1982: 623; Paton 1903: 56; Wawn 1973: 28).

It is also crucial to consider the question of the Tannese attitudes towards their own social arrangements, and whether the new ideas brought by the missionaries and other Europeans enabled the Tannese to codify, articulate and legitimize attitudes which previously may have existed only in an inchoate state. Here I have in mind Barth's fascinating discussion of the disjunction between the Baktaman practice of violence and apparent individual feelings about it, a disjunction which he suggests is due to the lack of 'generalized propositions about man as a social and moral person' (1975: 153).

Of course, this is by no means an easy question to answer. Nevertheless, the available evidence strongly suggests that the Tannese, or at least many of them, were not as enamoured with their own institutions as Adams seems to assume.

Insofar as contemporary informants can be any guide, there can be no doubt that an enormous sense of relief followed the successful establishment of peace in 1907. Indeed, many of Barth's comments about the ideology of Baktaman warfare apply equally to Tanna. Although people express admiration for those who are strong, it is not possible to identify any elements of a cult of warriorhood or bravery. People make few attempts to

destruction in the latter part of the nineteenth century may be a more appropriate reflection of the earlier situation than I have thought necessary to assume.

hide fear: the phrase 'mifela fraet tumas, mifela ronwe'[1] occurs frequently. Certainly their attitudes cannot be divorced from the appalling loss of life in warfare around the turn of the century. But there is no sense of a harking back to the time when only traditional weapons were used. Although informants were adamant that firearms increased the mortality rate and the frequency of fighting, they did not think that the *range* of hostile and potentially hostile relations was really changed. In other words, the accounts of men being killed by fellow *yimwayim* members, or at the request of a close *taniel*, are not different in kind from what occurred before.

Gray wrote that 'rumour of war fills the Tannese with unspeakable dread . . . [they] really hate war [and] recognise the benefits of peace' (1892: 650), although in a later note he suggested that there were situations in which war was unavoidable and 'beyond the control of everyone' (ibid.: 663). There are many references in the nineteenth-century literature to Tannese wishing to end fighting (F. Paton 1903: 83, 97; J. Paton 1965: 109, 132–3; Watt 1896: 282). In 1852, before European weapons had come into widespread use, a Tannese group from Anuikaraka (or Iuakaraka) led by Yaresi visited Aneityum. Geddie suggested that they walk around the island.

They hesitated at first lest they should be killed, but I assured them that there was no danger . . . Then most of them made up their minds to go but some of them were afraid. I told them that they might leave their clubs and spears behind them as there was no use for them now on this island. I shall never forget the impression made by this visit on the minds of these poor natives. They came directly to my house on their return . . . [I] asked Yaresi if he now believed in the change which the Gospel had effected on this island. He burst into tears and said that it was the first time that ever he knew that any people could live without fighting.

(1848–58, entry for 30 August 1852; see also Hardie 1854: 8).

Although he does not recount this particular episode, Adams treats similar incidents simply as attempts to manipulate Europeans and involve them in local intrigues and personal ambitions (e.g. 1984: 104). There can be no doubt that such intentions played their part in Tannese relations with the missionaries and their response to Christianity. But the motivations of a collectivity of human beings are rarely single-stranded or uniform. By ignoring the possibility that a moral component may have been involved, or that missionaries and other Europeans may have been perceived as possessing the means of addressing inadequacies of Tannese society, Adams has allowed a sentimental view of traditional culture to give rise to a caricature as one-dimensional in its own way as those of the Europeans that he scorns.[2]

[1] 'We were very frightened and we fled.'
[2] Adams' perspective also leads him into some striking inconsistencies. Thus he interprets the denunciations of fighting, sorcery and other practices by a number of chiefs at a meeting in 1860 at which Paton was present 'as being a typical display of Melanesian good manners' (1984: 104). Yet only a few pages later he describes vitriolic attacks on Christianity by men from the

I have already suggested that a number of apparent institutional innovations can best be interpreted as attempts to create a firmer basis of unity and reduce the level of strife in Tannese society. A brief and rather cryptic reference in Turner's journal points to efforts at limiting the murderousness of warfare, even before Christianity had had any influence. He states that an agreement had been reached in his part of the island some time previously to end the practice of fighting at night (1842–3: 6). Yet such agreements must have been fragile, and certainly broke down after European weapons were adopted, if not before. (See, for instance, John Paton's reports of attacks while men lay drunk on kava, 1965: 92, 180.)

Perhaps the most striking illustration of my suggestion can be given by considering the role of the *kouatkasua*. In contemporary usage a *kouatkasua* is someone who 'steals talk', providing an opposing group with information detrimental to his own group. Yet at the same time there are *kouatkasua* titles, and these are usually important. Yahoi of Loutahiko and Mowiagin of Lomtihekel, two of the most influential men in the area in which I worked, were both *kouatkasua* because they held the appropriate titles, and so too was Manga of Lamwinaura, who was responsible for the ritual innovations described in the last chapter.

Guiart states that *kouatkasua* comprised a third 'moiety' which could act as intermediaries between Numrukuen and Koiameta, or go from one side to another as they liked according to the fortunes of war. He suggests that the role may have arisen during the troubled military situation of the last century, possibly out of the activities of *yeniniko* attempting to extend their authority over both moieties in their area, as a number of *yeniniko* are also *kouatkasua* (1956a: 94–5). However, it must be pointed out that the great majority of *kouatkasua* are not *yeniniko* (and vice versa), and that *kouatkasua* appear to be considerably more numerous, certainly in the area in which I worked.

There are some interesting puzzles in the comments informants make about the actions of *kouatkasua* in the past (see also Lindstrom 1981a: 73). They say that his talk was bad, that he was a traitor who would warn his own side's enemies of impending attack, or who would try to stir up trouble by separately telling two hostile groups of the machinations of the other. The curious aspect about this is that men became *kouatkasua* by virtue of possessing the appropriate title. An obvious question arises, and it is one that I asked many times: if the talk and actions of the *kouatkasua* were so bad, why did such titles exist in the first place, and why were they perpetuated?

The typical response to this question was that, although the *kouatkasua* could create a lot of trouble for his group, he could also assist it. While he

same area, following the outbreak of serious illness and death, for which Paton and the new religion were blamed (ibid.: 109).

might betray his people, at other times he might warn them of danger. A number of men said that the *kouatkasua* remained in the middle, and that he tried to help both sides. They added that he attempted to maintain a flow of information between the enemies, so that each knew what the other was doing, and that he would try to ensure that fighting would not get out of hand. Informants said that there was a *kouatkasua* at every *yimwayim* at which both *niko* were present,[1] and they were usually able to name the appropriate titles. There was no agreement as to whether the *kouatkasua* retained their moiety affiliation; some men thought that they did, others denied this. Finally, it was generally agreed that it was a relatively recent development, 'put by man'. Most, but not all, informants also thought that it pre-dated the use of European weapons.

There is really only one interpretation that makes sense of this extraordinary amalgam of positive and negative elements. The origins of the *kouatkasua* lay in attempts at mediation, in efforts to reduce the level of violence between the *niko* and create a domain of relatively secure relations, at least at the local level. Even if it were claimed that the Tannese rejoiced in warfare – which, as I have shown, does not accord with the available evidence – it is still true that the shifting axes of violence created a high degree of insecurity at the level of a primary local group – the *yimwayim* – as well as constantly threatening relationships necessary for marriage, and life-cycle rituals and exchanges. As these were dependent on a fixed number of theoretically unchangeable *suatu*, the incentive to limit fighting between groups in any given neighbourhood must have been substantial.

Yet, as is obvious from the statements about betrayal, the *kouatkasua* turned out to offer an inadequate mechanism for mediation. He could not refer to any significant external sources of authority, and consequently he was unable to overcome the deep suspicion which was generated by the whole pattern of conflict. Whatever the specific actions of an individual, it was not possible for him to establish his neutrality. The varying information other anthropologists and I were given about whether *kouatkasua* retained their moiety membership or formed a third moiety illustrates this (cf. Guiart 1956a: 94; Lindstrom 1981a: 73). Just as the women who were passed between the *niko* in compensation for previous killings could never be trusted, the *kouatkasua* had no way of convincing others that he was not acting treacherously. It was not possible to establish and maintain boundaries between mediation and betrayal. The peacemaker was always a potential double agent.[2]

However, once an effective and continuous source of external power

---

[1] In fact, at some *yimwayim* there were more than one.
[2] See Greenhouse 1985 for a discussion of the limits of mediation in autonomous societies, and the problems of establishing neutrality under these conditions.

became available, Tanna changed, with remarkable suddenness, from being a society characterized by extreme violence to one in which violence virtually disappeared. According to my informants, in the latter part of the nineteenth century the whole population of Irakik, with the exception of one man, was killed in fighting. The situation in neighbouring *yimwayim* was not much better, and in many only a handful of people escaped a violent death. At the 1905 Synod of the Presbyterian Mission it was reported that in the fifteen months to February that year, seventy Tannese had died in fighting (New Hebrides Presbyterian Mission 1857–1938, vol. 3: 111; see also Grimshaw 1907: 287). At this time the total population of the island was around 7,000 (McArthur and Yaxley 1968: 4). This gives an annual homicide rate of 0.8 per cent, which is extraordinarily high. (See the comparative table in Knauft 1985: 379.)

The turnaround came after two visits from men-of-war in 1906 and 1907. In the first visit, by two ships – one British and one French – from the Joint Naval Commission, meetings were held between the captains and commissioners and Tannese representatives from many parts of the island. Dr Nicholson reported that at one meeting with Captain D'Oyly from HMS *Pegasus*, 'several of the chiefs who had long been at enmity, of their own accord desired to shake hands and make friends' (Nicholson 1907b: 40), and this accords with what I was told by informants.[1] Almost immediately, fighting ceased all over the island, although the following year a man was killed in the Port Resolution area (Watt 1907). When HMS *Cambrian* visited soon after, the culprits were captured, tried, and punished, 'the first time on Tanna that natives have been punished for inter-tribal fighting' (Macmillan 1907: 24).[2] Soon after this, fighting came to a complete halt. In December 1908 Nicholson was able to write that the end of the year had been reached 'without the slightest whisper of inter-tribal fighting' (1909a: 12; see also 1913a: 7; Humphreys 1926: xiii; Macmillan 1922: 7).

While the murderousness of war fought with European weapons provided a powerful motivation for peace, these motivations had existed for a long time, but without being effective. The new element was almost certainly the intrusion of European power into the context of local conflicts, and the likelihood that this would be continuous rather than intermittent. In the past, naval intervention occurred only if Europeans were attacked, and even then it was not guaranteed (MacClancy n.d.: 62, 68; Adams 1984: 128–33). There had long been attempts to use missionaries as mediators (ibid.: 103–5). But these could not achieve any lasting success because of apparent shortcomings in their access to convincing sources of power, as

---

[1] I referred to this in my 1981 article, but wrongly thought that the meeting had been with the captain of HMS *Cambrian* (1981a: 375).

[2] But cf. Paton 1903: 198–9 for reference to the earlier burning of a village by a joint British–French party after the killing of a Tannese Christian.

evidenced by their inability to bring down inevitable retribution for attacks on them and those who heeded their rulings (e.g. Watt 1895b: 11; Paton 1965: 109–11, 129, 169, 183–4, 193). The fears that my older informants expressed from the mid-1970s onwards, once Independence seemed likely, made it quite clear that they believed that the sole guarantor of peace on Tanna had been the European presence. As one man told me, 'We Tannese will listen to the whites because we are frightened of them. But we won't listen to black men from the New Hebrides.' These were not the remarks of sycophants. The same men frequently expressed their bitterness at colonial excesses, such as the repression that followed the John Frum movement, and the unwillingness to return *all* alienated land to the rightful owners.

Religious volatility, power and taboo

In the previous chapter I referred to the frequent changes in religious affiliation that have been evident since the times of 'Tanna Law'. Some of the older men that I knew had made up to five such changes. One man, for instance, had initially been brought up as a pagan, but was then encouraged to join the Presbyterians in his teens when his grandfather decided to convert.[1] A few years later, in the mid–1930s, he joined the Seventh-day Adventists, and was sent to Port Resolution to be trained as a teacher. Although he did not complete his training, he remained with the Adventists until the outbreak of the John Frum movement, when he became 'a man of John'. Later, like nearly all of the people from the Lomtihekel area, he had great faith in a secondary movement which was sparked by the visions of two local women in 1951–2 (see Guiart 1956a: 209–12), although afterwards he came to regard these visions as 'lies'. During the time that I knew him, from 1972 until his death in 1976, he presented himself as a follower of *tru kastom*. He saw the original appearance of John Frum at Green Point as being the only legitimate one, and claimed that the only purpose of this appearance had been to restore *kastom* and return its power. He rejected all the cargoist promises, although he admitted that he had once believed in them. And then, within five years of his death, his son, who had been as committed to *kastom* as his father, joined the charismatic New Life movement.

This volatility is not new, although if Tannese religious engagement is

---

[1] The conversion of his grandfather was itself quite remarkable. During the 'Tanna Law' days he had become involved in a dispute with a Christian over a woman the Christian owed him, but refused to transmit. When he inisted on his rights, a party of Christian 'policemen' captured him and a close *taniel* from Loutahiko, forced them to eat fowl manure, and took them in chains to a jail on the coast. So that this outrage would never be forgotten, a tree was planted on the *yimwayim* at Lomtihekel, where it took place. The tree is still there, and its story was one of the first things that I was ever told on Tanna. It was only much later that I learnt that he decided to convert some years after this event.

seen simply in terms of actual membership or non-membership of a church, it may not be so obvious. As it took over forty years for the first baptisms to take place, and over sixty before there were significant numbers of Christians, it was not surprising that the island was seen as 'dark Tanna' by missionaries (Macmillan 1935; New Hebrides Presbyterian Mission 1908; Nicholson 1909d; Wilson 1948). In reality, however, as will have been apparent from material already presented, there had always been many who were attracted by the missionaries' teaching, but who sooner or later became discouraged by its failure to meet their expectations in terms of its power, or their inability to maintain safe access to that power. Adams' work is full of such examples (e.g. 1984: 53–55, 58, 69, 71, 103–6, 132–3, 137, 144). In other words, from 1839 until the present, Tannese attachment to Christianity has been characterized by a continual ebb and flow, varying only in its magnitude. These continuities offer some degree of assurance that we can bypass the difficulties of recapturing the motivations of previous generations of Tannese, by using contemporary evidence as a key to the past.

Lindstrom noted early in his fieldwork that the Bislama word *paoa* (power) 'is a favourite word for the Tannese' (1979: 42). I had the same experience with the people in my area; *paoa* was a word frequently used, in a wide variety of contexts, and a number of grammatical forms. It was spoken of as an attribute of Europeans and the Condominium Government, or as something that they actually possessed. *Paoa* was a state attainable through knowing the English language, through performing magic and drinking kava and by following the restrictions laid down by a particular tradition – *kastom*, the John Frum movement, a Christian church. There does not seem to be a precise Lenakel equivalent; the closest words are *nasaninaan* or *ausikausik*, but in both cases the range of meanings appears rather narrower, focusing more on 'strength' with the former, and 'hardness' or 'difficulty' with the latter.[1] Lindstrom found a similar situation with the Kwamera language, and was given two possible synonyms, one meaning 'soul, spirit, shadow', and the other meaning 'strength, hardness' (1981a: 106).

The absence of an exact equivalent in indigenous languages does not reduce the importance of considering just what the Tannese are referring to with the word *paoa*. There are other frequently used Bislama words, such as

[1] In his discussion of *mana*-like concepts in Vanuatu, MacClancy gently taunts an unnamed anthropologist (almost certainly Lindstrom) who had unsuccessfully searched for the Tannese equivalent of *mana* without realizing that the word *teskasik* (Lenakel: *ausikausik*), meaning 'strong, difficult', was the one he was looking for (1986: 144–5, 151). However, insofar as the Lenakel word can be taken as a guide, this does not adequately encompass the range of meanings of *paoa*. MacClancy does not indicate which language *teskasik* is taken from, but it is most probably White Sands and, strangely, given that a discussion of the grammatical status of *mana*-like words in other Vanuatu languages immediately follows, he does not indicate that *teskasik* is an adjective with a third-person singular verbal affix.

trabol (trouble), which also seem to lack a precise equivalent, yet whose applicability to traditional situations is beyond question. Camden's dictionary of Bislama gives the following gloss for *paoa*:

Power. Traditionally conceived as ultimately originating from spirit beings. To varying degrees this concept persists as the root sense of the word. Rarely used for physical power ... Power in the area of leadership, ability to command respect, obedience etc. Authority. (1977: 80–1)

These meanings focus on *paoa* as socially operative. Although the Tannese also use the word to refer to individual efficacy or success,[1] it is these social aspects that are relevant to the present discussion. *Paoa* is manifested in such things as the ability to maintain social harmony, and the control of disease, fertility and the elements. In the Tannese view, there are significant interconnections between these phenomena (Lindstrom 1981a: 205–9; Wilkinson 1979: 156–66, 241).

The prominence of the John Frum movement creates the danger of placing too much analytical emphasis on Tannese resistance to colonial excesses, or envy of western material achievements (e.g. Gregory and Gregory 1984; Guiart 1956a; 1956b; Lindstrom 1981c). Certainly, these have been important elements in Tannese history. But so too is an envy of western social achievements, of Europeans' proficiency in social co-ordination, and their apparent ability to put aside their differences and act in unison when necessary. In the mid-1970s when people in the Irakik area were fretting about the introduction of political party organizations to Tanna, an old pagan said to me: 'Parties are okay for you white people. You can deal with them. You don't always disagree amongst yourselves.'

This is a major theme in the syncretic myth of Moses on the mountain. It was the Tannese inability to abide by a restriction that had been placed on their behaviour, their unwillingness to listen to authority or accept a united course of action, that led to their worship of the bull, and their subsequent punishment of the loss of power, which simply perpetuates the weaknesses of Tannese society. The narrator was explicit: the disaster had been caused because there was 'tumas agens, mo jelas, mo toktok long Tanna' (too much division, jealousy and disputation on Tanna). This was a constant complaint. The often expressed ideal is for 'wan tingting, wan tok long Tanna' (one mind – or heart, the seat of thought and emotion – one speech on Tanna). The words are a direct echo of those John Paton recorded at a large feast in October 1860 at which a number of groups promised to give up fighting and live in peace. 'Our leading chief said ... "Let us have one talk, and one conduct, and one heart" ' (cited in Adams 1984: 105). These are

---

[1] In these contexts, however, there appears to be a stronger notion of *paoa* as a fixed resource – as evidenced by the possibility of transferring the power of one's kava to another man – than is the case with *mana* (Keesing 1984, MacClancy 1986).

the sentiments at the core of the *niproou* ideal, the time when there was no dissension or division on Tanna (see also Wilkinson 1979: 279–83; Lindstrom 1981a: 276–7).

Yet it is important to exercise caution when considering what 'wan tingting' really means. Certainly, there has long been competition between different ideological organizations on Tanna (ibid.: 286–301). But there is other evidence to suggest that there is more to Tannese aspirations than a simple desire for ideological uniformity. Wilkinson describes a remarkable case that occurred in the White Sands area. When five people in the Christian *yimwayim* of Louniel died within two months of each other, the remaining members followed customary practice and requested the assistance of people from neighbouring *yimwayim*, who were mainly John Frum supporters. The Christians had thought that one of their number was performing sorcery, but the leaders of the John Frum movement claimed that this was not the problem. The deaths were a result of the people of Louniel contaminating their Christianity with *kastom*: they had taken kava into the church, performed *kastom* dances on a ground consecrated to Christianity and carried out traditional magic before a Christian festival. The John Frum people then told the Christians that they should *abandon* such *kastom* practices and return to the purity of the early days of Tannese Presbyterianism (1979: 233–54, 259).

Surprising as this case may seem, there are a number of other parallels. In 1931 Macmillan wrote of a meeting at which a pagan criticized Christians for not taking sufficient steps to prevent their young men from drinking kava, and 'he asked if that was a right example to set' (1931b: 10–11). Frank Paton reported a meeting between Christians and pagans in 1899 at which Iemakia, an influential pagan, stated 'The worship must not be given up. Numakia has died for it, Seimata has died for it, and now Numanian[1] has died for it. We must not lose what so many have died to gain for us' (1903: 203). This was not a statement made as a prelude to conversion, for Iemakia was still pagan when Paton wrote his book. My informants told me of a number of instances in pre-John Frum times when prominent Christians would send secret messages to pagans, urging them to retain their *kastom*. A message is said to have come even from Yavis, who was one of the stalwarts of Presbyterianism in the Lenakel area (see e.g. Nicholson 1909a: 10–11). One of these messages is also supposed to have played a major role in the pagans' realization that 'Tanna Law' was locally inspired, rather than originating from the metropolitan powers (Brunton 1981a: 369). It is possible that this apparent willingness to encourage pluralism, even during times of intense ideological conflict, may derive from a traditional experience in which *niko* were characterized by different cultural practices. I think

---

[1] It was the shooting of Numanian that resulted in the punitive burning of a village by a joint British–French party referred to earlier.

it is more likely, however, that it is a result of uncertainty as to whether the course of action currently being followed is really the one that is 'true' – i.e. more efficacious (cf. Sahlins 1983: 519) – and a corresponding fear that the 'true' one might be lost. Thus, the desire for ideological unity may coexist or be in tension with a concern to keep open options that might turn out to be more powerful.

The first two examples also underline the importance of obeying all the restrictions appropriate to a specific cultural 'package' if it is to work. The Tannese supposition that if something is to be powerful it must be arduous, demanding pains-taking adherence to taboos, is evident in material I have presented in this and the previous chapter. It is also confirmed by Wilkinson (1979: 188–9, 210, 216–17, 258) and MacClancy (1986: 145). Of course, there is nothing remarkable in the association between restriction and power; it is a common Pacific, even universal phenomenon. The Tannese assumption is similar to what has been noted, for example, by Barth for the Baktaman (1975: 170), or by Kahn for the Wamirans (1986: 117–18): taboo both protects power from contamination and protects people from the power. And as Rieff has stated, 'every structure of authority, of which culture is compound, has, at its topmost and controlling level, interdictory motifs – a *not* – a *no*' (1980: 1).

If the powers that a people may conjecture are to be more than just vague and idiosyncratic notions, if there is to be a potential for humans to harness these powers and channel them so that they become socially operative, there must be a certain degree of cultural formalization and structure. This point can be made by considering those hunting and gathering peoples who approach an extreme of cultural amorphousness such as the Hill Panderam of South India. As described by their ethnographer, they have few prohibitions on behaviour[1] and they display a general indifference to classifications and boundaries. Morris found it 'difficult to get a clear idea of a generally accepted moral order' (1982a: 161). Social relationships are ephemeral, and above the level of the nuclear family there are no groupings with any degree of stability (ibid.: 112; 1982b: 454). Powers certainly exist in their world, but they are idiosyncratic, rather than subject to any general agreement, and the ability of humans to utilize or channel them into any collective activity seems rudimentary (Morris 1976: 544).

The organization of human experience that a culture achieves is realized through the separation of domains, through mechanisms that prevent certain cultural spheres from interpenetrating. Through these mechanisms the world is differentiated and order imposed. This is precisely the function of taboos, whether they relate to sex, kinship, death or food (e.g. Douglas

---

[1] Although they consider a number of animals inedible, there is a fair degree of individual variation and, more importantly, there is no symbolic import to these restrictions (Morris 1976: 544–6).

1966: 94; Kahn 1986: 114–22; Schieffelin 1976: 65; Steiner 1967: 116). In Wagner's words, these taboos 'are the means of social self-invention' (1981: 121), and they produce 'a manageable power as well as the social institutions and situations in which that power is applied' (ibid.: 122).

However, if we are to explain the religious volatility of the Tannese we need to go further. Certainly, the association between power and taboo explains the appeal of cultural packages which are perceived as requiring an exacting observance of prohibitions, such as the Seventh-day Adventists, the Assembly of God, the Sulphur Bay version of the John Frum movement, or even *kastom* itself. But while there may be a tendency among some Tannese to join sects which involve progressively more extensive and onerous restrictions, it would be misleading to see their inconstancy as being simply unidirectional in this sense. For it is possible to discern sideways movements, and even conversions to packages which, at least from the outside, do not appear to have as extensive a set of restrictions as the one being abandoned. Thus pagans have converted to Catholicism, Presbyterians have joined Bahai, and John Frum cultists have returned to Presbyterianism. Perhaps the most appropriate way of describing the situation is to say that, for most Tannese, after a while any cultural package seems to lose its allure. In the words of an old man, 'Eventually we Tannese tire of these things.'

I intend to commence my explanation of this in formal terms, by developing Barth's point about the dual nature of taboo as protecting the strength of power, and protecting people from this strength (1975: 170). I think it is necessary to realize that its *effectiveness* as a means of protection is not guaranteed. Rather, it depends on people having some degree of confidence that taboos will be generally observed. I would suggest that this is conditional both on a substantial degree of trust amongst the people who are reliant on the powers, and on the belief that the appropriate categories of people possess all the necessary knowledge of the required behaviour. On Tanna the poorly developed structures of authority and leadership, the high level of social fragmentation, and the role of secrecy in the transmission of significant information, make these conditions very difficult to achieve.

Without this confidence, however, two interdependent – though analytically separate – consequences may follow. Stated baldly, and in the most obvious terms, neither power nor people are safe. In the long run, the powers may be relativized and weakened by contamination (cf. Sahlins 1981a: 44–8, 51–6, 62; Wagner 1981: 58–9, 105). But before they have been exhausted, if people believe – as they do on Tanna, and many other Melanesian societies – that breaches of taboo can harm others, as well as oneself, considerable suffering may be inflicted on a community as a punishment for the derelictions of individual members (e.g. Barth 1975:

113–15, 240; Fortune 1935: 3, 28, 47; Keesing 1982a: 36, 44, 236; Knauft 1985: 89, 405; Lewis 1975: 186; Lindstrom 1981a: 205–6; Wilkinson 1979: 51, 160, 209). Either consequence tends to promote a situation where an existing cultural package will be abandoned and another one adopted. In the first case the reason is obvious: there is no point in following something which is no longer efficacious. In the second case people hope that by placing themselves under the aegis of a different source of power they will be protected from the depredations of the existing one.[1]

The Tannese etiology of disease and misfortune is multi-faceted. Suffering may be a result of supernatural punishment, acts of capriciousness by ancestors or spirits, or the direct results of specific imbalances or lack of harmony, either physical or social (Wilkinson 1979: 156–66; Lindstrom 1981a: 205–9). At the core of these explanations is the notion of a failure to follow the appropriate restrictions on behaviour. This is partly true of sorcery as well, which is another possible explanation of adversity. Although some sorcery is due to malicious intent, it may also be the outcome of the social disharmony brought about by the unwillingness of people to observe the proper rules of behaviour.[2] Social disharmony can also produce illness independently of any sorcery being performed (see e.g. Wilkinson 1979: 241).

Where institutions of leadership are weak and individual autonomy is emphasized, the joint observance of restrictions on behaviour may provide one of the few effective mechanisms of social co-ordination (e.g. Barth 1975: 163–4; Errington 1974: 59, 243–50; Jennings 1985: 59–60). But the belief that inappropriate behaviour by an individual may cause relatives or neighbours to become ill as well as, or instead of, the transgressor can be a double-edged sword. On the one hand it expresses the idea that all those who can be affected are 'socially substitutable' (Knauft 1985: 405), and thus promotes cohesion through the awareness that certain categories of people have responsibilities towards each other. But on the other hand, when serious misfortune occurs – as it always does, for the events that a system of taboo is supposed to protect people from are invariably those things that are beyond human control – it has a tendency to amplify whatever distrust is already present in the community: people are not observing the pro-

---

[1] Wilkinson presents some striking instances of Tannese faith in the ability of a new religion to counter the dangers of the old in her account of attempts to explain the series of deaths in Louniel, e.g.: 'When prayer arrived these [taboo places where people could not go on pain of sickness or death] became free, any one could walk there, and our fathers cleared the bush, and made the village a clear place with grass, where people mixed' (1979: 251). 'He was afraid of kava because he thought it would make taboo places come alive again. While we were Christian it was as if they were dead and we could walk on them' (ibid.: 252; cf. Keesing 1982a: 234; Strathern 1984: 35).

[2] As discussed earlier, my informants claim that traditionally sorcery (i.e. *netik*) was used *only* to punish refractory behaviour, although the documentary evidence suggests that this is an idealization.

hibitions after all. And as we have seen, a number of elements of Tannese social organization tend to militate against a high degree of trust in the first place, even among those people in close everyday relations.

The result is a downward spiral of weakening powers and supernatural retaliation. In some societies this may be arrested by *inverting* key prohibitions in a ritual context: the well-known rituals of rebellion or reversal (e.g. Gluckman 1970: 109–36; Norbeck 1967; Turner 1969: 155–93; Vogt 1976: 201–10). These rituals may function not only to discharge individual tension and disaffection. By collapsing the normal orders of reality, by allowing the interpenetration of cultural domains to occur within precise and controlled bounds, they may create the conditions for a new cycle to start afresh as it were, with the contaminations of the past totally dissipated. This is a point that Wagner makes, although his indifference to any kind of sociological framework, and his unwillingness to distinguish between 'tribal people' (1981: 120) or 'tribal and religious peoples' (ibid.: 59), compromises the value of his presentation. As Handelman points out, rituals of reversal tend to occur in societies which strongly emphasize group boundaries (1982: 172). Despite Wagner's use of the Daribi *habu* as an example (1981: 120), well-developed rituals of inversion do not appear common amongst Melanesians (but cf. Allen 1981b: 112–26; Bateson 1958; Oosterwal 1976: 325–7; Wagner 1986: xviii, 197–210). To the best of my knowledge, they did not occur in traditional Tannese culture.[1]

Explanations I was given of particular misfortunes left me in no doubt that the Tannese suspect each other of disregarding important prohibitions, either wilfully or through carelessness and – as the secret drinking of kava by Christians referred to in the previous chapter indicates – their suspicions are far from groundless (see also Brunton 1981a: 371). A striking example in support of their fears is provided by an incident involving my first wife. As a courtesy, she publicly observed the Tannese menstrual taboos. Once, however, in the company of some women, she forgot herself and picked up a loaf of bread belonging to the husband of one of them. Horrified, she asked what she could do. The owner's wife smiled and said not to worry; her husband would not find out about it and so it did not matter.

This downward spiral of entropy may be illustrated by the apparent inability of Presbyterianism before the Second World War to fulfil its earlier promise of social harmony and health. In the early years of the century the successful establishment of peace and the construction of a hospital at

---

[1] Some writers have claimed that themes of inversion were prominent in some stages of the John Frum movement, as they were in other Melanesian cargo movements (e.g. Steinbauer 1979: 85–7; Wilson 1975: 323; Worsley 1968: 164–5). Wilkinson refers to a belief that when *niproou* returns, the mountains will fall and the land of the dead will be above the ground rather than below. She states that it is a traditional belief (1979: 180). I would be less certain about this, especially given the extensive acculturation in the White Sands area in which she worked.

162

Lenakel, staffed by a medical missionary who was able to achieve significant advances in health and a reversal of the population decline, appear to have made a profound impression. In particular, the use of anaesthetics in operations and the later introduction of a cure for yaws seem to have been important (Anonymous 1917: 3; Macmillan 1923b: 13–15; Nicholson 1909b: 11–12; 1916a: 10; Speiser 1922). The improvements in health meant that the fears of sorcery, and the suspicion and conflict they engendered, declined (Nicholson 1913a: 7; Rae 1919: 12). Initially, there was obviously a widespread belief that conversion to Christianity effectively put an end to a sorcerer's activities, as there are at least three instances around the turn of the century in which supposed sorcerers were offered a choice by their pagan neighbours: either become Christians, or be killed (Nicholson 1907a: 9–10; Paton 1903: 253, 286). Dr Nicholson noted that, with few exceptions, pagans who had been treated at the hospital began to attend Sunday services regularly and that, in a reversal of the previous situation, pagans were pleading for teachers to be installed in their villages. They were also contributing substantial sums of money for the hospital (1909a: 9; 1910a: 11).

Nevertheless, there were major reverses in the health of the Tannese in the 1920s, coinciding with the introduction of a new, virulent form of sorcery known as *su* from the northern islands (Guiart 1956a: 73–5; Macmillan 1925: 7–9; 1927b: 5–6; 1929: 6–7; 1931a: 10–11). By the end of the decade the social euphoria that had followed the earlier conversions (cf. Nicholson 1910a: 11) seems to have been dissipated in the face of the cycles of disease, sorcery suspicions – and loss of faith in the earlier belief that Christians would not perform sorcery – and the inevitable social tensions that these produced. A number of the Christian villages had already begun to fragment as a result of the increased conflicts, and the process continued throughout the 1930s. Some of the inhabitants returned to paganism, others turned to the Seventh-day Adventists (Guiart 1956a: 148–50, 226–7). Although there were still some pagans converting to Presbyterianism, the high point of the church's influence was over by the end of the 1920s (Guiart 1956b: 110). Wilkinson reports that her John Frum informants claimed that they originally abandoned the Presbyterian church because of its inability to protect them from disease (1979: 233). From the Tannese perspective, it must have seemed as though the power of Presbyterianism was waning, but that it still had enough strength to inflict punishments on those who claimed to be Presbyterians for the known and inferred breaches of church prohibitions.

From the pagan point of view, the breaking of traditional taboos by Presbyterians and other Christians also appears to have weakened *kastom*. In the early 1970s – before the current wave of Christian enthusiasm had even commenced in the area in which I worked – I was told that during the period of Christian pre-eminence on Tanna many of the spirits moved away because of the violations that were occurring, and that while John Frum brought power back to *kastom*, some of the spirits had never returned.

Informants also offer another explanation for the reduced power available at present compared to the past: loss of knowledge of the appropriate taboos and techniques needed to gain access to it (cf. e.g. Wilkinson 1979: 247). Older informants claimed that soon after the return to *kastom* at the beginning of the John Frum movement, there was a substantial increase in illness. They said that this happened because, although people were following the traditional spirits, many of them had forgotten, or had not learnt, their 'law'. Of course, this served to legitimize the return, and in itself did not present much of a long-term threat. This was because the taboos seem to have related to everyday activities such as the specific restrictions associated with kava preparation at particular *yimwayim*, or the need for certain categories of people to avoid particular places, and the appropriate knowledge was usually readily available from those who had remained pagan. Much more serious is the loss of specialized knowledge relating to the activities associated with individual titles. While contemporary Tannese see this as having resulted from the extensive depopulation of the last century and the success of Christianity in the earlier years of this century, to a considerable degree the process is inherent in the way in which the transmission of important knowledge is organized.

This specialized knowledge is usually taught by existing titleholders to their successors in secret, without witnesses. But the process is not automatic. If a youth does not look after the needs of his father or grandfather – chewing and preparing his kava, fetching his water and firewood – the man may threaten to withhold the knowledge, and give it to someone else in trust. This may also occur if a man is dying, and his heir is too young to understand. In such cases, the expectation is that the proper heir will eventually be taught; I was told that the person who held the information in trust could not refuse this, but obviously there is a fair amount of room for manoeuvre here. During my visit to Tanna in 1973 there was a major quarrel involving the co-occupants of the side of a *lauanu* at Inapukil. A rightful heir had not shown the proper concern for his grandfather, who punished him by telling him nothing, and giving everything to another man, who had looked after the grandfather when he was dying. Although this man had begun to teach the rightful heir, he was doing this slowly. The ostensible reason was that the rightful heir was doing little to assist him with exchanges and other tasks, although it was also made clear that a man who controlled the flow of information in this situation was 'on top of' the other, and that when all the information had been handed over the position would be reversed. During the quarrel the rightful heir also accused the other man of keeping back some aspects of even the knowledge he had supposedly given.

Two points need to be made here. The first is that the secrecy surrounding specialized knowledge, and the fact that it is transmitted over a period of time, means that sudden deaths, either of titleholders, or of men holding knowledge in trust, make it inevitable that loss will occur.[1] And what is crucial, given the argument I am proposing, is that this loss is *believed* to take place, so that many men feel that they do not have the power of their predecessors (cf. Rubinstein 1981: 156). The situation is very similar to that described by Errington and Gewertz for the Chambri, with one possible difference: that, in cases where an heir has been diligent in performing his duties, and knowledge is transmitted to him directly, men do not seem as concerned with retaining exclusive possession,[2] because while they are alive they are still 'on top of' their heirs (1986: 102–3). The second point is that while the depopulation of the last century and large-scale conversions to Christianity would have exacerbated the problem, quite obviously it was something that could, and almost certainly did occur, before any contact with Europeans.

At the beginning of this section I mentioned that the son of an old *kastom* man had become a Christian within five years of his father's death. I strongly suspect that it was his fear that he had lost crucial *kastom* knowledge that played a major role in this decision,[3] although my evidence is circumstantial. In November 1975 his father confided to me that he was worried about his son, who had a poor memory, and did not seem to be retaining what he was being taught. He said that he intended to tape-record all the necessary *kastom* so that it would not be lost. But as far as I have been able to discover, he had not got around to doing this before he died suddenly only a few months later. The father's death was one of four in the immediate family within the period of a couple of years: first his younger brother died, to be followed by his grandson, the father himself, and finally his other younger brother.[4] In 1986, while staying in Vila after my visit to

---

[1] While such knowledge may be individually held, its loss may have serious social consequences, given the high degree of magical specialization. Thus I was told that two men from Lounapektuan, who performed the magic for certain kinds of kava, left their village rather than join the Assembly of God. It was not that they were particularly against the new religion, but they were frightened that they might be held responsible for the failure of kava over a wide area of the island if they abandoned the magic, which they would have to do if they converted.

[2] This is my impression; I do not have enough information to state this with certainty. Nevertheless, men told me that an heir was always inferior to his predecessor while the latter was alive.

[3] It is true that in doing so he was acting no differently from many of his neighbours. But as he had been so staunch in his opposition to the church up until the late 1970s, and as some of his close brothers and *taniel* were still holding out in 1986, his conversion nonetheless came as a surprise.

[4] The father would have been around sixty when he died. While this is hardly young, he had appeared very healthy right until his death which, judging from what I was told, was probably from a heart attack. One of his brothers died just as suddenly, but the other died after a couple

Tanna, I met a man from Lomtihekel whom I knew very well. I told him I was surprised that the man in question had become a Christian. The Lomtihekel man said that there was a simple explanation. The convert had been very scared by the four deaths in his family, and so he had joined the New Life movement. In other words, he does not seem to be confident that he has the resources to remain safely under the aegis of *kastom*.

My argument about the causes of Tannese religious volatility can be restated and summarized as follows. Because institutions of authority and social co-ordination were weak, traditional society was marked by a high level of social divisiveness, suspicion and individual autonomy. While certain features of the Tannese situation should be interpreted as attempts to transcend this fragmentation – the recourse to external powers whose potency is embodied in the prohibitions that they demand, and the creation of new social categories whose membership cut across existing loyalties – these attempts invariably prove ineffectual because of the very problems that they are meant to overcome. When adversity strikes, the mechanisms that could protect the integrity of the current interpretive system – or 'cultural package' as I have called it – and assure its continuity tend to fail. Suspicious of each other's behaviour, and open to doubt that they actually possess all the resources required to access the package properly, the Tannese fear that the powers they seek are being diminished by ineluctable contamination, but that before they are dissipated they will be punished for the refractory behaviour of those in their midst. This opens the way for the enthusiastic adoption of a new package – or a return, dispirited or enthusiastic, depending on the circumstances, to a previous one that had been prematurely rejected – that can protect them from the dangers of the one they are abandoning. This serves to frustrate further the development of stable and effective institutions of leadership and so perpetuates the whole cycle.

It is important to emphasize that, at least *in the short term*, adversity need not undermine the commitment of people to a new avenue of power. On the contrary, as is shown by the example of the increased disease following the return to *kastom* in the 1940s, this commitment may initially be reinforced. The actual outcome will be determined by the skills and manoeuvrings of those with an interest in promoting or denigrating a particular interpretive system, people's perceptions about their ability to secure reasonably safe access to the power in the long run, and the extent to which the adversity continues and affects the overall tenor of social relations. Where there is an established and effective structure of human authority, whose position

---

of years of illness. The grandson – who was the son of the man with the poor memory – almost certainly died from dehydration following a severe attack of gastroenteritis which was treated by forbidding him fluids (to restore the balance – his faeces were liquid; cf. Lindstrom 1981a: 209).

derives from the existing interpretive system, the process of entropy may be inhibited. Greater credence is likely to be attached to the rationalizations of those with authority, as they attempt to turn untoward events to their own advantage. The classic Melanesian example comes from the Trobriands, where the Tabalu chiefs of Omarakana claim power over the sun and the rain. Favourable weather confirms this, but so too do droughts or washouts which, far from being an indication of the failure of power, are an expression of the chief's displeasure with his people, and the insufficient loyalty they have shown him (Malinowski 1932: 113; 1966: 78, 163; Weiner 1976: 30, 204; cf. the situation in Dobu, Fortune 1963: 131–2). If an accepted structure of authority exists, there is also a greater likelihood of maintaining social cohesion and averting the deterioration of social relations that may follow serious misfortune – thus reducing some of the incentive for turning to an alternative. It is all a matter of degree: in Tanna – and many other Melanesian societies – cultural packages are very vulnerable. But as our own history shows, even the most hierarchical and all-embracing systems cannot resist the onslaught of sustained suffering indefinitely.

8

Conclusion

Before discussing the applicability of my analysis of the Tannese case to other parts of Melanesia,[1] it is appropriate to retrace the steps of my argument. The starting point was the observation that the known distribution of kava drinking in the Pacific is puzzling. If the properties of *Piper methysticum* were independently discovered in a number of places there would be no problem. But the accumulated weight of botanical, linguistic and ethnological evidence indicates that this is extremely unlikely. There are very strong grounds for believing that kava drinking had a single source, and that its known distribution is a consequence of diffusion from this place of origin. Yet the distances which separate some of the kava-using regions are such that direct links between them before the period of European contact seem out of the question. And while such links could have been established in the decades after European contact, all the evidence suggests that kava drinking predated contact in the crucial regions of New Guinea. So we are left with the conclusion first put forward by W. H. R. Rivers in a paper to the British Association for the Advancement of Science over three-quarters of a century ago (1910), and developed in *The History of Melanesian Society:* kava was once drunk over a much wider area of Melanesia, but it was abandoned before European contact by many of the people who used it. However, the major reason that Rivers proposed to account for this disappearance – that kava was replaced by betel – is not particularly compelling, and there are no good grounds for accepting it as a general explanation.

I suggested that it would be more productive to consider an alternative line of inquiry, one that was also present – although in a rudimentary and not clearly distinguished form – in Rivers' work.[2] The ritual and religious

---

[1] I am using the term 'Melanesia' to apply to the area covered by present-day Vanuatu, Solomon Islands and Papua New Guinea. Although, as I noted in Chapter 3, some reports suggest that kava may have been present in parts of New Caledonia, these have been questioned by Lebot and Cabalion. The real puzzle with the distribution of kava drinking centres on the region north-west from Vanuatu.

[2] Although, as I also noted, it was more clearly stated in his paper attempting to account for the disappearance of the canoe, etc. from some Oceanic societies (1978 [1912]).

significance of kava made it vulnerable to disappearance, because of the religious instability of many Melanesian societies. I developed this suggestion through a detailed examination of the effects of changes in religious affiliation on the consumption of kava in the post-contact period on Tanna. I then attempted to account for the volatility of Tannese religious behaviour by arguing that the integrity and accessibility of existing sources of ritual power were never assured. The divisiveness and distrust produced by ineffective institutions of leadership and social co-ordination led to a spiral of entropy, to which many Tannese responded by rejecting their current cultural 'package' in favour of another.

However, if the Tannese case is to serve as a general model for kava's disappearance from other Melanesian societies, two issues have to be confronted. Firstly, it is necessary to consider the argument's dependence on the assumption that kava drinking was of similar religious or ritual significance in the – unknown – societies which abandoned it. Secondly, we need to ask whether we are justified in thinking that these societies were also characterized by a high degree of religious volatility. After all, we are talking about processes that may have occurred at any time during the past 3,500 or so years, and we cannot even presume that those responsible for the original diffusion of kava drinking in Melanesia were a single, culturally homogeneous people (see e.g. Terrell 1986: 252–3).

The matter of the religious significance of kava can be dealt with quite readily, by taking two different, though complementary, approaches. Firstly, the available ethnographic evidence suggests it is reasonable to think both that kava drinking was nearly everywhere a predominantly ritual activity and that, with one qualification, kava would have been more vulnerable to abandonment the more it was confined to specific ritual or religious contexts. The second approach is to focus on this qualification, and argue that in cases where the excesses of predominantly secular patterns of kava drinking might have been causing problems, the most likely way of responding would have been through ritual or religious innovation.

There are many parts of the Pacific where the contemporary use of kava is primarily, or solely, secular (Marshall 1987: 26). But, while it is possible to point to a number of cases of kava drinking in secular contexts traditionally, in hardly any of these cases does it appear that secular use predominated over ritual or religious use (e.g. Haddon 1916: 146; Serpenti 1969: 34; Williamson 1939: 51, 70). Certainly, Nevermann stated that the Kanum Irebe of Irian Jaya drank kava on a regular basis without any special occasion (1938: 184). However, given that Nevermann was engaged in survey work, rather than any intensive fieldwork, it is not unlikely that he would have missed any magical or ritual use. He may also have been unable to distinguish contemporary from traditional patterns of consumption. And while van Baal states that kava drinking among the Marind-anim 'is not a ritual, as it is among the Kiwai' (1966: 21), he adds that 'it is closely associated with every ceremony' (ibid.). Furthermore, kava was used to make magic effective (ibid.: 877), and was mixed with cadaveric fluid and drunk to divine the identity of the sorcerer responsible for a death. For Tahiti, Oliver claims that he was unable to find any mention of kava drinking as part of religious ritual (1974: 258). However, this claim appears to be contradicted by his reference to an annual ceremony on Huahine in which idols were decorated, and large quantities of kava were consumed (ibid.: 885–6). He also states that the person of a chief under the influence of kava was sacred (ibid.: 980).

Thus the available data indicate that the major significance of kava in virtually all the societies in which it was drunk was ritual or religious. Furthermore, with the exception of Tahiti, where intense missionary pressure led to its early abandonment (Handy 1930: 21), in the societies from which kava is known to have disappeared at one stage or other, and where some information exists about its pattern of use, secular consumption appears to have been of little significance. Examples are Kosrae, Niue, Tikopia, Santa Maria (Gaua) Island in the Banks Group, West Aoba, Erakor,[1] Arosi, Bagabag Island and other parts of the Madang area, and Boazi (Burrows 1970: 114; Riesenberg 1968: 103; Loeb 1926: 9, 27–8, 71–2; Kirch and Yen 1982: 36–7; Rivers 1914, vol. 1: 86; Michael Allen, personal communication; Philibert 1981: 325; Fox 1919: 167; 1924: 216–17; Louise Morauta, personal communication; Stephanie Fahey, personal communication; Mark Busse, personal communication).

Indeed, if Kirk Huffman is correct in his belief that kava was once drunk in south-west Malekula by men who held the rank of *muluwun* or above in the graded society (personal communication) – a belief given additional credence by Deacon's references to the use of the kava plant in the ritual of some high *mangki* grades in Seniang, and the 'making of man' rites in Mewun (1934: 318, 373, 650) – it provides a good illustration of the vulnerability of kava when restricted to a narrow range of contexts. The graded societies were labile institutions, not only under conditions of missionary influence, but also in the past. Individual grades, particularly at the higher levels, might be lost as a result of demographic circumstances, or as grades imported from neighbouring peoples took their place (see e.g. Deacon 1934: 278–80; Layard 1942: 696, Table XI). In addition, a specific graded society might decline in favour of one more recently adopted from neighbours. During fieldwork in south-west Malekula in 1970, I was told by Mbotgote people from the interior who had recently settled in the coastal village of Lawa that this had occurred in a number of interior villages.

[1] The people of Erakor commenced drinking kava again around the time of Vanuatu's Independence (Philibert 1986: 6), and I imagine that the same would have occurred in the other areas of Vanuatu included in this list.

Commenting about a generation previously – predating the period of intensive European contact with the people of the interior – an older system of *mangki* grades had been superseded by the *nimangki mielmiele*, which had been introduced from the district of Wien in south Malekula (see also Muller 1972: 159–60). Deacon refers to what appears to have been a similar situation with the *nalawan* in Mewun district (1934: 430–1). Obviously, any practices exclusively associated with the superseded graded societies or lost individual grades most probably would have disappeared as well. This can be seen from another example – though one from the post-contact period – taken from the island of Aoba in Vanuatu. In the west part of the island, the graded society (*hungwe*) was abandoned in the first part of this century, and so too was kava drinking, which was closely associated with the *hungwe*. But in east Aoba, both the graded society and kava drinking have continued to be present without substantial interruption (Michael Allen, personal communication).

The examples of betel and tobacco both suggest that extensive secular consumption of a drug facilitates continuity of use, and – with one qualification, to be dealt with below – there is no reason to think that the situation would be any different with kava. It is true that many Pacific peoples use betel and tobacco in ritual as well as secular contexts (Burton-Bradley 1979: 483–5; Knauft 1987: 75–82; Lepowsky 1982: 333–42; Marshall 1987: 16, 20–1, 32, 36–7; Michel 1981; Poole 1987: 154, 175–82; Schwimmer 1982: 322–3). Nevertheless, it is the latter contexts that appear to predominate. While part of the explanation may lie in the fact that betel and tobacco have generally been subject to less hostile pressure (Forman 1982: 113–14), their fortunes have been quite different from those of kava, and the areas in which they are consumed have tended to increase, rather than contract (Black 1984: 476–7; Marshall 1987: 16, 30–2).[1] Certainly, maps depicting the distribution of their use do not suggest the kind of puzzling gaps – and hence the likelihood that they were abandoned in a number of areas – that are evident in the geographical distribution of kava drinking (Hays 1984; Riesenfeld 1947, 1951; Theodoratus 1953: 4, 85).

Of course, it might be retorted that we can know only about those cases where kava drinking persisted until after European contact. The common element amongst those peoples who abandoned it earlier may have been a

[1] But cf. my comments in Chapter 4 about the possibility of previous betel use in Tanna at some time in the distant past. However, as I pointed out, there are also other explanations for the linguistic evidence I referred to when suggesting this possibility. The reader may also recall that I noted that the area in which kava is drunk has started to expand in the past decade – in Vanuatu, where it has been taken up by people in Ambrym and Malekula, who were not known to have been drinkers traditionally (Bob Tonkinson, personal communication; Kirk Huffman, personal communication), and Australia, where it is rapidly spreading among Aborigines. Yet such are the concerns about the supposed abuse of kava among Aborigines that this spread may soon be checked (Ayris 1987; Graham 1987; Hogarth 1987; Mathews *et al.* 1988).

mainly secular pattern of use. Such a pattern of consumption could have brought about the kinds of excesses and abuses that the Tannese have experienced, and that have been recorded in a few other parts of the Pacific where predominantly secular drinking was adopted some time after contact (e.g. Cawte 1988: 545; Dening 1980: 240; Ferdon 1981: 184; Smith 1984; 46–7). But while profligate consumption may have provided a motivation for giving up kava drinking, it is difficult to see how the custom could have been effectively abandoned before European contact other than through religious innovation, such as the imposition of a supernaturally sanctioned blanket prohibition, just as has occurred in historic times on Tanna (or Tahiti, see above). Codrington provided an example of a traditional mechanism for introducing a taboo on a significant consumption item. The people from a part of Ulawa, in the Solomons, refused to eat bananas, which grew in profusion. This had commenced within living memory, after an influential man 'made it known before his death that after he died he would be in a banana' (1890: 614).[1] Codrington also claimed that the specific food taboos associated with each of the exogamous divisions of Bogutu on Santa Isabel had similarly been introduced within living memory, and thought that the underlying reason was probably the same (1891: 32).

An alternative response to intemperate secular use of kava might be to restrict consumption to particular occasions or categories of people. Again the Tannese case provides a model: recall the reference in Chapter 6 to a man claiming to have received instructions from the spirits in 1952 that the drinking of kava during the day should end. Where this may have occurred, it is possible that notions of kava as a substance of supernatural power had previously existed only in a rudimentary form. But given the drink's psychoactive properties, interdictions on the contexts in which it could be drunk, and/or those who could participate, are likely to have facilitated the further elaboration of such notions, and increasing ritualization of its use.

The outcome of the above discussion is that, although we cannot know whether any of the peoples who once used kava had a predominantly secular pattern of consumption, the consequences of this ignorance for my

---

[1] Ivens, working on Ulawa nearly forty years after Codrington left the region, describes a more complex situation. The taboo covered all of Ulawa. In two villages it was said to have been instituted by 'E'ewa, their 'chief ghost' (1927: 269), but with no indication that ghost and banana were interchangeable. Although Ivens asserts ' 'E'ewa is no modern ghost' (ibid.: 271), his account is quite consistent with Codrington's despite differences in the reasons offered. In the other villages, bananas were originally consumed, but only after a priest had offered them to the ghosts. Following the death of many of the priests in an 1869 epidemic, 'the eating of bananas, already a matter of severe restrictions . . . cease[d] entirely' (ibid.), although no one claimed bananas had caused the epidemic. Rather, it appears as though the rationale was one discussed in the last chapter: with the death of the priests, people no longer had access to the ritual required for safe use. It is significant in this regard that 'the eating of bananas in the earlier days of mission work on Ulawa was always preparatory to the acceptance of a mission school' (ibid.: 269).

argument are not as serious as might first appear. The thornier issue is whether it is justifiable to use the Tannese evidence as an illustrative case study.

The question can be broken down into two parts. Firstly, is the religious instability I have described for Tanna typical of at least a substantial number of Melanesian societies? Secondly, how legitimate is it to think that the ethnographic materials available to us can be taken as representative of the distant past?

In discussing the Tannese case, I spoke of *kastom*, Presbyterianism, the Sulphur Bay-based John Frum cult, etc. as cultural 'packages' which are perceived as requiring observance *in toto*, although people's actual behaviour may be very different. The contemporary expectation was neatly expressed by the comments of a young English-speaking man from Lounekeuk who accompanied me to Vila after my first visit to Tanna in 1972. Obviously thinking that I, as a European, would be well disposed towards Christianity, and concerned that I might have formed an unfavourable impression of his people, he told me:

> You think that no one knows God at Lounekeuk and Laruanu and Lomtihekel. Oh, they know God all right. But they are frightened to join the Church. If they do, and they do something that breaks God's law, like work in their gardens on Sunday, God will punish them.[1]

But this contrasts with the traditional attitude towards customs as comprising separately detachable elements, an attitude which was apparent in the early years of contact with missionaries. Individual Christian rites were adopted for varying periods of time and Tannese ones abandoned (see e.g. Adams 1984: 58, 65, 71, 75), just as individual dances, songs, and certain kinds of magic were – and still are. There can be little doubt that the notion of unified cultural 'packages' gradually developed in the post-contact period, as a response to European categorization and opposition. Previously – both on Tanna and elsewhere – the ritual elements that made up the largest coherent complex which might be taken up or discarded are likely to have been far fewer (Brunton 1983; Keesing 1982b; Larcom 1982; Tonkinson 1982: 304).

With this one proviso, my account of Tannese religious volatility does not portray a situation which is in any way exceptional for Melanesia. I have already referred to the obsolescence of previous graded-society institutions and the adoption of new ones in south-west Malekula. There are numerous other instances of people adopting and – much more importantly for our purposes – abandoning or modifying major ritual complexes, either before European contact or, if after, under circumstances which

---

[1] Cf. my reference in Chapter 6 to pagan men in the mid-1970s who expressed their scorn of God's power by forming groups to work in each other's gardens on Sundays.

highlight the brittle nature of their former adherents' commitment to them.

Watson, depicting the Northern Tairora as 'highly receptive to novelty and change' (1983: 325), states that 'even from ethnohistorical enquiries that were not exhaustive or systematic' (ibid.) he obtained ample evidence of the abandonment of important rituals, which occurred without any Christian interference or responsibility. His major – though not sole – example is of the *ihalabu*, an annual ritual of growth and renewal. His older informants explained that it was displaced by the *orana*, a renewal ceremony which came from the Agarabi or Gadsup to their north (ibid.: 324).

Schieffelin provides an account of the demise of the *bau a*, a Kaluli bachelor's ceremonial hunting lodge which was 'believed to promote the growth of the young boys . . . and induce strength for the youths and bachelors . . . ward off sickness and death by quieting the appetites of witches in the surrounding communities . . . [and which] represented a special relationship between men and the *memul* spirits of Mount Bosavi' (1982: 158–9). This was abandoned in 1964, when two European missionaries and a party of workmen arrived in the area to build a station and airstrip while two communities were holding the ceremony. Although 'the missionaries never knew about the lodges' (1976: 17), the Kalulu feared that the integrity of the *bau a* would be violated, and hurriedly terminated it. 'In most men's minds that was the end of the old way' (ibid.). 'The Kaluli themselves quietly discontinued their most dramatic ritual institution' (1982: 200). In attempting to explain why the *bau a* was such a 'fragile institution' (ibid.: 199), Schieffelin claims that it depended on a delicate balance of understandings between Kaluli communities to provide social support and maintain its ritual sanctity, and 'when this balance was disturbed, the *bau a* collapsed' (ibid.). Previously there had been changes to the form of the *bau a*, most obviously in the architectural style of the lodge, but also in 'magic and ritual details' (ibid.: 158), with the new form adopted from the west about a generation earlier.

Many researchers provide evidence of conscious ritual obsolescence and/or innovation – seemingly independent of any European influence – amongst Melanesians, without necessarily attempting to offer possible explanations (e.g. Bulmer 1965; Gell 1975: 331; Harrison 1987; Hays 1986: 437, 449; Hilliard 1978: 198; Larcom 1982: 333–5; Lowman-Vayda 1971: 351–5; McArthur 1971: 189; Strathern and Strathern 1971: 129, 192; Tonkinson 1981: 79). But present in a number of accounts are indications of motives similar to those of the Tannese discussed in the previous chapter, although, not unexpectedly, the details and the ways in which they are combined and related to other processes differ. Thus circumstances may develop which make rituals too powerful, or dangerous, for people to perform; or they may be thought to lose their power over time. Alternatively, the transmission of ritual knowledge or paraphernalia may be organized in a way that makes it particularly vulnerable to demographic misfortune.

For the Northern Tairora, Watson states 'it is suggested, that the people have now abandoned the *ihalabu*, because of its danger' (1983: 142). While he is not as clear about the precise nature of this danger as he could be, it appears to have arisen from fears that sexual intercourse during this time was particularly hazardous, as well as being associated with the notion that women, either through carelessness or maliciousness, posed the major threat. Williams recorded that although the Western Elema gave a number of reasons for not continuing the *hevehe* ritual cycle after the Vailala Madness – including the one that he believed was decisive, that it was too much trouble to put on – the reason most commonly given was its danger; it caused too many deaths. 'The supposed agent of death is the sorcerer; the reason, some breach of procedure, a slight upon some member of the *avai* [the self-selecting group of old men, who were the supposed guardians of tradition], a too-small pig, a default in paying over the ornaments, or, above all, the witting or unwitting observation of forbidden mysteries' (1940: 423; see also p. 219). Even among villages which were still performing the *hevehe*, sorcery threats and fears usually caused the cycle to be drawn out over many years, a situation that was independent of modern influences (ibid.: 186–9).

Wagner provides details of the adoption and subsequent decline of two rituals for promoting the health of people and pigs among the Daribi. The first, called *waianu*, was adopted from the north-west at around the turn of the century, and then replaced in the mid-1930s, after it had lost its power, by the *gerua*, which came from the east. By the time of Wagner's fieldwork, the *gerua* was undergoing a similar deterioration: 'Daribi say that the *gerua* was "strong" and effective when it was first adopted . . . but that now it has become ineffective' (1972: 165). Ryan writes that the Mendi 'appear to tire' of their cults directed at propitiating ghostly malice after a time, and abandon them for new ones (1961: 270). He reports that a leader of the latest cult, the *timp*, told him that he expected some new kind of ritual to arrive later from the south, but that he had no idea what it might be (ibid.: 285).

Barth states that the Augobmin, neighbours of the Baktaman, used to have an initiation cycle which probably comprised four grades. But some years before his fieldwork all the knowledgeable men died as a result of warfare and other causes. 'They have since had to abandon their temples and practice only a truncated 1st degree initiation' (1975: 260). Barth also notes a sense of the entropy of ritual traditions – though one which is subject to differing expression and degrees of conceptualization – among the number of Mountain Ok peoples (1987: 48–50). Errington and Gewertz explain the Chambri predilection for adopting rituals from the Iatmul and

175

other neighbours, and their willingness to acknowledge this foreign origin, in terms of the Chambri belief that the processes of competition among males are such that power is inevitably lost in each generation. Transmitting the appropriate knowledge to an heir diminishes the existing holder's access to ancestral power, thus quickening his decline. Although it is in the holder's interests to ensure that the knowledge is eventually transmitted, many men hold off too long, and it is lost, either through the weakening powers of memory, or through death (1986: 99–106).

Despite the great diversity of Melanesian cultures and societies, there is an ever-present tendency for anthropologists to overgeneralize about the region. It would be foolish to think that there was a uniform propensity for cultural obsolescence and innovation to occur in Melanesia. Differences are apparent even in the examples I have just discussed. The degree to which the integrity of existing cults and rituals could be protected, and their successful transmission from generation to generation ensured, will vary. It follows from my argument in the previous chapter that this variation will depend on the strength of institutions of social co-ordination and authority, the degree of trust within local communities, and the extent to which the requisite ritual knowledge is dispersed, all of which will affect the believed capacity of the rituals to cope with the inescapable vicissitudes and afflictions of human existence.[1]

Nevertheless, there is enough evidence from a number of regions in Melanesia to justify the conclusion that the abandonment of existing ritual practices – from either desire or necessity – and the adoption of new ones – either locally developed or borrowed from neighbours – was widespread. Other anthropologists have felt confidence in drawing similar conclusions. Schwartz, while admitting that his view 'is strongly affected by [his four years of] research in the Admiralty Islands . . . with briefer fieldwork in New Hanover and the Upper Sepik River area' (1973: 154), emphasizes 'the general Melanesian openness to cultural importation . . . [in which] whole ceremonial complexes and much of another group's art may be adopted, replacing their own' (ibid.: 159). And sixty years ago Williams, reflecting on the Orakaiva's rapid adoption of the Taro cult and its variants, and the way that these had 'overwhelmed' (1928: 97) the older ceremonies, wrote: 'we may suppose that native life in the past has from time to time been subject to

---

[1] Additionally, there may be alternative institutions which act to arrest the downward spiral. One example appears to be the *yasolu* exchange cycle among the Anganen of the Southern Highlands of Papua New Guinea. The *yasolu* culminates in a huge pig kill every fifteen years or so, when men exchange equivalent sides of pork. Transactions in which outstanding debts are acquitted also take place. According to Nihill, during this time ordinary relations and their associated frustrations and tensions are transcended. It is a time of harmony, 'without sickness', when 'bad thoughts' are constrained, and 'new men' created (1988: 260–4). Nihill compares *yasolu* to cargo cults and other radical social movements, claiming that it gives 'rise to a vision of a "new society", and with it new notions of morality, the individual, even time' (ibid.: 270).

sudden and even revolutionary change. Nor is it perhaps necessary to assume that such changes always take place in the phase of social unrest which accompanies the clash of cultures' (ibid.: 80).

The precise form of Tannese social organization may be distinctive, but the problems of divisiveness and distrust that it both generates and attempts to resolve are not. A number of the anthropologists I have just cited also refer to the fragility of the social order, and the prevalence of suspicion and uncertainty, even within the context of close relationships, although they have not necessarily made any links between social conditions and the increasing relativization and/or inaccessibility of supernatural power (Barth 1975: 134–5; Errington and Gewertz 1986: 111; Schwartz 1973; Watson 1983: 214, 237). These themes are also frequently found in other anthropological literature of the region (e.g. Errington 1974: 13, 112, 216–18; Forge 1970; Gordon 1983: 207–8; Hallpike 1977: 77–83, 237; O'Hanlon 1983: 324–9; Salisbury 1964: 226–7; Schieffelin 1976: 121; Young 1971: 133–4, 177–81).[1]

A significant amount of this evidence comes from societies soon after contact, or else appears to provide a reasonable depiction of the situation before contact. I would not deny that some pre-contact Melanesian societies may have been more hierarchical than anthropologists have tended to recognize (Douglas 1979: 5). Nor do I doubt the possibility that parts of western Melanesia may have been subject to a greater degree of socio-political complexity during some periods in the past (Friedman 1982: 182–93; Pawley 1982: 45–7; Lilley 1985: 63–4; 1988: 514–16). I would simply point out that there are no good reasons for thinking that either religious volatility or the precariousness of social relations is a relatively recent phenomenon in Melanesia, however much the intensity or direction may have been affected by pacification and missionization.[2] Certainly, given that the time scale for agriculture, at least in New Guinea, is as long as the scale for the major Old World centres of civilization (Golson 1977: 612–19; 1982: 119), the absence of complex, hierarchical, large-scale political units represents a theoretical problem. Furthermore, there is no evidence of anything approaching a political trajectory comparable to those found in other fertile regions which have a great time depth for agriculture (Allen

---

[1] Certainly, however, some Melanesian communities appear to have been relatively successful in developing mechanisms to contain internal social divisiveness (e.g. the Ilahita Arapesh – Tuzin 1976: 297–302; 1980: 284–310; and, to a lesser extent, the Marind-anim – van Baal 1966: 689–95; Ernst 1979).

[2] Some anthropologists would place a much greater emphasis on post-contact transformations relating to social cohesiveness. Thus Lindenbaum refers to 'the degree of mutual trust and support which magnetised communities from within' (1981: 122), and argues that 'endo-sorcery' did not occur traditionally. I suspect that such statements are more the expression of an excessively sentimental perspective than a true reflection of the general pattern. For criticisms of Lindenbaum's ideas about 'endo-sorcery' see Chowning 1987: 174–5; Stephen 1987: 9–10.

1985: 50–6; Yoffee 1985: 45–7). Whatever the ultimate explanation, the problems of authority legitimation which underlie and exacerbate the cultural instability of Melanesia (cf. M. R. Allen 1984; Chowning 1979: 78) almost certainly are of an antiquity sufficient to account for the loss of kava along the lines I have suggested.

As I indicated in the early part of this book, the problematical distribution of kava in Melanesia contrasts markedly with its distribution in Polynesia. With perhaps only one or two exceptions, the only parts of Polynesia from which kava disappeared traditionally were islands which were environmentally unsuitable for growing *Piper methysticum*. This contrast is completely in line with the argument I have developed. Anthropological characterizations and analyses of Polynesian political systems may have tended to stress ideology at the expense of their actual workings (Douglas 1979: 27). But the ideology is itself an important social fact, and there can be no doubt that for the great majority of Polynesian societies the legitimation of authority did not present the difficulty that it presented throughout most of Melanesia. Nor can there be much quarrel with a depiction of Polynesian polities – and cultures – as comparatively more stable than those of Melanesia, however much one can point to individual exceptions on both sides.[1]

The problem of the geographical distribution of kava drinking is an instance of a broader range of problems arising from the existence of widely dispersed cultural items in the western Pacific. The extravagance of some of the claims made by those who have written about diffusion caused most social and cultural anthropologists to shy away from these problems for a long time. This was despite the fact that the wide distribution of certain complexes raised important questions about the extent to which similarities in the symbolic elements occurring in specific kinds of situations were indicative of a limited range of possible psychological or cultural responses to such situations. Many examples can be given; for instance, the *sangguma* or assault sorcery found in Melanesia and Australia (Codrington 1891: 206–7; Patterson 1974–5: 142–3; Elkin 1964: 308–9), the sacred flute complex in New Guinea and nearby islands (Hays 1986; Gourlay 1975), and the rainbow serpent myths of New Guinea and Australia (Brumbaugh 1987). In this book I believe I have shown that such questions are not just matters of culture history, but involve issues that have long been topics of primary concern to social anthropologists: ritual power, social order, and cultural stability.

---

[1] Over fifty years ago, at the suggestion of Margaret Mead, van Briessen carried out an investigation of the relation between kava drinking and hereditary chieftainship (1935). Not surprisingly, given the distribution of kava in Melanesia, he concluded that they were not connected. But the insight which triggered the study was sound, and was compromised by a static distributional analysis, rather than an analysis based on social processes.

References

AJCP Australian Joint Copying Project
ANU Australian National University
ASA Association of Social Anthropologists
ASAO Association for Social Anthropology in Oceania
IASER Institute of Applied Social and Economic Research (Papua New Guinea)
NSW New South Wales
UPNG University of Papua New Guinea

Abel, P. 1906. 'Knabenspiele auf Neu Mecklenburg'. *Anthropos* 1: 818–23.
   1907. 'Knabenspiele auf Neu Mecklenburg'. *Anthropos* 2: 219–29, 708–14.
Adams, R. 1977 'In the land of strangers and degraded human beings. A culture
   contact history of Tanna to 1865, with particular reference to the Rev. John
   G. Paton'. Ph.D. thesis, La Trobe University.
   1984. *In the land of strangers: a century of European contact with Tanna, 1774–
   1874*. Canberra, ANU. (Pacific Research monograph no. 9.)
   1987. 'Homo anthropologicus and man-Tanna'. *Journal of Pacific History* 22:
   3–14.
Aitken, R. T. 1930. *Ethnology of Tubuai*. Honolulu, Bernice P. Bishop Museum,
   bulletin no. 70.
Alexander, K. 1985. *Kava in the north: a study of kava in Arnhem Land Aboriginal
   communities*. Darwin, ANU North Australia Research Unit.
Allen, J. 1977. 'Sea traffic, trade and expanding horizons'. In J. Allen, J. Golson
   and R. Jones (eds.), *Sunda and Sahul*. London, Academic Press, pp. 387–
   417.
   1984. 'In search of the Lapita homeland'. *Journal of Pacific History* 19: 186–201.
   1985. 'Comments on complexity and trade: a view from Melanesia'. *Archaeology in Oceania* 20: 49–57.
Allen, J., M. Latu, M. Koesana and M. Tsirumits. 1982. *Halia dictionary*. Ukarumpa, Summer Institute of Linguistics. (Dictionaries of Papua New Guinea,
   vol. 6.)
Allen, M. R. n.d. 'Origin tales, Aoba'. Unpublished MS.
   1981a. 'Rethinking old problems: matriliny, secret societies and political evolution'. In M. Allen (ed.), *Vanuatu: politics, economics and ritual in island
   Melanesia*. Sydney, Academic Press, pp. 9–34.
   1981b. 'Innovation, inversion and revolution as political tactics in West Aoba'.
   In M. Allen (ed.), *Vanuatu: politics, economics and ritual in island Melanesia*.
   Sydney, Academic Press, pp. 105–34.
   1984. 'Elders, chiefs and big men: authority legitimation and political evolution
   in Melanesia'. *American Ethnologist* 11: 20–41.

References

Allen, M. S. 1984. 'A review of archeobotany and paleoethnobotany in Hawaii'. *Hawaiian Archaeology* 1: 19–30.

Altschul, S. von Reis. 1973. *Drugs and foods from little-known plants: notes in Harvard University Herbaria*. Cambridge, Mass., Harvard University Press.

Ambrose, W. 1978. 'The loneliness of the long distance trader in New Guinea'. *Mankind* 11: 326–33.

Anonymous. 1894. 'Better than prohibition – abolition'. *Quarterly Jottings from the New Hebrides* 5: 17.

Anonymous. 1916. 'Darkness and light on Aneityum'. *Quarterly Jottings from the New Hebrides* 93: 19–21.

Anonymous. 1917. 'Jottings'. *Quarterly Jottings from the New Hebrides* 98: 3–4.

Anonymous. 1947. 'News from the field: Tanna'. *Quarterly Jottings from the New Hebrides* 213: 10.

Anson, D. 1986. 'Lapita pottery of the Bismarck Archipelago and its affinities'. *Archaeology in Oceania* 21: 157–65.

Armstrong, W. 1939. 'From Dr William Armstrong'. *Quarterly Jottings from the New Hebrides* 186: 6–8.

1940. 'From Dr William Armstrong'. *Quarterly Jottings from the New Hebrides* 187: 4–6.

Aufenanger, H. and G. Höltker. 1940. *Die Gende in Zentral-Neu Guinea. Vom Leben und Denken eines Papua-stammes im Bismarck Gebirge*. Vienna, Modling.

Aufinger, A. 1939. 'Wetterzauber auf den Yabob Inseln in Neuguinea'. *Anthropos* 34: 277–91.

1950. 'Mythological fragments from the small islands near Madang (New Guinea)'. *Anthropos* 45: 779–86.

Ayers, W. S. and R. Mauricio. 1987. 'Stone adzes from Pohnpei, Micronesia'. *Archaeology in Oceania* 22: 27–31.

Ayris, C. 1987. 'Curse of the kava: Fiji's "happy drink" threatens Australia's Aboriginal communities'. *Australasian Post*, 14 May, pp. 4–5.

Baal, J. van 1966. *Dema*. The Hague, Martinus Nijhoff.

1982. *Jan Verschueren's description of Yei-nan culture*. The Hague, Martinus Nijhoff.

Baker, J. R. 1929. *Men and animals in the New Hebrides*. London, George Routledge and Sons.

Baker, J. R. and I. Baker. 1936. 'The seasons in tropical rain-forest, New Hebrides, Part II. Botany'. *Journal of the Linnean Society, Zoology* 39: 507–19.

Baldwin, J. n.d. 'Plants'. Unpublished MS in possession of Michael Wood.

Barrau, J. 1957. 'A propos du piper methysticum'. *Journal d'Agriculture et de Botanique Appliquée* 5–8: 270–4.

Barth, F. 1975. *Ritual and knowledge among the Baktaman of New Guinea*. New Haven, Yale University Press.

1987. *Cosmologies in the making: a generative approach to cultural variation in inner New Guinea*. Cambridge, Cambridge University Press.

Bastin, R. 1981. 'Economic enterprise in a Tannese village'. In M. Allen (ed.), *Vanuatu: politics, economics and ritual in island Melanesia*. Sydney, Academic Press, pp. 337–55.

Bateson, G. 1958. *Naven: a survey of the problems suggested by a composite picture of the culture of a New Guinea tribe drawn from three points of view*. 2nd edn. Stanford, Stanford University Press.

Beaglehole, E. 1957. *Social change in the South Pacific: Rarotonga and Aitutaki*. London, Allen and Unwin.

Beaglehole, E. and P. Beaglehole 1938. *Ethnology of Pukapuka*. Honolulu, Bernice P. Bishop Museum, bulletin no. 150.

Beardmore, E. 1890. 'The natives of Mowat, Daudai, New Guinea'. *Journal of the Royal Anthropological Institute* 19: 459–66.

Beaumont, C. H. 1972. 'New Ireland languages: a review'. In *Papers in Linguistics of Melanesia no. 3*. Canberra, ANU, Pacific Linguistics A–35, pp. 1–41.

——— 1979. *The Tigak language of New Ireland*. Canberra, ANU, Pacific Linguistics B–58.

Beckett, J. 1987. *Torres Strait Islanders: custom and colonialism*. Cambridge, Cambridge University Press.

Bell, H. M. 1938. 'From the Rev. H. M. Bell'. *Quarterly Jottings from the New Hebrides* 180: 7 –9.

——— 1941. 'From the Rev. H. M. Bell'. *Quarterly Jottings from the New Hebrides* 194: 8–11.

Bellwood, P. 1978. *Man's conquest of the Pacific*. Auckland, Collins.

Bennett, J. A. 1987. *Wealth of the Solomons*. Honolulu, University of Hawaii Press. (Pacific Islands monograph series 3.)

Biggs, B. 1978. 'The history of Polynesian phonology'. In S. A. Wurm and L. Carrington (eds.), *Second International Conference on Austronesian linguistics: proceedings*. Canberra, ANU, Pacific Linguistics C–61, vol. 2, pp. 691–716.

Biro, L. 1901. *Beschreibender Catalog der ethnographischen Sammlung Ludwig Biro's aus Deutsch Neu Guinea (Astrolabe Bai)*. Budapest, Ethnographische Sammlung des Ungarischen Nationalmuseums III.

Black, P. W. 1984. 'The anthropology of tobacco use: Tobian data and theoretical issues'. *Journal of Anthropological Research* 40: 475–503.

Bloch, M. and J. Parry. 1981. 'Introduction: death and the regeneration of life'. In M. Bloch and J. Parry (eds.), *Death and the regeneration of life*. Cambridge, Cambridge University Press, pp. 1–44.

Bluhme, H. 1970. 'The phoneme system and its distribution in Roro'. In S. A. Wurm and D. C. Laycock (eds.), *Pacific linguistic studies in honour of Arthur Capell*. Canberra, ANU, Pacific Linguistics C–13, pp. 867–77.

Boelaars, J. H. M. C. 1981. *Head hunters about themselves: an ethnographic report from Irian Jaya*. The Hague, Martinus Nijhoff.

Bogesi, G. 1948. 'Santa Isabel, Solomon Islands'. *Oceania* 18: 208–32.

Bonnemaison, J. 1975. *New Hebrides*. Translated by W. Reed, photography by B. Herman. Papeete, Les Editions du Pacifique.

——— 1985a. 'Les fondements d'une identité: territoire, histoire et société dans l'archipel de Vanuatu (Mélanésie)'. Ph.D. thesis, Université de Paris IV.

——— 1985b. 'The tree and the canoe: roots and mobility in Vanuatu societies'. *Pacific Viewpoint* 26: 30–62.

Bott, E. 1972. 'Psychoanalysis and ceremony'. In J. S. La Fontaine (ed.), *The interpretation of ritual*. London, Tavistock, pp. 205–37.

Bourgarel, A. 1865. 'Des races de l'Océanie française, de celles de la Nouvelle-Calédonie'. *Mémoire de la Société d'Anthropologie de Paris* 2: 375–416.

Bowden, R. 1983. *Yena: art and ceremony in a Sepik society*. Oxford, Pitt Rivers Museum.

Brewster, A. B. 1922. *The hill tribes of Fiji*. London, Lippincott.

Briessen, H. van, II. 1935. 'Hereditary chieftainship and kava in Melanesia'. M.A. thesis, Columbia University.

Brooker, S., R. Cambie and R. Cooper. 1981. *New Zealand and medicinal plants*. Auckland, Heinemann.

References

Brown, F. B. H. 1935. *Flora of Southeastern Polynesia, III, dicotyledons*. Honolulu, Bernice P. Bishop Museum, bulletin no. 130.

Brown, G. 1908. *George Brown, D.D., pioneer missionary and explorer: an autobiography*. London, Hodder and Stoughton.

Brumbaugh, R. 1987. 'The rainbow serpent on the Upper Sepik'. *Anthropos* 82: 25–33.

Brunton, R. 1971. 'Cargo cults and systems of exchange in Melanesia'. *Mankind* 8: 115–28.

1974. 'John Frum and custom on Tanna, New Hebrides'. Unpublished paper presented to Macquarie University anthropology seminar, April.

1975. 'Why do the Trobriands have chiefs?' *Man* 10: 544–58.

1979. 'Kava and the daily dissolution of society on Tanna, New Hebrides'. *Mankind* 12: 93–103.

1980. 'Misconstrued order in Melanesian religion'. *Man* 15: 112–28.

1981a. 'The origins of the John Frum movement: a sociological explanation'. In M. Allen (ed.), *Vanuatu: politics, economics and ritual in island Melanesia*. Sydney, Academic Press, pp. 357–77.

1981b. 'Nias's story'. *Quadrant* 164: 34–6.

1983. 'Tradition and power in Melanesia'. Unpublished paper presented to Research School of Pacific Studies anthropology seminar, ANU, September.

1988. 'The disappearing narcotic: kava and cultural instability in Melanesia'. Ph.D. thesis, La Trobe University.

Buck, P.H., *see* Te Rangi Hiroa.

Buckley, J. P., A. R. Furgiuele and M. J. O'Hara. 1967. 'Pharmacology of kava'. In D. H. Efron (ed.), *Ethnopharmacologic search for psychoactive drugs*. Washington, US Department of Health, Education and Welfare, pp. 141–51.

Bühler, A. 1935. 'Versuch einer Bevölkerungs und Kulturanalyse auf den Admiralitätsinseln'. *Zeitschrift für Ethnologie* 67: 1–32.

Bulmer, R. N. H. 1965. 'The Kyaka of the Western Highlands'. In P. Lawrence and M. J. Meggitt (eds.), *Gods, ghosts and men in Melanesia*. Melbourne, Oxford University Press, pp. 132–61.

Burkill, I. H. 1966. *A dictionary of the economic products of the Malay Peninsula*. Kuala Lumpur, Ministry of Agriculture and Co-operatives.

Burridge, I. O. L. 1960. *Mambu: a Melanesian millennium*. London, Methuen.

1965. 'Tangu, northern Madang District'. In P. Lawrence and M. J. Meggitt (eds.), *Gods, ghosts and men in Melanesia*. Melbourne, Oxford University Press, pp. 224–49.

Burrows, E. G. 1936. *Ethnology of Futuna*. Honolulu, Bernice P. Bishop Museum, bulletin no. 138.

1937. *Ethnology of Uvea (Wallis Island)*. Honolulu, Bernice P. Bishop Museum, bulletin no. 145.

1970. *Western Polynesia: a study of cultural differentiation*. Dunedin, University Book Shop.

Burton-Bradley, B. G. 1966. 'Papua and New Guinea transcultural psychiatry: some implications of betel chewing'. *Medical Journal of Australia* 2: 744–6.

1972. 'Betel chewing'. In *Encyclopaedia of Papua and New Guinea*. Melbourne, Melbourne University Press, vol. 1, pp. 66–7.

1979. 'Arecaidinism: betel chewing in transcultural perspective'. *Canadian Journal of Psychiatry* 24: 481–8.

Camden, B. 1977. *A descriptive dictionary: Bislama to English*. Vila, Maropa Bookshop.

Campbell, S. F. 1983. 'Kula in Vakuta: the mechanics of keda'. In J. W. Leach and

E. Leach (eds.), *The kula: new perspectives on Massim exchange.* Cambridge, Cambridge University Press, pp. 201–27.

Capell, A. 1951–2. 'Languages of Bogia District, New Guinea'. *Oceania* 22: 130–47, 178–207, 317.

1960. *Anthropology and linguistics of Futuna-Aniwa.* Sydney, Oceania Linguistic monograph no. 5.

Capell, A. and J. Lynch 1983. 'Sie vocabulary'. In J. Lynch (ed.), *Studies in the languages of Erromanga.* Canberra, ANU, Pacific Linguistics C–79, pp. 75–147.

Cawte, J. 1986. 'Parameters of kava used as a challenge to alcohol'. *Australian and New Zealand Journal of Psychiatry* 20: 70–6.

1988. 'Macabre effects of a "cult" for kava'. *Medical Journal of Australia* 148: 545–6.

Chalmers, J. 1903. 'Notes on the natives of Kiwai Island'. *Journal of the Royal Anthropological Institute of Great Britain and Ireland* 33: 117–24.

Chamisso, A. von 1986. *A voyage around the world with the Romanzov exploring expedition in the years 1815–1818.* Translated and edited by H. Kratz. Honolulu, University of Hawaii Press.

Chew, W.-L. 1972. 'The genus Piper (Piperaceae) in New Guinea, Solomon Islands, and Australia, 1'. *Journal of the Arnold Arboretum* 53: 1–25.

Chinnery, E. W. P. 1922. 'Piper methysticum in betel chewing'. *Man* 22: 24–7.

Chowning, A. 1963. 'Proto-Melanesian plant names'. In J. Barrau (ed.), *Plants and the migration of Pacific peoples.* Honolulu, Bishop Museum Press, pp. 39–44.

1979. 'Leadership in Melanesia'. *Journal of Pacific History* 14: 66–84.

1987. 'Sorcery and the social order in Kove'. In M. Stephen (ed.), *Sorcerer and witch in Melanesia.* Melbourne, Melbourne University Press, pp. 149–82.

Christian, F. W. 1897. 'On the distribution and origin of some plant and tree names in Polynesia and Micronesia'. *Journal of the Polynesian Society* 6: 123–40.

1899. *The Caroline Islands.* London, Methuen.

Churchill, W. 1916. *Sissano: movements of migration within and through Melanesia.* Washington, Publications of the Carnegie Institute no. 244.

Churchward, C. M. 1939. 'Rotuman legends'. *Oceania* 9: 462–73.

1959. *Tongan dictionary.* London, Oxford University Press.

Clark, R. 1979. 'Language'. In J. D. Jennings (ed.), *The prehistory of Polynesia.* Cambridge, Massachusetts, Harvard University Press, pp. 249–70.

Clunie, F. 1986. *Yalo i Viti.* Suva, Fiji Museum.

Cochran, A. M. 1978. 'A comparative study of Milne Bay phonology'. In S. A. Wurm and L. Carrington (eds.), *Second International Conference on Austronesian linguistics: proceedings.* Canberra, ANU, Pacific Linguistics C–61, vol. 2, pp. 851–66.

Codrington, R. H. 1890. 'Totems in Melanesia'. *Reports of the Australasian Association for the Advancement of Science* 2: 611–15.

1891. *The Melanesians.* Oxford, Clarendon Press.

Codrington, R. H. and J. Palmer. 1896. *A dictionary of the language of Mota.* London, Society for Promoting Christian Knowledge.

Collocott, E. E. V. 1921. 'Notes on Tongan religion'. *Journal of the Polynesian Society* 30: 152–63, 227–40.

1927. 'Kava ceremonial in Tonga'. *Journal of the Polynesian Society* 36: 21–47.

Conrad, R. and W. Dye. 1975. 'Some language relations in the Upper Sepik region of Papua New Guinea'. In *Papers in New Guinea Linguistics No. 18.* Canberra, ANU, Pacific Linguistics A–40, pp. 1–35.

Conton, L. 1977. 'Women's roles in a man's world: appearance and reality in a lowland New Guinea village'. Ph.D. thesis, University of Oregon.

References

Cook, J. 1961. *The journals of Captain James Cook on his voyages of discovery,* Vol. 2: *The voyage of the Resolution and Adventure 1772–1775.* Edited by J. C. Beaglehole. Cambridge, Cambridge University Press.

Copeland, J. 1861. 'Letter to J. Kay, 28 November 1860'. *Reformed Presbyterian Church Magazine,* May, pp. 169–71.

Cordy, Ross. 1982. 'Archaeological research on Kosrae (E. Caroline islands)'. *Bulletin of the Indo-Pacific Prehistory Association* 3: 129–34.

Counts, D. R. 1969. *A Grammar of Kaliai-Kove.* Honolulu, University of Hawaii Press. (Oceanic Linguistics special publication no. 6.)

Craib, J. L. 1983. 'Micronesian prehistory: an archeological overview'. *Science* 219: 922–7.

Crawford, A. L. 1981. *Aida: life and ceremony of the Gogodala.* Port Moresby, National Cultural Council of Papua New Guinea in association with R. Brown and Associates.

Crystal, D. 1985. *A dictionary of linguistics and phonetics.* 2nd edn. Oxford, Basil Blackwell.

Cuzent, G. 1858. 'Du kawa, kava ou hava de Tahiti et des îles Marquises'. *Revue Coloniale* 20: 630–46.

1860. *Iles de la Société.* Rochefort, Imprimerie Thèze.

D'Albertis, L. M. 1880. *New Guinea, what I did and what I saw.* London, Sampson, Low, Marston, Searle and Livingstone.

Darlington, C. D. 1973. *Chromosome botany and the origins of cultivated plants.* 3rd edn. London, George Allen and Unwin.

Davenport, W. H. 1968. 'Social organization notes on the southern Santa Cruz Islands: Utupua and Vanikolo'. *Baessler-Archiv* (N.S.) 16: 207–75.

Davis, D. R. 1968. 'Wantoat–English dictionary'. Unpublished MS. Summer Institute of Linguistics, Kangaroo Ground, Victoria.

Deacon, A. B. 1929. 'Notes on some islands of the New Hebrides'. *Journal of the Royal Anthropological Institute of Great Britain and Ireland* 59: 461–515.

1934. *Malekula: a vanishing people in the New Hebrides.* London, G. Routledge and Sons.

Deane, W. 1921. *Fijian society.* London, Macmillan and Co.

Degener, O. 1940. *Flora Hawaiiensis,* vol. 4. Honolulu, privately published by the author.

Dempwolff, O. 1911. 'Sagen und Märchen aus Bilibili'. *Baessler Archiv* 1: 63–102.

Dening, G. 1974. *The Marquesan journal of Edward Robarts.* Canberra, ANU Press.

1980. *Islands and beaches.* Melbourne, Melbourne University Press.

Dobkin de Rios, M. 1984. *Hallucinogens: cross-cultural perspectives.* Albuquerque, University of New Mexico Press.

Dornstreich, M. D. 1973. 'An ecological study of Gadio Enga (New Guinea) subsistence'. Ph.D. thesis, Columbia University.

Douglas, B. 1979. 'Rank, power, authority: a reassessment of traditional leadership in South Pacific societies'. *Journal of Pacific History* 14: 2–27.

Douglas, M. 1966. *Purity and danger.* London, Routledge and Kegan Paul.

Duffield, A. M. and D. D. Jamieson. 1988. 'Chemistry and pharmacology of kava'. Unpublished paper presented to the Centre for South Pacific Studies and National Drug and Alcohol Research Centre symposium on kava, University of NSW, November.

Durrad, W. J. 1940–1. 'Notes on the Torres Islanders'. *Oceania* 11: 75–109, 186–201.

Dutton, T. 1969. *The peopling of Central Papua.* Canberra, ANU, Pacific Linguistics B–9.

1971. 'Languages of South-east Papua'. In *Papers in New Guinea Linguistics no. 14*. Canberra, ANU, Pacific Linguistics A–28, pp. 6–46.

1973. ' "Cultural" items of basic vocabulary in the Gulf and other districts of Papua'. In K. J. Franklin (ed.), *The linguistic situation in the Gulf and adjacent areas, Papua New Guinea*. Canberra, ANU, Pacific Linguistics C–26, pp. 411–592.

1975. 'A Koita grammar sketch and vocabulary'. In T. Dutton (ed.), *Studies in languages of Central and South-East Papua*. Canberra, ANU, Pacific Linguistics C–29, pp. 281–412.

1982a. 'Towards a history of the hiri'. In T. Dutton (ed.), *The hiri in history: further aspects of long distance Motu trade in Central Papua*. Canberra, ANU, pp. 65–98. (Pacific Research monograph no. 8.)

1982b. 'Borrowing in Austronesian and non-Austronesian languages of coastal South-east mainland Papua New Guinea'. In A. Halim, L. Carrington and S. A. Wurm (eds.), *Papers from the 3rd International Conference on Austronesian linguistics*. Canberra, ANU, Pacific Linguistics C–74, vol. 1, pp. 109–77.

Duve, R. N. 1976. 'Highlights of the chemistry and pharmacology of yaqona'. *Fiji Agricultural Journal* 38: 81–4.

1981. 'Gas–liquid-chromatographic determination of major constituents of piper methysticum'. *Analyst* 106: 160–5.

Dye, W., P. Townsend and W. Townsend. 1968. 'The Sepik Hill languages – a preliminary report'. *Oceania* 29: 146–56.

Eckardt, M. 1881. 'Die Salomo-Inseln'. *Globus* 39: 349–51.

Egloff, B. J. and R. Kaiku. 1978. *An archaeological and ethnographic survey of the Purari River (Wabo) dam site and reservoir*. Papua New Guinea, Office of Environment and Conservation and Department of Minerals and Energy. (Purari River (Wabo) Hydroelectric Scheme environmental studies vol. 5.)

Eisler, D. C. 1979. 'Continuity and change in a Lowland political system in Papua New Guinea'. Ph.D. thesis, University of Oregon.

Elbert, S. H. 1975. *Dictionary of the language of Rennell and Bellona: Rennellese–English*. Copenhagen, The National Museum of Denmark.

Elkin, A. P. 1964. *The Australian Aborigines: how to understand them*. 4th edn. Sydney, Angus and Robertson.

Ellis, J.-A. 1984. 'Looking at kava as an export crop'. *Pacific Islands Monthly*. February: 27–8.

Emerson, O. P. 1903. 'The awa habit of the Hawaiians'. *The Hawaiian Annual* (Honolulu), pp. 130–40.

Emory, K. 1940. 'Tuamotuan concepts of creation'. *Journal of the Polynesian Society* 49: 69–136.

1947. *Tuamotuan religious structures and ceremonies*. Honolulu, Bernice P. Bishop Museum, bulletin no. 191.

1975. *Material culture of the Tuamotuan archipelago*. Honolulu, Bernice P. Bishop Museum. (Pacific anthropological records 22.)

1979. 'The Societies'. In J. D. Jennings (ed.), *The prehistory of Polynesia*. Cambridge, Massachusetts, Harvard University Press, pp. 200–21.

Ernst, T. 1979. 'Myth, ritual and population among the Marind-anim'. *Social Analysis* 1: 34–53.

1987. 'Empirical attitudes among the Onabasulu'. Unpublished paper presented to Australian Anthropological Society annual conference, Monash University, August.

Errington, F. 1974. *Karavar: masks and power in a Melanesian ritual*. Ithaca, Cornell University Press.

185

References

Errington, F. and D. Gewertz. 1986. 'The confluence of powers: entropy and importation among the Chambri'. *Oceania* 57: 99–113.

Errington, S. 1977. 'Order and power in Karavar'. In R. D. Fogelson and R. N. Adams (eds.), *The anthropology of power*. New York, Academic Press, pp. 23–43.

Erskine, J. E. 1853. *Journal of a cruise among the islands of the Western Pacific, including the Feejees and others inhabited by the Polynesian negro races, in her Majesty's ship 'Havannah'*. London, J. Murray.

Facey, E. F. 1981. 'Hereditary chiefship in Nguna'. In M. Allen (ed.), *Vanuatu: politics, economics and ritual in island Melanesia*. Sydney, Academic Press, pp. 295–313.

Farnworth, E. R. 1976. 'Betel nut – its composition, chemistry and uses'. *Science in New Guinea* 4: 85–90.

Feil, D. 1984. *Ways of exchange: the Enga tee of Papua New Guinea*. St Lucia, University of Queensland Press.

Ferdon, E. N. 1981. *Early Tahiti: as the explorers saw it, 1767–1797*. Tucson, University of Arizona Press.

Finney, B. R. 1985. 'Anomalous westerlies, El Niño, and the colonization of Polynesia'. *American Anthropologist* 87: 8–26.

Firchow, I., J. Firchow and D. Akoitai. 1973. *Vocabulary of Rotokas-Pidgin-English*. Ukarumpa, Summer Institute of Linguistics.

Firth, R. 1954. 'Anuta and Tikopia: symbiotic elements in social organization'. *Journal of the Polynesian Society* 63: 87–131.

1967. *The work of the gods in Tikopia*. 2nd edn. London, Athlone.

1970. *Rank and religion in Tikopia*. Boston, Beacon.

Fleischmann, L. and S. Turpeinen. 1976. 'A dialect survey of Eastern Trans-Fly languages'. In *Papers in New Guinea Linguistics no. 19*. Canberra, ANU, Pacific Linguistics A-45, pp. 39–76.

Foley, W. A. 1986. *The Papuan languages of New Guinea*. Cambridge, Cambridge University Press.

Ford, C. S. 1967. 'Ethnographic aspects of kava'. In D. H. Efron (ed.), *Ethnopharmacologic search for psychoactive drugs*. Washington, US Department of Health, Education and Welfare, pp. 162–73.

Forge, A. 1970. 'Prestige, influence, and sorcery: a New Guinea example'. In M. Douglas (ed.), *Witchcraft confessions and accusations*. London, Tavistock, pp. 257–75. (ASA monographs 9.)

Forman, C. W. 1982. *The island churches of the South Pacific*. Maryknoll, NY, Orbis Books. (American Society of Missiology series no. 5.)

Forster, G. 1968. *A voyage round the world*. Berlin, Akademie Verlag.

Forster, J. R. 1982. *The Resolution journal of Johann Reinhold Forster 1772–1775*, vol. 4. Edited by M. E. Hoare. London, The Hakluyt Society.

Fortune, R. 1935. *Manus religion: an ethnological study of the Manus natives of the Admiralty Islands*. Philadelphia, Memoirs of the American Philosophical Society 3.

1942. *Arapesh*. New York, J. J. Augustin. (Publications of the American Ethnological Society vol. 19.)

1963. *Sorcerers of Dobu*. Revised edn. London, Routledge and Kegan Paul.

Fox, C. E. 1917. 'Some notes on Taumako relationship names'. *Journal of the Polynesian Society* 26: 190.

1919. 'Social organization in San Cristobal, Solomon Islands'. *Journal of the Royal Anthropological Institute* 49: 95–179.

1924. *Threshold of the Pacific*. London, Routledge.

186

1978. *Arosi dictionary*. Revised edn. Canberra, ANU, Pacific Linguistics C-57.

Franklin, K. J. 1973. 'Appendices'. In K. J. Franklin (ed.), *The linguistic situation in the Gulf and adjacent areas, Papua New Guinea*. Canberra, ANU, Pacific Linguistics C-26, pp. 541–92.

Franklin, K. J. and C. L. Voorhoeve. 1973. 'Languages near the intersection of the Gulf, Southern Highlands and Western Districts'. In K. J. Franklin (ed.), *The linguistic situation in the Gulf and adjacent areas, Papua New Guinea*. Canberra, ANU, Pacific Linguistics C-26, pp. 151–86.

Frater, A. S. 1952. 'Medical aspects of yaqona'. *Transactions and Proceedings of the Fiji Society* 5: 31–9.

Freund, P. 1977. 'Social change among the Kasua, Southern Highlands, Papua New Guinea'. Ph.D. thesis, University of Iowa.

Freund, P. and M. Marshall. 1977. 'Research bibliography of alcohol and kava studies in Oceania: update and additional items'. *Micronesica* 13: 313–17.

Friedman, J. 1982. 'Catastrophe and continuity in social evolution'. In C. Renfrew, M. J. Rowlands and B. A. Segraves (eds.), *Theory and explanation in archaeology*. London, Academic Press, pp. 175–96.

Furst, P. T. 1976. *Hallucinogens and culture*. San Francisco, Chandler and Sharp.

Gajdusek, D. C. 1967. 'Recent observations of the use of kava in the New Hebrides'. In D. H. Efron (ed.), *Ethnopharmacologic search for psychoactive drugs*. Washington, US Department of Health, Education and Welfare, pp. 119–25.

Gardiner, J. S. 1898. 'The natives of Rotuma'. *Journal of the Royal Anthropological Institute* 27: 396–435, 457–524.

Gatty, R. 1956. 'Kava – Polynesian beverage shrub'. *Economic Botany* 10: 241–9.

Geddie, J. 1848–58. New Hebrides diaries. Pacific Manuscripts Bureau 418 (Manuscripts series).

Geerts, P. 1970. *'Are'are dictionary*. Canberra, ANU, Pacific Lingustics C-14.

Geertz, C. 1966. 'Religion as a cultural system'. In M. Banton (ed.), *Anthropological approaches to the study of religion*. London, Tavistock, pp. 1–46. (ASA monographs 3.)

Gell, A. 1975. *Metamorphosis of the cassowaries: Umeda society, language and ritual*. London, Athlone.

Gerstner, A. 1954. 'Die glaubensmässige Einstellung der Wewak-Boikin-Leute zu den Krankheiten und deren Heilung (Nordost-Neuguinea)'. *Anthropos* 49: 460–80.

Gewertz, D. B. 1983. *Sepik River societies*. New Haven, Yale University Press.

Gifford, E. W. 1924. *Tongan myths and tales*. Honolulu, Bernice P. Bishop Museum, bulletin no. 8.

1929. *Tongan society*. Honolulu, Bernice P. Bishop Museum, bulletin no. 61.

Gluckman, M. 1970. *Custom and conflict in Africa*. Oxford, Basil Blackwell.

Golson, J. 1977. 'No room at the top: agricultural intensification in the New Guinea Highlands'. In J. Allen, J. Golson and R. Jones (eds.), *Sunda and Sahul*. London, Academic Press, pp. 601–38.

1982. 'The Ipomoean revolution revisited: society and the sweet potato in the upper Waghi valley'. In A. Strathern (ed.), *Inequality in the New Guinea Highlands*. Cambridge, Cambridge University Press, pp. 109–36.

Gordon, R. 1983. 'The decline of the kiapdom and the resurgence of "tribal fighting" in Enga'. *Oceania* 53: 205–23.

Gourlay, K. A. 1975. *Sound-producing instruments in traditional society: a study of esoteric instruments and their role in male–female relations*. Port Moresby, New Guinea Research Unit bulletin no. 60.

References

Graham, D. 1987. 'Battle to keep kava out will go on, says blacks' group'. *The Age*, 14 June, p. 4.

Gray, W. M. 1892. 'Some notes on the Tannese'. *Reports of the Australasian Association for the Advancement of Science* 4: 645–80.

1899. 'Notes on the natives of Tanna'. *Journal of the Anthropological Institute* 28: 127–32.

Green, R. 1979. 'Lapita'. In J. D. Jennings (ed.), *The prehistory of Polynesia*. Cambridge, Massachusetts, Harvard University Press, pp. 27–60.

1981. 'Location of the Polynesian homeland'. In J. Hollyman and A. Pawley (eds.), *Studies in Pacific languages and cultures*. Auckland, Linguistic Society of New Zealand, pp. 133–58.

Greenhouse, C. J. 1985. 'Mediation: a comparative approach'. *Man* 20: 90–114.

Gregory, R. J. and J. E. Gregory. 1984. 'John Frum: an indigenous strategy of reaction to mission rule and the colonial order'. *Pacific Studies* 7: 68–90.

Gregory, R. J., J. E. Gregory and J. G. Peck. 1981. 'Kava and prohibition in Tanna, Vanuatu'. *British Journal of Addiction* 76: 299–313.

Grimshaw, B. 1907. *From Fiji to the Cannibal Islands*. London, G. Bell and Sons.

Guiart, J. 1953. 'Native society in the New Hebrides: the Big Nambas of northern Malekula'. *Mankind* 4: 439–46.

1956a. *Un siècle et demi de contacts culturels à Tanna, Nouvelles-Hébrides*. Paris, Musée de l'Homme.

1956b. 'Culture contact and the "John Frum" movement on Tanna, New Hebrides'. *Southwestern Journal of Anthropology* 12: 105–16.

1958. *Espiritu Santo*. Paris, Librairie Plon.

Guillaumin, A. 1938. 'A florula of the island of Espiritu Santo, one of the New Hebrides'. *Journal of the Linnean Society, Botany* 51: 547–66.

1948. *Flore analytique et synoptique de la Nouvelle-Calédonie (Phanérogames)*. Paris, ORSC.

Guppy, H. B. 1887. *The Solomon Islands and their natives*. London, Swan Sonnenschein, Lowrey and Co.

Haddon, A. C. 1912. 'Food and its preparation, and narcotics'. In A. C. Haddon (ed.), *Reports of the Cambridge Anthropological Expedition to Torres Straits*. Cambridge, Cambridge University Press, vol. 4, pp. 130–43.

1916. 'Kava-drinking in New Guinea'. *Man* 16: 145–52.

1920. *Migrations of cultures in British New Guinea*. London, Royal Anthropological Institute.

1947. 'Smoking and tobacco pipes in New Guinea'. *Royal Society of London Philosophical Transactions* series B, 232: 1–278.

Hagen, B. 1899. *Unter den Papua's*. Wiesbaden, C. W. Kreidel.

Hallpike, C. R. 1977. *Bloodshed and vengeance in the Papuan mountains: the generation of conflict in Tauade society*. Oxford, Clarendon.

Hambruch, P. 1932–6. *Ponape*. Hamburg, Friederichsen, de Gruyter and Co., 3 vols. (G. Thilenius (ed.), *Ergebnisse der Südsee Expedition 1908–1910*, vol. II-B7.)

Handelman, D. 1982. 'Reflexivity in festival and other cultural events'. In M. Douglas (ed.), *Essays in the sociology of perception*. London, Routledge and Kegan Paul, pp. 162–90.

Handy, E. S. C. 1923. *The native culture of the Marquesas*. Honolulu, Bernice P. Bishop Museum, bulletin no. 9.

1930. *History and culture in the Society Islands*. Honolulu, Bernice P. Bishop Museum, bulletin no. 79.

Hannemann, E. F. 1944. 'Village life and social change in Madang society'. Mimeo.

Hardie, C. 1854. 'Voyage to New Hebrides, New Caledonia and Savage Island'. London Missionary Society, South Seas Journals no. 148. (AJCP microfilm, box 10, Victorian State Library.)

1981. '1849'. Extracts from *Samoan Reporter* 1845–61. La Trobe University, Department of History.

Harding, T. G. 1970. 'Trading in northeast New Guinea'. In T. G. Harding and B. J. Wallace (eds.), *Cultures of the Pacific*. New York, The Free Press, pp. 94–111.

Harrison, S. 1987. 'Cultural efflorescence and political evolution on the Sepik River'. *American Ethnologist* 14: 491–507.

Harrisson, T. 1936a. 'Living in Espiritu Santo'. *Geographical Journal* 88: 243–61.

1936b. 'The New Hebrides people and culture'. *Geographical Journal* 88: 332–41.

Hays, T. 1984. 'Tobacco in the New Guinea Highlands'. Unpublished paper delivered at 13th annual meeting of the Association for Social Anthropology in Oceania, 1984.

1986. 'Sacred flutes, fertility, and growth in the Papua New Guinea Highlands'. *Anthropos* 81: 435–53.

Healey, P. and A. Healey. 1977. *Telefol dictionary*. Canberra, ANU, Pacific Linguistics C-46.

Hide, R. *et al.* 1979. A checklist of some plants in the territory of the Sinasina Nimai (Simbu Province, Papua New Guinea), with notes on their uses. University of Auckland, Department of Anthropology. (Working papers in anthropology no. 54.)

Hilliard, D. 1978. *God's gentlemen: a history of the Melanesian Mission 1849–1942*. St Lucia, University of Queensland Press.

Hiroa, Te Rangi, *see* Te Rangi Hiroa

Hocart, A. M. 1929. *Lau Islands, Fiji*. Honolulu, Bernice P. Bishop Museum, bulletin no. 62.

1952. *The northern states of Fiji*. London, Royal Anthropological Institute occasional publication no. 11.

Hogarth, M. 1987. 'Aborigines seek ban on "killer" kava'. *Times on Sunday* 22 March, p. 5.

Hogbin, I. 1970. *The island of menstruating men*. Scranton, Chandler.

Holmes, L. D. 1967. 'The function of kava in modern Samoan culture'. In D. H. Efron (ed.), *Ethnopharmacologic search for psychoactive drugs*. Washington, US Department of Health, Education and Welfare, pp. 107–18.

1973. 'The kava complex in Oceania'. Paper read at 72nd annual meeting of the American Anthropology Association, New Orleans.

1979. 'The kava complex in Oceania'. *New Pacific* 4: 30–1.

Hughes, I. 1977. *New Guinea stone age trade*. Canberra, ANU, Department of Prehistory, Research School of Pacific Studies. (*Terra Australia* vol. 3.)

Huisman, R. and J. Lloyd. 1981. 'Angaatiha tone, stress and length'. In P. M. Healey (ed.), *Angan languages are different*. Huntington Beach, Summer Institute of Linguistics, pp. 63–82. (Language data, Asian Pacific series no. 12.)

Humphreys, C. B. 1926. *The southern New Hebrides; an ethnological record*. Cambridge, Cambridge University Press.

Iamo, W. 1987. 'One of the things that brings good name is betel: a Keakalo conception of betel use'. In L. Lindstrom (ed.), *Drugs in western Pacific societies*. Lanham, University Press of America, pp. 135–48. (ASAO monograph 11.)

im Thurn, E. 1922. 'Piper methysticum in betel chewing'. *Man* 22: 57.

Ivens, W. G. 1927. *Melanesians of the South-east Solomon Islands*. London, Kegan Paul, Trench and Trubner.

References

1930. *The island builders of the Pacific*. London, Seeley, Service and Co.

1940. *A dictionary of the language of Bugotu*. London, The Royal Asiatic Society.

Jenness, D. and A. Ballantyne. 1928. *Language, mythology and songs of Bwaidoga*. New Plymouth, Avery and Sons.

Jennings, S. 1985. 'Temiar dance and the maintenance of order'. In P. Spencer (ed.), *Society and the dance: the social anthropology of process and performance*. Cambridge, Cambridge University Press, 1985, pp. 47–63.

Jett, S. C. 1971. 'Diffusion versus independent development: the bases of controversy'. In C. L. Riley, J. C. Kelley, C. W. Pennington and R. L. Rands (eds.), *Man across the sea*. Austin, University of Texas Press, pp. 5–53.

1984. 'Comments on Mundkur: The bicephalous "animal style" on northern Eurasian religious art and its western hemisphere analogues'. *Current Anthropology* 25: 474–5.

Johannes, A. 1975. 'Medicinal plants of the Nekematigi of the Eastern Highlands of New Guinea'. *Economic Botany* 29: 268–77.

Kahn, M. 1986. *Always hungry, never greedy: food and the expression of gender in a Melanesian society*. Cambridge, Cambridge University Press.

Kasprus, A. 1942–5. 'The languages of the Mugil district, NE New Guinea'. *Anthropos* 37–40: 711–78.

Keesing, R. 1982a. *Kwaio religion*. New York, Columbia University Press.

1982b. 'Kastom in Melanesia: an overview'. *Mankind* 13: 297–301.

1984. 'Rethinking mana'. *Journal of Anthropological Research* 40: 137–56.

1987. 'Anthropology as interpretive quest'. *Current Anthropology* 28: 161–76.

Keesing, R. and P. Corris. 1980. *Lightning meets the west wind*. Melbourne, Oxford University Press.

Kirch, P. V. 1979. *Marine exploitation in prehistoric Hawaii: archaeological investigations at Kalahuipua'a, Hawaii Island*. Honolulu, Bernice P. Bishop Museum. (Pacific anthropological records 29.)

1984. *The evolution of the Polynesian chiefdoms*. Cambridge, Cambridge University Press.

Kirch, P. V., M. S. Allen, V. L. Butler and T. L. Hunt. 1987. 'Is there an early Far Western Lapita province? Sample size effects and new evidence from Eloaua Island'. *Archaeology in Oceania* 22: 123–7.

Kirch, P. V. and D. E. Yen. 1982. *Tikopia: the prehistory and ecology of a Polynesian outlier*. Honolulu, Bernice P. Bishop Museum, bulletin no. 238.

Kirtley, B. F. 1971. *A motif-index of traditional Polynesian narratives*. Honolulu, University of Hawaii Press.

Knauft, B. 1985. *Good company and violence: sorcery and social action in a lowland New Guinea society*. Berkeley, University of California Press.

1987. 'Managing sex and anger: tobacco and kava use among the Gebusi of Papua New Guinea'. In L. Lindstrom (ed.), *Drugs in western Pacific societies*. Lanham, University Press of America, pp. 73–98. (ASAO monograph 11.)

Koch, G. 1981. 'Kawa in Polynesien'. *Ethnologica* 9: 194–9.

Kwapena, N. 1974. 'Preliminary survey on wild plant utilization in Papua New Guinea'. *Science in New Guinea* 2: 246–53.

Laba, B. 1974. *Waidoro: isolation and change in a Western District village*. Port Moresby, UPNG, Department of Geography. (Student papers no. 1.)

Landtman, G. 1917. *The folktales of the Kiwai Papuans*. Helsingfors, Societas Scientarum Fennica.

1927. *The Kiwai Papuans of British New Guinea*. London, Macmillan.

Lanyon-Orgill, P. A. 1950. 'A comparative vocabulary of the language of the island of Choiseul, British Solomon Islands, Melanesia'. *Anthropos* 45: 57–80.

190

Larcom, J. 1982. 'The invention of convention'. *Mankind* 13: 330–7.

Lawrence, P. 1964. *Road belong cargo*. Melbourne, Melbourne University Press.

1984. *The Garia*. Melbourne, Melbourne University Press.

Lawrie, J. H. 1895. 'Aneityum'. *'Dayspring' and New Hebrides mission: report for year 1894*, p. 10.

Lawrie, M. 1970. *Myths and Legends of Torres Strait*. Brisbane, University of Queensland Press.

Layard, J. 1942. *Stone men of Malekula*. London, Chatto and Windus.

Laycock, D. 1984. 'Betel chewing etc. in Sepik languages'. Unpublished MS.

Lebot, V. 1983. 'The kava'. In *Vanuatu: tri independens selebresen*. Vila, Independence Committee, pp. 77–106.

1986. 'Differentiation of local kava cultivars on the basis of their total kavalactone content and their composition'. Portion of annual report to the Department of Agriculture, Vanuatu.

n.d. 'Background and rationale [for study of kava]'. Unpublished MS.

Lebot, V. and R. Brunton n.d. 'Traditional plants as cash crops: a survey of kava in Vanuatu'. Unpublished MS.

Lebot, V. and P. Cabalion. 1986. *Les kavas de Vanuatu*. Paris, Editions de l'Orstom. (Collection travaux et documents no. 205.)

Lebot, V., P. Cabalion and J. Levesque n.d. 'Le "kava des ancêtres" (Piper wichmannii C.DC) est-il l'ancêtre du kava (P. methysticum Forst. f.)?' Vila, mimeo.

Lebot, V. and J. Levesque n.d. 'The chemical types of kava'. Unpublished paper translated by E. Rod.

Leenhardt, M. 1946. 'Le ti en Nouvelle-Calédonie'. *Journal de la Société des Océanistes* 2: 192–3.

Lemert, E. M. 1967. *Human deviance, social problems and social control*. Englewood Cliffs, Prentice-Hall.

Lepowsky, M. 1982. 'A comparison of alcohol and betelnut use on Vanatinai (Sudest Island)'. In M. Marshall (ed.), *Through a glass darkly: beer and modernization in Papua New Guinea*. Boroko, IASER, pp. 325–42.

Lester, R. M. 1941–2. 'Kava drinking in Vitilevu, Fiji'. *Oceania* 12: 97–121, 226–54.

Lewis, G. 1975. *Knowledge of illness in a Sepik society*. London, Athlone.

1980. *Day of shining red*. Cambridge, Cambridge University Press.

Lewis, W. H. and M. P. F. Elvin-Lewis. 1977. *Medical botany*. New York, John Wiley and Sons.

Lilley, I. 1985. 'Chiefs without chiefdoms? Comments on prehistoric sociopolitical organization in western Melanesia'. *Archaeology in Oceania* 20: 60–5.

Lilley, I. 1988. 'Prehistoric exchange across the Vitiaz Strait, Papua New Guinea'. *Current Anthropology* 29: 513–16.

Lindenbaum, S. 1981. 'Images of the sorcerer in Papua New Guinea'. *Social Analysis* 8: 119–28.

Lindstrom, L. 1979. 'Americans on Tanna: an essay from the field'. *Canberra Anthropology* 2: 37–46.

1980. 'Spitting on Tanna'. *Oceania* 50: 228–34.

1981a. 'Achieving wisdom: knowledge and politics on Tanna (Vanuatu)'. Ph.D. thesis, University of California, Berkeley.

1981b. 'Speech and kava on Tanna'. In M. Allen (ed.), *Vanuatu: politics, economics and ritual in island Melanesia*. Sydney, Academic Press, pp. 379–93.

1981c. 'Cult and culture: American dreams in Vanuatu'. *Pacific Studies* 4: 101–23.

1982. 'Grog blong yumi: alcohol and kava on Tanna, Vanuatu'. In M. Marshall (ed.), *Through a glass darkly: beer and modernization in Papua New Guinea.* Boroko, IASER, pp. 421–32. (IASER monograph 18.)

1984. 'Doctor, lawyer, wise man, priest: big-men and knowledge in Melanesia'. *Man* 19: 291–309.

1985. 'Personal names and social reproduction on Tanna, Vanuatu'. *Journal of the Polynesian Society* 94: 27–45.

1987. 'Drunkenness and gender on Tanna, Vanuatu'. In L. Lindstrom (ed.), *Drugs in western Pacific societies.* Lanham, University Press of America, pp. 99–118. (ASAO monograph 11.)

Linton, R. 1923. *The material culture of the Marquesas Islands.* Honolulu, Bernice P. Bishop Museum, memoir VIII, no. 5.

Lithgow, D. and O. Claassen. 1968. *Languages of the New Ireland District.* Port Moresby, Department of Information and Extension Services.

Loeb, E. M. 1926. *History and traditions of Niue.* Honolulu, Bernice P. Bishop Museum, bulletin no. 32.

Lowman-Vayda, C. 1971. 'Maring big men'. In R. M. Berndt and P. Lawrence (eds.), *Politics in New Guinea.* Nedlands, University of Western Australia Press, pp. 317–61.

Ludvigson, T. 1981. 'Kleva: some healers in Central Espiritu Santo, Vanuatu'. Ph.D. thesis, University of Auckland.

Lynch, J. 1977. *Lenakel dictionary.* Canberra, ANU, Pacific Linguistics C–55.

1978a. 'Proto-South Hebridean and Proto-Oceanic'. In S. A. Wurm and L. Carrington (eds.), *Second International Conference on Austronesian linguistics: proceedings.* Canberra, ANU, Pacific Linguistics C–61, vol. 2, pp. 717–79.

1978b. *A grammar of Lenakel.* Canberra, ANU, Pacific Linguistics B-55.

MacAndrew, C. and R. B. Edgerton. 1969. *Drunken comportment: a sociological explanation.* Chicago, Aldine.

McArthur, M. 1971. 'Men and spirits in the Kunimaipa Valley'. In L. R. Hiatt and C. Jayawardena (eds.), *Anthropology in Oceania.* Sydney, Angus and Robertson, pp. 155–89.

McArthur, N. and J. F. Yaxley. 1968. *A report on the first census of the population 1967.* Condominium of the New Hebrides.

McCarthy, F. D. 1939. 'Trade in aboriginal Australia and trade relationships with Torres Strait, New Guinea and Malaya'. *Oceania* 10: 171–95.

MacClancy, J. 1986. 'Mana: an anthropological metaphor for island Melanesia'. *Oceania* 57: 142–53.

n.d. *To kill a bird with two stones: a short history of Vanuatu.* Vila, Vanuatu Cultural Centre.

MacDonald, D. 1889. *New Hebrides linguistics*, vol. 1. Melbourne, Edgerton and Moore.

1892. 'Efate, New Hebrides'. *Reports of the Australasian Association for the Advancement of Science* 4: 720–35.

1898. 'Mythology of the Efatese'. *Reports of the Australasian Association for the Advancement of Science* 7: 759–68.

McGrath, T. B. 1973. 'Sakau in towm. Sarawi in towm'. *Oceania* 44: 64–7.

Macgregor, G. 1937. *Ethnology of Tokelau Islands.* Honolulu, Bernice P. Bishop Museum, bulletin no. 146.

Macleod, D. 1937. 'Dr Macleod's letter'. *Quarterly Jottings from the New Hebrides* 175: 10–11.

Macmillan, T. 1907. 'Synod and Tanna news'. *Quarterly Jottings from the New Hebrides* 58: 24–6.

1922. 'From our Tanna Island mission'. *Quarterly Jottings from the New Hebrides* 118: 6–9.

1923a. 'From our Tanna Island mission'. *Quarterly Jottings from the New Hedbrides* 119: 13–16.

1923b. 'From our Tanna Island mission'. *Quarterly Jottings from the New Hebrides* 122: 12–15.

1925. 'From our Tanna Island mission'. *Quarterly Jottings from the New Hebrides* 129: 5–9.

1927a. 'From our Tanna Island mission'. *Quarterly Jottings from the New Hebrides* 135: 5–10.

1927b. 'From our Tanna Island mission'. *Quarterly Jottings from the New Hebrides* 138: 5–8.

1929. 'From our Tanna Island mission'. *Quarterly Jottings from the New Hebrides* 145: 6–11.

1931a. 'Tanna's welcome to their new doctor and his wife'. *Quarterly Jottings from the New Hebrides* 151: 7–12.

1931b. 'The Rev. Thomson Macmillan's report'. *Quarterly Jottings from the New Hebrides* 152: 5–11.

1935. 'Koukarei, an old warrior of east Tanna'. *Quarterly Jottings from the New Hebrides* 167: 14–16.

Mager, J. F. 1952. *Gedaged–English dictionary*. Columbus, Ohio, Board of Foreign Missions of the American Lutheran Church.

Malinowski, B. 1932. *The sexual life of savages in north-western Melanesia*. 3rd edn. London, Routledge and Kegan Paul.

1966. *Coral gardens and their magic*, vol. 1. 2nd edn. London, George Allen and Unwin.

Mandelbaum, D. G. 1979. 'Alcohol and culture'. In M. Marshall (ed.), *Beliefs, behaviours and alcoholic beverages: a cross-cultural survey*. Ann Arbor, University of Michigan Press, pp. 14–30.

Mariner, W. 1818. *An account of the natives of the Tonga Islands*. 2nd edn. Compiled by John Martin. London, John Murray, 2 vols.

Markham, A. H. 1873. *The cruise of the 'Rosario' amongst the New Hebrides and Santa Cruz Islands*. London, Sampson Low, Marston, Low and Searle.

Marshall, M. 1976. 'A review and appraisal of alcohol and kava studies in Oceania'. In M. W. Everett, J. O. Waddell and D. B. Heath (eds.), *Cross-cultural approaches to the study of alcohol*. The Hague, Mouton, pp. 103–18.

1979. 'Introduction'. In M. Marshall (ed.), *Beliefs, behaviours and alcoholic beverages: a cross-cultural survey*. Ann Arbor, University of Michigan Press, pp. 1–11.

1981. 'Kava and betel'. In R. D. Craig and F. P. King (eds.), *Historical dictionary of Oceania*. Westport, Greenwood Press, pp. 145–6.

1982. 'Introduction: twenty years after deprohibition'. In M. Marshall (ed.), *Through a glass darkly: beer and modernization in Papua New Guinea*. Boroko, IASER, pp. 3–13. (IASER monograph 18.)

1983. ' "Four hundred rabbits": an anthropological view of ethanol as a disinhibitor'. In R. Room and G. Collins (eds.), *Alcohol and disinhibition: nature and meaning of the link*. Maryland, National Institute on Alcohol Abuse and Alcoholism, pp. 186–232.

1984. 'Structural patterns of sibling classification in Island Oceania: implications for culture history'. *Current Anthropology* 25: 597–637.

1987. 'An anthropological view of drugs in Oceania'. In L. Lindstrom (ed.),

Drugs in western Pacific societies. Lanham, University Press of America, pp. 13–49. (ASAO monograph 11.)

Mathews, J. D., M. D. Riley, L. Fejo, E. Munoz, N. R. Milns, I. D. Gardner, J. R. Powers, E. Ganygulpa and B. J. Gununuwawuy. 1988. 'Effects of the heavy usage of kava on physical health: summary of a pilot survey in an Aboriginal community'. *Medical Journal of Australia* 148: 548–55.

Mead, M. 1930. *Social organization of Manu'a*. Honolulu, Bernice P. Bishop Museum, bulletin no. 76.

1934. 'Kinship in the Admiralty Islands'. *Anthropological Papers of the American Museum of Natural History* 34: 181–354.

1970 [1940]. *The Mountain Arapesh*, vol. 2: *Arts and supernaturalism*. New York, The Natural History Press.

1971 [1947]. *The Mountain Arapesh*, vol. 3: *Streams of events in Alitoa*. New York, The Natural History Press.

Meggers, B. J. 1975. 'The transpacific origin of Mesoamerican civilization: a preliminary review of the evidence and its theoretical implications'. *American Anthropologist* 77: 1–27.

Metraux, R. 1940. *Ethnology of Easter Island*. Honolulu, Bernice P. Bishop Museum, bulletin no. 160.

Meyer, H. J. 1967. 'Pharmacology of kava'. In D. H. Efron (ed.), *Ethnopharmacologic search for psychoactive drugs*. Washington, US Department of Health, Education and Welfare, pp. 133–40.

Michel, T. 1981. 'Tabak in Neuguinea'. *Ethnologica* 9: 258–62.

Miklouho-Maclay, N. N. 1886a. 'List of plants in use by the natives of New Guinea'. *Proceedings of the Linnean Society of NSW for 1885*, 10: 346–58.

1886b. 'Note on the "keu" of the Maclay-Coast, New Guinea'. *Proceedings of the Linnean Society of NSW for 1885*, 10: 687–95.

1951. *Sobranie Sochenenii*, vol. 3. Moscow, Academy of Sciences. (Extracts translated by Don Laycock.)

1975. *New Guinea diaries 1871–1883*. Translated by C. L. Sentinella. Madang, Kristen Press.

Mills, A. R. 1961. 'Ritual circumcision on Tanna, New Hebrides'. *Man* 61: 185.

Morris, B. 1976. 'Whither the savage mind? Notes on the natural taxonomies of a hunting and gathering people'. *Man* 11: 542–57.

1982a. *Forest traders*. London, Athlone.

1982b. 'Economy, affinity and inter-cultural pressure: notes around Hill Pandaram group structure'. *Man* 17: 452–61.

Mosko, M. S. 1985. *Quadripartite structures; categories, relations and homologies in Bush Mekeo culture*. Cambridge, Cambridge University Press.

Muller, K. 1972. 'Field notes on the Small Nambas'. *Journal de la Société des Océanistes* 35: 153–67; 36: 239–51.

Nachman, S. 1981. 'Buai: expressions of sorcery in the dance'. *Social Analysis* 8: 42–57.

Needham, R. 1978. *Primordial characters*. Charlottesville, University Press of Virginia.

Neuhauss, R. 1911. *Deutsch Neu-Guinea*, vol. 1. Berlin, Dietrich Reimer.

Nevermann, H. 1934. *Admiralitäts-Inseln*. Hamburg, Friederichsen, de Gruyter und Co. (G. Thilenius (ed.), *Ergebnisse der Südsee Expedition 1908–1910*, vol. II–A3.)

1938. 'Kawa auf Neuguinea'. *Ethnos* 3: 179–92.

1939. 'Die Kanum-irebe und ihre Nachbarn'. *Zeitschrift für Ethnologie* 71: 1–70.

1940. 'Die Sohur'. *Zeitschrift für Ethnologie* 72: 169–96.

New Hebrides Presbyterian Mission. 1857–1938. Minutes of synod. Pacific manuscripts Bureau 31 (Manuscripts series).

1908. 'Synod's minute on reports of stations'. *New Hebrides Magazine* 29: 31–2.

1909. 'Synod's minute on reports of stations'. *New Hebrides Magazine* 33: 5.

Newell, W. H. 1947. 'The kava ceremony in Tonga'. *Journal of the Polynesian Society* 56: 364–417.

Nicholson, J. C. 1907a. 'From our first mission station'. *Quarterly Jottings from the New Hebrides* 55: 9–13.

1907b. 'From our first mission station'. *Quarterly Jottings from the New Hebrides* 56: 39–43.

1908. 'From our first mission station'. *Quarterly Jottings from the New Hebrides* 62: 8–12.

1909a. 'From our first mission station'. *Quarterly Jottings from the New Hebrides* 64: 8–14.

1909b. 'From our first mission station'. *Quarterly Jottings from the New Hebrides* 65: 9–12.

1909c. 'From our first mission station'. *Quarterly Jottings from the New Hebrides* 66: 6–14.

1909d. 'Reports of stations: Tanna'. *New Hebrides Magazine* 32: 20.

1910a. 'From our first mission station'. *Quarterly Jottings from the New Hebrides* 67: 6–13.

1910b. 'From our first mission station'. *Quarterly Jottings from the New Hebrides* 69: 7–19.

1913a. 'From our first mission station'. *Quarterly Jottings from the New Hebrides* 79: 6–9.

1913b. 'From our first mission station'. *Quarterly Jottings from the New Hebrides* 81: 7–12.

1913c. 'From our first mission station'. *Quarterly Jottings from the New Hebrides* 82: 8–14.

1914. 'From our first mission station'. *Quarterly Jottings from the New Hebrides* 85: 11–17.

1916a. 'From our first mission station'. *Quarterly Jottings from the New Hebrides* 91: 6–11.

1916b. 'From our first mission station'. *Quarterly Jottings from the New Hebrides* 92: 4–13.

Nihill, M. 1988. ' "Worlds at war with themselves": notions of the antisociety in Anganen ceremonial exchange'. *Oceania* 58: 255–74.

Nisbet, H. 1840–51. Diary, 8 September 1840 – 3 January 1851. In Journals and other papers 1836–76. Pacific Manuscripts Bureau 417 (Manuscripts series).

Norbeck, E. 1967. 'African rituals of conflict'. In J. Middleton (ed.), *Gods and rituals: readings in religious beliefs and practices*. New York, Natural History Press, pp. 197–226.

O'Hanlon, M. 1983. 'Handsome is as handsome does: display and betrayal in the Waghi'. *Oceania* 53: 317–33.

Oliver, D. L. 1955. *A Solomon Island society*. Boston, Beacon.

1974. *Ancient Tahitian society*. Canberra, ANU Press, 3 vols.

Oosterwal, G. 1976. 'The role of women in the male cults of the Soromaja in New Guinea'. In A. Bharati (ed.), *The realm of the extra-human: agents and audiences*. The Hague, Mouton, pp. 323–34.

Oram, N. n.d. 'Areca nut chewing among Motu-speaking peoples'. Unpublished MS.

Ortner, S. 1978. *Sherpas through their rituals*. Cambridge, Cambridge University Press.

References

Parham, B. E. V. 1972. *Plants of Samoa*. Wellington, Department of Scientific and Industrial Research.

Parkinson, R. 1907. *Dreissig Jahre in der Südsee*. Stuttgart, Strecker und Schroder.

Paton, F. 1897. 'Lenakel news no. 8'. *Quarterly Jottings from the New Hebrides* 18: 11–12.

1903. *Lomai of Lenakel: a hero of the New Hebrides*. London, Hodder and Stoughton.

Paton, J., ed. 1965. *John G. Paton: missionary to the New Hebrides*. 12th edn. London, The Banner of Truth Trust.

Paton, W. F. 1973. *Ambrym (Lonwolwol) dictionary*. Canberra, ANU, Pacific Linguistics C–21.

1979. *Customs of Ambrym (texts, songs, games and drawings)*. Canberra, ANU, Pacific Linguistics D-22.

Patterson, M. 1974–5. 'Sorcery and witchcraft in Melanesia'. *Oceania* 45: 132–60, 212–34.

Pawley, A. K. 1972. 'On the internal relationships of Eastern Oceanic languages'. In R. C. Green and M. Kelly (eds.), *Studies in Oceanic culture history*. Honolulu, Bernice P. Bishop Museum, vol. 3, pp. 1–142. (Pacific anthropological records 13.)

1982. 'Rubbish-man commoner, big man chief? Linguistic evidence for hereditary chieftainship in Proto-Oceanic society'. In J. Siikala (ed.), *Oceanic studies: essays in honour of Aarne A. Koskinen*. Helsinki, Finnish Anthropological Society, pp. 33–52. (Transactions no. 11.)

Pawley, A. K. and R. C. Green. 1971. 'Lexical evidence for the Proto-Polynesian homeland'. *Te Reo* 14: 1–35.

1973. 'Dating the dispersal of the Oceanic languages'. *Oceanic Linguistics* 12: 1–67.

1984. 'The Proto-Oceanic language community'. *Journal of Pacific History* 19: 123–46.

Philibert, J.-M. 1981. 'Living under two flags: selective modernization in Erakor village, Efate'. In M. Allen (ed.), *Vanuatu: politics, economics and ritual in island Melanesia*. Sydney, Academic Press, pp. 315–36.

1986. 'The politics of tradition: toward a generic culture in Vanuatu'. *Mankind* 16: 1–12.

Poole, F. J. P. 1982. 'Cultural significance of "drunken comportment" in a non-drinking society: the Bimin-Kuskusmin of the West Sepik'. In M. Marshall (ed.), *Through a glass darkly: beer and modernization in Papua New Guinea*. Boroko, IASER, pp. 189–210. (IASER monograph 18.)

1987. 'Ritual rank, the self, and ancestral power: liturgy and substance in a Papua New Guinea society'. In L. Lindstrom (ed.), *Drugs in western Pacific societies*. Lanham, University Press of America, pp. 149–96. (ASAO monograph 11.)

Pospisil, L. 1969. 'Structural change and primitive law: consequences of a Papuan legal case'. In L. Nader (ed.), *Law in culture and society*. Chicago, Aldine, pp. 208–29.

Powell, J. 1976. 'Ethnobotany'. In K. Paijmans (ed.), *New Guinea vegetation*. Canberra, Commonwealth Scientific and Industrial Research Organization, pp. 106–83.

Queensland Herbarium. Distribution of Pipers. Herbrecs Computer Printout prepared for Ron Brunton, 1986.

Rae, J. C. 1919. 'From our first mission station'. *Quarterly Jottings from the New Hebrides* 105: 8–15.

1920a. 'From our first mission station'. *Quarterly Jottings from the New Hebrides* 108: 7–10.

1920b. 'From our first mission station'. *Quarterly Jottings from the New Hebrides* 109: 10–12.

Raghavan, V. and H. K. Baruah. 1958. 'Arecanut: India's popular masticatory – history, chemistry and utilization'. *Economic Botany* 12: 315–45.

Ramsey, E. M. 1975. *Middle Waghi dictionary*. Mt Hagen, Church of the Nazarene.

Ranby, P. 1980. *A Nanumea lexicon*. Canberra, ANU, Pacific Linguistics C-65.

Rappaport, R. 1984. *Pigs for the ancestors*. Rev. edn. New Haven, Yale University Press.

Raven, P. H., R. F. Evert and H. Curtis. 1981. *Biology of plants*. 3rd edn. New York, Worth.

Ray, S. 1913–14. 'Languages of the Gulf District, Papua'. *Zeitschrift für Kolonialsprachen* 4: 20–67.

1916. 'Polynesian linguistics: III. Polynesian languages of the Solomon Islands'. *Journal of the Polynesian Society* 25: 44–52.

1923. 'The languages of the Western Division of Papua'. *Journal of the Royal Anthropological Institute* 53: 332–60.

Reesink, G. P. 1976. 'Languages of the Aramia River area'. In *Papers in New Guinea Linguistics no. 19*. Canberra, ANU, Pacific Linguistics A-45, pp. 1–37.

Reid, A. 1985. 'From betel-chewing to tobacco-smoking in Indonesia'. *Journal of Asian Studies* 44: 529–47.

Rhoads, J. W. 1982. 'Prehistoric Papuan exchange systems: the hiri and its antecedents'. In T. Dutton (ed.), *The hiri in history*. Canberra, ANU, pp. 131–51. (Pacific Research monograph 8.)

Rice E. 1974. *John Frum he come: cargo cults and cargo messiahs in the South Pacific*. New York, Doubleday and Co.

Rieff, P. 1980. 'Authority and culture'. Transcription of lecture delivered at the Conference on the sociology of culture, La Trobe University, August.

Riesenberg, S. H. 1968. *The Native Polity of Ponape*. Washington, Smithsonian Institution Press.

Riesenfeld, A. 1947. 'Who are the betel people?'. *Internationales Archiv für Ethnographie* 45: 157–215.

1950. *The megalithic culture of Melanesia*. Leiden, Brill.

1951. 'Tobacco in New Guinea and the other areas of Melanesia'. *Journal of the Royal Anthropological Institute* 81: 69–102.

Rivers, W. H. R. 1910. 'Kava drinking in Melanesia'. *Reports of the British Association*, p. 734.

1914. *The history of Melanesian society*. Cambridge, Cambridge University Press, 2 vols.

1978 [1912]. 'The disappearance of useful arts'. In R. Slobodin, *W. H. R. Rivers*. New York, Columbia University Press, pp. 193–207.

Rodman, W. L. 1973. 'Men of influence, men of rank: leadership and the graded society in Aoba, New Hebrides'. Ph.D. thesis, University of Chicago.

1985. ' "A law unto themselves": legal innovation in Ambae, Vanuatu'. *American Ethnologist* 12: 603–24.

Ross, M. 1987. 'Early Oceanic linguistic prehistory: a reassessment'. Unpublished paper presented to the Lapita homeland workshop, La Trobe University, December.

Royen, P. van. 1982. *The alpine flora of New Guinea*, vol. 3. Vaduz, J. Cramer.

Rubinstein, R. L. 1981. 'Knowledge and political process on Malo'. In M. Allen (ed.), *Vanuatu: politics, economics and ritual in island Melanesia.* Sydney, Academic Press, pp. 135–72.

Ryan, D. 1961. 'Gift exchange in the Mendi Valley'. Ph.D. thesis, University of Sydney.

Sahlins, M. 1981a. *Historical metaphors and mythical realities: structure in the early history of the Sandwich Islands kingdom.* Ann Arbor, University of Michigan Press. (ASAO special publication no. 1.)

1981b. 'The stranger king: or Dumezil among the Fijians'. *Journal of Pacific History* 16: 107–32.

1983. 'Other times, other customs: the anthropology of history'. *American Anthropologist* 85: 517–44.

Salisbury, R. F. 1964. 'Despotism and Australian administration in the New Guinea Highlands'. In J. B. Watson (ed.), *New Guinea: the Central Highlands* (special publication of *American Anthropologist* 66), pp. 225–39.

Sanders, A. G. 1977. 'Guidelines for conducting a lexicostatistic survey in Papua New Guinea'. In *Language variation and survey techniques.* Ukarumpa, Summer Institute of Linguistics. (Working papers in Papua New Guinea languages no. 21.)

Sauer, H. and R. Hansel. 1967. 'Kawalaktone und Flavonoide aus einer endemischen Piper-Art New Guineas'. *Planta Medica* 15: 443–58.

Savage, S. 1962. *A dictionary of the Maori language of Rarotonga.* Wellington, New Zealand Department of Island Territories.

Saville, W. J. V. 1959. 'Short English–Mailu vocabulary and appendices'. ANU, mimeo.

Schiefenhovel, W. 1970. *Ergebnisse ethnomedizinischer Untersuchungen bei den Kaluli und Waragu in Neu Guinea.* Erlangen and Nuremberg, Friedrich Alexander University.

Schieffelin, E. L. 1976. *The sorrow of the lonely and the burning of the dancers.* New York, St Martin's Press.

1982. 'The *bau a* ceremonial hunting lodge: an alternative to initiation'. In G. H. Herdt (ed.), *Rituals of manhood: male initiation in Papua New Guinea.* Berkeley, University of California Press, pp. 155–200.

Schmitz, C. A. 1960. *Historische Probleme in Nordost-Neu Guinea.* Wiesbaden, Franz Steiner Verlag.

Schumann, K. and K. Lauterbach. 1976 [1901, 1905]. *Die Flora der Deutschen Schutzgebiete in der Südsee und Nachtrage.* Vaduz, J. Cramer, 2 vols.

Schutz, A. J. 1969. *Nguna texts.* Honolulu, University of Hawaii Press.

Schwartz, T. 1962. 'The Paliau Movement in the Admiralty Islands 1946–54'. *Anthropological Papers of the American Museum of Natural History* 49: 211–421.

1973. 'Cult and context: the paranoid ethos in Melanesia'. *Ethos* 1: 153–74.

Schwartz, T. and L. Romanucci-Ross. 1979. 'Drinking and inebriate behaviour in the Admiralty Islands, Melanesia'. In M. Marshall (ed.), *Beliefs, behaviours and alcoholic beverages: a cross-cultural survey.* Ann Arbor, University of Michigan Press, pp. 252–67.

Schwimmer, E. 1973. *Exchange in the social structure of the Orokaiva.* London, Hurst.

1982. 'Betelnut: the beer of the Orokaiva'. In M. Marshall (ed.), *Through a glass darkly: beer and modernization in Papua New Guinea.* Boroko, IASER, pp. 319–23. (IASER monograph 18.).

Scott, G. 1978. *The Fore language of Papua New Guinea.* Canberra, ANU, Pacific Linguistics B-47.

Serpenti, L. M. 1965. Cultivators in the swamps. Assen, Van Gorcum.
   1969. 'On the social significance of an intoxicant'. *Tropical Man* 2: 31–44.
   1972–3. 'Ndambu, the feast of competitive giving'. *Tropical Man* 5: 162–87.
Setchell, W. A. 1924. *American Samoa*. Washington, Carnegie Institution.
Shaw, R. D. 1975. 'Samo social structure'. Ph.D. thesis, University of Papua New
   Guinea.
   1981. 'Narcotics, vitality and honor'. Paper read at 80th annual meeting of the
   American Anthropological Association, Los Angeles.
Shineberg, D. 1967. *They came for sandalwood*. Melbourne, Melbourne University
   Press.
   1971. 'Guns and men in Melanesia'. *Journal of Pacific History* 6: 61–82.
Shulgin, A. T. 1973. 'The narcotic pepper – the chemistry and pharmacology of
   Piper methysticum and related species'. *Bulletin on Narcotics* 25: 59–74.
Siegel, S. and J. MacRae. 1984. 'Environmental specificity of tolerance'. *Trends in
   Neurosciences* 7: 140–3.
Sinoto, Y. H. 1983. 'An analysis of Polynesian migrations based on the archaeo-
   logical assessments'. *Journal de la Société des Océanistes* 39: 57–67.
Sizai, D. 1982. 'Stampa blong kava'. Unpublished MS. Vila Cultural Centre.
Skingle, D. C. 1970. 'Some medicinal herbs used by the natives of New Guinea'.
   Mankind 7: 223–5.
Smith, A. C. 1943. 'Studies of Pacific Island plants, II: notes on the Pacific species of
   piper'. *Journal of the Arnold Arboretum* 24: 347–61.
Smith, J. C. 1984. 'The impact of cultural expectation on kava-induced behavior'.
   M.A. thesis, University of Iowa.
Smith, R. M. 1979. 'Piper methysticine, a novel pyridone alkaloid from Piper
   methysticum'. *Oxford Tetrahedron* 35: 437–9.
   1983. 'Kava lactones in Piper methysticum from Fiji'. *Phytochemistry* 22: 1055–6.
Smythe, W. E. 1970. 'Melanesian, Micronesian, and Indonesian features in lan-
   guages of the Admiralty Islands'. In S. A. Wurm and D. C. Laycock (eds.),
   Pacific linguistic studies in honour of Arthur Capell. Canberra, ANU, Pacific
   Linguistics C-13, pp. 1209–34.
Smythe, W. E. and J. Z'graggen. 1975. 'Comparative wordlists of the Admiralty
   Islands languages'. In *Comparative wordlists 1*. Ukarumpa, Summer Institute of
   Linguistics, pp. 117–216. (Workpapers in Papua New Guinea languages no. 14.)
Somerville, B. T. 1894. 'Ethnological notes on New Hebrides'. *Journal of the
   Anthropological Institute* 23: 363–93.
Sørum, A. 1980. 'In search of the lost soul: Bedamini spirit seances and curing rites'.
   Oceania 50: 273–97.
   1982. 'The seeds of power: patterns in Bedamini male initiation'. *Social Analysis*
   10: 42–62.
Sparrman, A. 1944. *A voyage round the world with Captain James Cook in HMS
   Resolution*. London, Golden Cockerel Press.
Speiser, F. 1913. *Two years with the natives in the Western Pacific*. London, Mills and
   Boon.
   1922. 'Decadence and preservation in the New Hebrides'. In W. H. R. Rivers
   (ed.), *Essays on the depopulation of Melanesia*. Cambridge, Cambridge University Press, pp. 25–61.
   1923. *Ethnographische materialien aus den Neuen Hebriden und der Banks Inseln*.
   Berlin, C. W. Kreidel.
   1934. 'Versuch einer Kulturanalyse der zentralen Neuen Hebriden'. *Zeitschrift
   für Ethnologie* 66: 128–86.
Spriggs, M. 1984. 'The Lapita cultural complex'. *Journal of Pacific History* 19: 202–23.

References

Staalsen, P. 1962. 'The dialects of Iatmul'. In *Papers in New Guinea Linguistics no. 10*. Canberra, ANU, Pacific Linguistics A-22, pp. 69–84.

Steinbauer, F. 1979. *Melanesian cargo cults: new salvation movements in the South Pacific*. Translated by M. Wohlwill. St Lucia, University of Queensland Press. 1934–5.

Steinen, K. von den. 'Marquesanische Mythen'. *Zeitschrift für Ethnologie* 66:191–240.

Steiner, F. 1967. *Taboo*. Harmondsworth, Penguin.

Steinmetz, E. F. 1960. *Piper methysticum (kava) famous drug plant of the South Sea Islands*. Amsterdam, privately published by the author.

Stephen, M. 1987. 'Introduction'. In M. Stephen (ed.), *Sorcerer and witch in Melanesia*. Melbourne, Melbourne University Press, pp. 1–14.

Sterly, J. 1967a. 'Kawa in Melanesien'. *Ethnos* 32: 97–121.
  1967b. 'Gelbwurz (Curcuma spp.) als Ritual- und Heilmittel in Melanesien'. *Anthropos* 62: 239–40.

Stimson, J. F. with D. S. Marshall. 1964. *A dictionary of some Tuamotuan dialects of the Polynesian language*. The Hague, Martinus Nijhoff.

Stokes, J. F. G. 1930. Ethnology of Rapa Island. Unpublished MS, Bernice P. Bishop Museum, Honolulu.

Stokhof, W. A. L. 1983. *Holle lists: vocabularies in languages of Indonesia*, vol. 5/2: *Irian Jaya: Papuan languages, northern languages, Central Highlands languages*. Canberra, ANU, Pacific Linguistics D-53. (Materials in languages of Indonesia no. 19.)

Strathern, A. 1984. *A line of power*. London, Tavistock.

Strathern, A. and M. Strathern. 1971. *Self-decoration in Mount Hagen*. London, Gerald Duckworth and Co.

Strauss, W. P. 1963. *Americans in Polynesia 1783–1842*. East Lansing, Michigan State University Press.

Stringer, M. D. and J. M. Hotz. 1979. *Dictionary of Waffa Tok Pisin English*. Ukarumpa, Summer Institute of Linguistics. (Dictionaries of Papua New Guinea, vol. 3.)

Te Rangi Hiroa (P. H. Buck). 1930. *Samoan material culture*. Honolulu, Bernice P. Bishop Museum, bulletin no. 75.
  1932a. *Ethnology of Tongareva*. Honolulu, Bernice P. Bishop Museum, bulletin no. 92.
  1932b. *Ethnology of Manihiki-Rakanga*. Honolulu, Bernice P. Bishop Museum, bulletin no. 99.
  1934. *Mangaian society*. Honolulu, Bernice P. Bishop Museum, bulletin no. 122.
  1938. *Ethnology of Mangareva*. Honolulu, Bernice P. Bishop Museum, bulletin no. 157.
  1944. *Arts and crafts of the Cook Islands*. Honolulu, Bernice P. Bishop Museum, bulletin no. 179.
  1945. *An introduction to Polynesian anthropology*. Honolulu, Bernice P. Bishop Museum, bulletin no. 187.

Terrell, J. 1986. *Prehistory in the Pacific Islands*. Cambridge, Cambridge University Press.

Theodoratus, R. J. 1953. 'Betel chewing'. M.A. thesis, University of Washington.

Thompson, L. 1940. Southern Lau: an ethnography. Honolulu, Bernice P. Bishop Museum, bulletin no. 162.

Thomson, B. 1901. 'Note upon the natives of Savage Island, or Niue'. *Journal of the Royal Anthropological Institute* 31: 137–45.
  1908. *The Fijians: a study of the decay of custom*. London, Heinemann.

Tippett, A. R. 1967. *Solomon Islands Christianity*. London, Lutterworth Press.

Titcomb, M. 1948. 'Kava in Hawaii'. *Journal of the Polynesian Society* 57: 105–71.

Tonkinson, R. 1981. 'Sorcery and social change in Southeast Ambrym, Vanuatu'. *Social Analysis* 8: 77–88.

1982. 'Kastom in Melanesia: introduction'. *Mankind* 13: 302–5.

Tregear, E. 1969. *The Maori–Polynesian comparative dictionary*. Ooosterhout, Anthropological Publications.

Tryon, D. T. 1976. *New Hebrides languages: an internal classification*. Canberra, ANU, Pacific Linguistics C-50.

1984. 'The peopling of the Pacific: a linguistic appraisal'. *Journal of Pacific History* 19: 147–59.

Tryon, D. T. and B. D. Hackman. 1983. *Solomon Islands languages: an internal classification*. Canberra, ANU, Pacific Linguistics C–72.

Turner, G. 1842–3. Journal, New Hebrides. London Missionary Society, South Seas Journals no. 134. (AJCP microfilm, box 9, Victorian State Library.)

1861. *Nineteen years in Polynesia*. London, John Snow.

Turner, J. W. 1986. ' "The water of life": kava ritual and the logic of sacrifice'. *Ethnology* 25: 203–14.

Turner, V. 1967. *The forest of symbols*. Ithaca, Cornell University Press.

1969. *The ritual process*. Harmondsworth, Penguin.

Tuzin, D. F. 1976. *The Ilahita Arapesh: dimensions of unity*. Berkeley, University of California Press.

1980. *The voice of the tambaran: truth and illusion in Ilahita Arapesh religion*. Berkeley, University of California Press.

1984. 'Fighting for their lives: the problem of cultural authenticity in today's Sepik region'. Unpublished paper presented to Wenner-Gren Foundation symposium, 'Sepik research today', Basle, August.

Urbanowicz, C. F. 1975. 'Drinking in the Polynesian kingdom of Tonga'. *Ethnohistory* 22: 33–50.

Veur, P. W. van der. 1966a. *Search for New Guinea's boundaries*. Canberra, ANU Press.

Veur, P. W. van der, compiler. 1966b. *Documents and correspondence on New Guinea's boundaries*. Canberra, ANU Press.

Vicedom, G. F. and H. Tischner. 1983. *The Mbowamb*. Translated by H. M. Groger-Wurm. Sydney, Oceania monograph no. 25.

Vogt, E. 1976. 'Rituals of reversal as a means of rewiring social structure'. In A. Bharati (ed.), *The realm of the extra-human: ideas and actions*. The Hague, Mouton, pp. 201–11.

Voorhoeve, C. L. 1965. *The Flamingo Bay dialect of the Asmat language*. The Hague, Martinus Nijhoff. (Verhandleingen van het Koninklijk Instituut voor Taal-, Land-, and Volkenkunde, vol. 46.)

1970. 'Some notes on the Suki-Gogodala subgroup of the Central and South New Guinea Phylum'. In S. A. Wurm and D. C. Laycock (eds.), *Pacific linguistic studies in honour of Arthur Capell*. Canberra, ANU, Pacific Linguistics C-13, pp. 1246–70.

1971. 'Miscellaneous notes on languages in West Irian, New Guinea'. *Papers in New Guinea Linguistics no. 14*. Canberra, ANU, Pacific Linguistics A-28, pp. 47–114.

Waddell, E. 1974. 'Frost over Niugini'. *New Guinea and Australia, the Pacific and South-East Asia* 8/4: 39–49.

Wagner, R. 1972. *Habu*. Chicago, University of Chicago Press.

1979. 'The talk of Koriki: a Daribi contact cult'. *Social Research* 46: 140–65.

1981. *The invention of culture*. Revised edn. Chicago, University of Chicago Press.

References

1986. *Asiwinarong: ethos, image and social power among the Usen Barok of New Ireland*. Princeton, Princeton University Press.

Wales, W. 1961. 'Journal of William Wales'. In J. C. Beaglehole (ed.), *The journals of Captain James Cook on his voyages of discovery*. Vol. 2: *The voyage of the Resolution and Adventure 1772–1775*. Cambridge, Cambridge University Press, pp. 776–869.

Warburg, O. 1890. 'Beiträge zur Kenntnis der Papuanischen Flora'. *Englers Botanische Jahrbücher* 13: 230–455.

Watson, J. B. 1983. *Tairora culture: contingency and pragmatism*. Seattle, University of Washington Press.

Watson, P. 1987. 'Drugs in trade'. In L. Lindstrom (ed.), *Drugs in western Pacific societies*. Lanham, University Press of America, pp. 119–34. (ASAO monograph 11.)

Watt, A. C. P. 1896. *Twenty-five years, mission life on Tanna, New Hebrides*. Paisley, J. and R. Parlane.

Watt, W. 1895a. 'Cannibalism as practised on Tanna'. *Journal of the Polynesian Society* 4: 226–30.

1895b. 'Kwamera and Port Resolution'. *'Dayspring' and New Hebrides Mission: Report for Year 1894*, pp. 10–11.

1907. 'Reports of stations: Port Resolution and east Tanna'. *New Hebrides Magazine* 25: 23.

1908. 'Missionaries and native courts'. *New Hebrides Magazine* 27: 21–3.

Wawn, W. T. 1973. *The South Sea islanders and the Queensland labour trade*. Edited by P. Corris. Canberra, ANU Press.

Weiner, A. B. 1976. *Women of value, men of renown*. Austin, University of Texas Press.

Weiner, J. F. 1988. *The heart of the pearl shell*. Berkeley, University of California Press.

Werner, E. 1911. *Kaiser-Wilhelms-Land*. Freiburg, Herdersche Verlagshandlung.

Wetherell, D. 1977. *Reluctant mission: the Anglican Church in Papua New Guinea 1891–1942*. St Lucia, University of Queensland Press.

White, J. P. and J. F. O'Connell. 1982. *A prehistory of Australia, New Guinea and Sahul*. Sydney, Academic Press.

Whitmore, T. C. 1966. *Guide to the forests of the British Solomon Islands*. London, Oxford University Press.

Wilkinson, J. 1979. 'A study of a political and religious division on Tanna, New Hebrides'. Ph.D. thesis, University of Cambridge.

Williams, F. E. 1924. *The natives of the Purari Delta*. Port Moresby, Territory of Papua, 1924. (Anthropology report no. 5).

1928. *Orokaiva magic*. Oxford, Clarendon.

1936. *Papuans of the Trans-Fly*. Oxford, Clarendon.

1940. *Drama of Orokolo: the social and ceremonial life of the Elema*. Oxford, Clarendon.

1976. *'The Vailala Madness' and other essays*. St Lucia, University of Queensland Press.

Williams, H. W. 1957. *A dictionary of the Maori language*. Wellington.

Williams, T. and J. Calvert. 1859. *Fiji and the Fijians*. New York, D. Appleton and Co.

Williamson, R. W. 1939. *Essays in Polynesian ethnology*. Edited by R. Piddington. Cambridge, Cambridge University Press.

Wilson, A. 1948. 'The fight for Tanna: the story of our mission's longest campaign'. *Quarterly Jottings from the New Hebrides* 220: 9–10.

Wilson, B. 1975. *Magic and the millennium.* St Albans, Paladin.

Wilson, P. 1976. 'Abulas dialect Survey'. In *Surveys in 5 PNG languages.* Ukarumpa, Summer Institute of Linguistics, pp. 51–79. (Workpapers in Papua New Guinea Languages no. 16.)

Wirz, P. 1922. *Die Marind-anim von Holländisch-Süd-Neu-Guinea.* Hamburg, L. Friederichsen und Co.

1934. 'Die Gemeinder der Gogodara'. *Nova Guinea* 16: 371–488.

Wolfers, E. P. 1975. *Race relations and colonial rule in Papua New Guinea.* Sydney, Australia and New Zealand Book Co.

Wood, M. 1982. 'Kamula social structure and ritual'. Ph.D. thesis, Macquarie University.

Worsley, P. 1968. *The trumpet shall sound.* 2nd edn. London, McGibbon and Kee.

Wurm, S. A. 1982. *Papuan languages of Oceania.* Tübingen, Gunter Narr.

Wurm, S. A. and S. Hattori. 1981. *Language atlas of the Pacific area: part 1.* Canberra, Australian Academy of the Humanities, Pacific Linguistics C-66.

Wurm, S. A. and B. Wilson. 1975. *English finderlist of reconstructions in Austronesian languages (post-Brandsetter).* Department of Linguistics, ANU, Pacific Linguistics C-33.

Yen, D. 1974. *The sweet potato and Oceania.* Honolulu, Bernice P. Bishop Museum, bulletin no. 236.

Yoffee, N. 1985. 'Perspectives on "trends towards complexity in prehistoric Australia and Papua New Guinea" '. *Archaeology in Oceania* 20: 41–9.

Young, M. W. 1971. *Fighting with food.* Cambridge, Cambridge University Press.

1983. *Magicians of manumanua.* Berkeley, University of California Press.

Zahn, H. 1982. *Jabem–English dictionary.* Canberra, ANU, Pacific Linguistics C-68.

Z'graggen, J. A. 1971. *Classificatory and typological studies in languages of the Madang District.* Canberra, ANU, Pacific Linguistics C-19.

1975. *The languages of the Madang District, Papua New Guinea.* Canberra, ANU, Pacific Linguistics B-41.

1980a. *A comparative word list of the Rai Coast languages, Madang Province, Papua New Guinea.* Canberra, ANU, Pacific Linguistics D-30.

1980b. *A comparative word list of the Northern Adelbert Range languages, Madang Province, Papua New Guinea.* Canberra, ANU, Pacific Linguistics D-31.

1980c. *A comparative word list of the Mabuso Languages, Madang Province, Papua New Guinea.* Canberra, ANU, Pacific Linguistics D-32.

1980d. *A comparative word list of the Southern Adelbert Range languages, Madang Province, Papua New Guinea.* Canberra, ANU, Pacific Linguistics D-33.

Zöller, H. 1891. *Deutsch-Neuguinea und meine Einsteigung des Finisterre-Gebirges.* Stuttgart, Union Deutsch Verlagsgesellschaft.

Glossary of Tannese words

These are from the Lenakel language spoken in the central west of the island, except for those marked (Bis.) which are from Bislama, the Vanuatu pidgin.

asuul Big, wide, important.

kapouaitai Shrub whose leaves curl up around the time of sunset. On Tanna it was once used on overcast days to determine when kava should be drunk.

kastom (Bis.) Tradition customs, traditional way of life.

kipwia Hairless pig. Such pigs are highly valued.

kouatkasua A traditional spy and possible mediator in conflicts between the political moieties.

kualinapwir A minor kind of *suatu*.

kueria Tall cylindrical feather head-dress, built on an armature of coconut palm ribs, worn on the shoulders of *yeremira* at *nikoviaar* ceremonies.

lauanu Hamlet

nahunu Food eaten after drinking kava.

nakamal (Bis.) Traditional men's house; kava drinking ground; by extension kava bars in urban centres.

namwipwi Grandchildren, descendants.

napwok Areca palm.

naupwinaan Final stage of circumcision ceremony.

nelual Kind of pudding made from one of the starch staples and baked in an earth oven.

netik Sorcery.

niel One of the major ritual exchanges.

niko Canoe, traditional kava bowl, political moiety, kind of *suatu*.

nikoviaar The most important of the ritual exchanges.

niproou The original pre-social state of peace said to have existed before the arrival of the political moieties.

nipwagniel 'True' *taniel*; *taniel* linked by a *nukulu* joining hamlets from separate clusters. Literally 'hole' *taniel*.

nipwagnoukausik Another term for 'true' *taniel*. Literally 'dry hole'.

nivhau Traditional strainer for kava, made from banana stem.

norhin Younger sibling of the same sex.

nousumiriang Kava grown over a wide piece of wood in order to make the root system grow parallel to the ground.

nukulu Kind of *suatu* linking two hamlets whose male residents are in a *taniel* relationship to each other.

paoa (Bis.) Power.

peraieuanhin A traditional prostitute.

pwian Older sibling of the same sex.

rol il nasis Supporter, witness.

stronghed (Bis.) A wilful or stubborn person.

suatu Road, relation of exchange and alliance between local groups.

taniel The relationship between male cross-cousins, who ideally exchange sisters in marriage.

timavha Invocation made by spitting out last mouthful of kava and uttering a statement.

topunga Kava grown inside a cylinder of tree fern in order to make the root long and straight.

uipil Flask made from coconut.

yeniniko The spokesman for the *yeremira*. Literally, 'spokesman of the canoe'.

yeremira Chief.

yimwa District.

yimwayim Cleared ground on which kava is drunk and dances and exchanges held.

yolatkokunar A man who assisted the *yeremira* by performing ritual and other services for him.

Index

206

214

Cambridge Studies in
Social Anthropology

General Editor: JACK GOODY

217